Charlotte Chandler is the author of several biographies of actors and directors, including Groucho Marx, Federico Fellini, Billy Wilder, Alfred Hitchcock, Bette Davis, and Ingrid Bergman. She lives in New York City.

Joan Crawford
A Personal Biography

Not the Girl Next Door

Charlotte Chandler

POCKET
BOOKS

LONDON • SYDNEY • NEW YORK • TORONTO

First published in Great Britain in 2008 by Simon & Schuster UK Ltd
This edition first published by Pocket Books, 2009
An imprint of Simon & Schuster UK Ltd
A CBS COMPANY

1 3 5 7 9 10 8 6 4 2

Simon & Schuster UK Ltd
1st Floor
222 Gray's Inn Road
London WC1X 8HB

www.simonandschuster.co.uk

Simon & Schuster Australia
Sydney

A CIP catalogue for this book is available
from the British Library.

ISBN: 978-1-84739-229-9

Book design by Ellen R. Sasahara

Printed and bound by CPI Group (UK) Ltd, Croydon, CR0 4YY

Acknowledgments

WITH SPECIAL APPRECIATION

Betty Barker, Bob Bender, George Cukor, Bette Davis, Douglas Fairbanks, Jr., Vera Fairbanks, Cathy Crawford LaLonde, Paul Morrissey, David Rosenthal, Vincent Sherman, Sean Sobeck, and John Springer.

WITH APPRECIATION

Michael Accordino, Enrica Antonioni, Michelangelo Antonioni, Amelia Antonucci, Jeanine Basinger, Marcella Berger, Fred Chase, Gypsy da Silva, Delmer Daves, Olivia de Havilland, Mitch Douglas, Lisa Drew, Mark Ekman, Jane Elias, Marie Florio, Henry Fonda, Leatrice Fountain, Joe Franklin, Steve Friedeman, Bob Gazzale, Tracey Guest, Dick Guttman, Robert Haller, Howard Hawks, Angela Herlihy, Peter Johnson, Van Johnson, Fay Kanin, Alexander Kordonsky, John Landis, Robert Lantz, Ted Landry, Johanna Li, Myrna Loy, Joseph Mankiewicz, Gummo Marx, Jeremiah Newton, Dale Olson, Otto Preminger, Elisa Rivlin, Robert Rosen, Isabella Rossellini, Ellen Sasahara, Jaime Sobeck, Carly Sommerstein, Steven Spielberg, Gary Springer, June Springer, Jeff Stafford, Brian Ulicky, Jack Valenti, King Vidor, John Wayne, Will Willoughby, and Billy Wilder.

The Academy of Motion Picture Arts and Sciences, the American Film Institute, Anthology Film Archives, the British Film Institute, the Film Society of Lincoln Center, illy, the Italian Cultural Institute of New York City, the Paul Morrissey Archive, the Museum of Modern Art, the Museum of Television and Radio, the New York Public Library for the Performing Arts, the Sean Sobeck Archive, Turner Classic Movies, and the UCLA Department of Theater, Film, and Television.

To Joan

CONTENTS

"People expect to see Joan Crawford, not the girl next door.
If they want to see the girl next door, let them go next door."

—JOAN CRAWFORD

Not the Girl Next Door

PROLOGUE

I was at Pickfair with Douglas to see a film," Joan Crawford told me. "It was one of the grandest evenings, when Douglas, Sr., and Mary Pickford were having guests in to see a new film, ahead of the time it would be seen in theaters.

"I took my knitting along so I could keep my hands busy, because I was so nervous. I just couldn't feel at ease when Douglas and I were invited to Pickfair by his father and Mary. I didn't drink then, but I couldn't even hold a glass of water because my hand would be shaking so much, and I didn't want people to notice my shaking hand.

"I could sit there and watch the film on the screen or I could watch the reactions of Charlie Chaplin, who was sitting a few feet away from me. The film hadn't started yet, because Douglas was still in the steam room with his father.

"I saw a lady enter and join Chaplin. I noticed her beautiful hands. They were soft and white. Clearly she had never washed a dish. She was wearing the most beautiful blouse with a jabot and ruffles and wonderful tucks. It wasn't a style I wore, but it was so beautiful. I thought about how difficult it must be to launder . . .

"That led my mind back to a childhood memory of myself and my mother working in a laundry, which was our home. My mother was hidden behind a pile of clothes, and all I could see were her small red, rough hands. For a few seconds those horrible smells that made me feel sick—lye, solvent, bleach, grease, and steam—came back to me.

"The memory flashback fortunately didn't last long, and I was again in the beauty of Pickfair with the scent of fragrant flowers, expensive ladies perfume, everything fresh and clean. I was glad to be far from the laundry and its smells.

"'Memory is so strange,' I thought. Sitting there and watching the film, I was certainly the only person at Pickfair who had that memory."

Introduction

NOT KNOWING HOW it all ends," Joan Crawford told us, "is the most important element in having a happy life. For me, knowing how one's life will end is the most terrible thing that could happen to anyone."

Joan was having lunch with her longtime friend and publicist, John Springer, and me. He had just asked Joan if she would like dessert, though he already knew the answer, based on the years of lunches they had eaten together.

"No, thank you, Johnny," she said. "As you know, I never, almost never, indulge in dessert. I always stop eating while the food still looks wonderful to me."

"I personally look forward most to the end of the meal," Springer said, "which I hope will be crème brûlée."

"Well, I'm still enjoying this delicious salad," Joan said. "I've had a wonderful meal, and a wonderful life, and I don't look forward to the end of either."

Springer was momentarily stopped by this unexpected train of thought. Then, he said, "You've had a *great* life, and you're going to *continue* having it!"

"Oh, I don't know, Johnny, about the future, I mean. I've lived a life that was *more* than I could ever have dreamed, more than I ever even could have imagined. But I'll tell you what I *do* know about the future: I feel very proud of my films, some better than others, but I'm at least a little bit proud of every one of them. They are my past *and* my future. They are forever. Nothing can change that."

Her confidence was based on the certainty that the legacy of her films and the image of Joan Crawford, the star, were secure, at least for as long as people cared about motion pictures. She didn't know yet about the book that her daughter would publish after her death.

"What people think," she said, "not only while I'm alive, but afterwards—I hope far into the future—really does matter to me."

"There's no actress whose reputation is more secure than yours," Springer said.

Joan smiled. "Does that include Bette?"

"You and Bette Davis are both secure in film history," Springer said.

"I can tell you one thing Bette and I had in common," Joan said. "Our roles put men off.

"Do you know, when we were making *Baby Jane*, Bette admitted to me she was 'absolutely smitten' with Franchot [Tone], who had made *Dangerous* with her, but Franchot and I were already very much involved. That proves that Bette *did* have some good taste in men. Franchot said he thought Bette was a good actress, but he never thought of her as a woman. Our marriage didn't last, but we had some wonderful years. I wouldn't give them back for anything, and we remained friends as long as he lived.

"Bette and I both played strong women, and I think it influenced our real-life relationships with men. I was somewhat typecast that way on the screen and in life. I suppose it had something to do with my chin and my eyes, physical attributes which had nothing to do with me, except for my genes.

"I did pay great attention to my posture. It came partly from my being a dancer, and partly because I wished to appear taller than I was. I always held my head looking up so I could be my full height and a bit more.

"In life, I have my weaknesses. I certainly do. On-screen, I'm told I radiate confidence in myself. In real life, I feel vulnerable. I lack that kind of perfect self-confidence. As you well know, Johnny, just the thought of a personal appearance, as myself, can turn me into a nervous wreck.

"I always tried hard, perhaps too hard. I cared too much about what other people thought from the time I was a child—my family, the men in my life, my children, and my audience."

"I've never known anyone to care about her fans the way you do," Springer said.

"Sometimes people question why I love my public so," Joan said. "It's because the studio didn't make me a star. They gave me the chance to *be* one. It's the audiences that made me a star. I never forget them or what I owe them.

"That's why I never get tired when I'm answering their letters to me, even when I have to work for more than sixteen hours doing it, even when I did it while I was waiting between takes on films or on the way to the studio in the morning, or on my way home at night.

"On the soundstage, we don't hear applause the way stage actors do, so being asked for my autograph and receiving fan mail, *that* is my applause. As an actress, I love applause, because, after all, I'm not performing just for myself. But I did not want to be on the stage. I loved the movies, so the fan mail, millions of pieces of it, yes, that's my applause.

"Can you guess how many letters I've answered?"

Springer shook his head.

"I don't know myself," Joan said, "but it must be tens of thousands."

"You don't *need* a publicist."

"I need you as a friend *and* as my publicist. The image of the star is so important. The public doesn't want warts. I think my public comes to dream, to identify with me, especially in my early pictures. They didn't come to see the warts, or the freckles.

"I think it's a shame to de-glamorize us, a trend these days. We actresses owe our own public something, but the press has to go along with us. The press has to be reminded that there is a human being, a person, inside the celebrity. You have to *work* with the press. Knowing them as individuals, understanding what they need and trying to give it to them. That's what a publicist like you does for a star.

"The life of a celebrity is not the way it was, especially with the photographers. It's essential to be able to figure out how to have and guard some personal privacy, or one would go mad. They used to be more respectful, and now there are so many *more* of them!

"Personally, I don't like candid camera shots in the bright sun showing my freckles. I think it shocks people to see how many freckles I have. I've never counted them. I tried, but I lost count.

"Even when I just walk out of my building, I feel I owe it to the doorman that I look like Joan Crawford. It's the least I can do. I overheard him once talking to another doorman, and he said with pride, 'Joan Crawford lives in my building.' So, if I can't look like Joan Crawford, I don't go out.

"My audience always deserves the best I have to give, and I give them everything I have. If anyone sees me, it's important they see Joan Crawford. That's why I dress up, even to throw out the garbage."

OUR LUNCH HAD been arranged to introduce me to Joan Crawford for some interviews I hoped to do with her for a chapter in a book. It was a perfect beginning for me, because she trusted her friend, John Springer, and had faith in anything he suggested. She spoke openly with him in my presence, and the three of us had lunch several times. Then I went to see her in her New York Imperial House apartment on the Upper East Side.

She greeted me at the front door, opening the door herself. She was wearing a black, clinging dress, with a diamond necklace and diamond earrings. Her hair and makeup were carefully and rather elaborately done. Her black shoes were the kind of high heels she wore in her films—thick, not spike-thin, with an elaborate ankle strap—dancer's shoes.

When I mentioned her lovely dress, she said, "People expect to see Joan Crawford, not the girl next door. If they want to see the girl next door, let them go next door."

There were parquet floors, the walls were white, and her modern sofa and chairs were yellow. She had some green, leafy plants and fresh gardenias, and pieces of valuable antique Chinese white porcelain.

Joan led me into the living room, where I sat on the sofa after she removed its plastic cover. Her Oscar was standing on the coffee table to greet me. She said she would be back in a moment and went to the kitchen.

She returned with a tray of crabmeat on crackers, palm hearts on pieces of toast, black beans in tiny pastries, cheese, and crackers. "These are delicious, from my favorite Brazilian restaurant," she said as she offered me the tray, setting it down on the table in front of me.

She left again, returning with a china pot of tea and matching cups. She removed the plastic cover and sat down in a yellow armchair beside me. She noticed that I was looking at her large collection of books.

"I've read them all," she said. "Well, not *all* of them, but most of them. I've always loved books. Many of them are signed by the authors who gave their books to me. The book on the table is signed by Noël Coward."

Her desk, which was by the window, was where she spent hours every day, faithfully doing her correspondence. There were dozens of letters, all fan mail, she said, neatly stacked on the desk in the order the envelopes had been received. Joan said she didn't like to fall behind, because people were waiting. "Maybe most of them might not really care much, but there are a few, I'm sure, who are waiting for my response and will be disappointed if they have to wait too long."

There were some scripts, as well. "I still get offers all the time for films and television, but nothing I want to do. I'd never do anything I thought would hurt the image of Joan Crawford."

As she poured tea for both of us, she encouraged me to fill my plate. After I did, she put a few more appetizers on my plate. She took only two crackers for herself, and then ate only a small bite of one.

"I think that the parts I played, especially Mildred Pierce, influenced people's perception of me as a person. The price you pay for those juicy parts is that if you do them well enough, instead of giving you credit as an actress, many people think that you really *are* that person!

"I always wanted to be so successful in my parts that audiences would forget I was an actress. It happened, but there was a price. They confused the character I was playing with *me*.

"Actually the part of Mildred itself deserved an Oscar. It's really a *film noir*, you know."

"The *film noir* usually has a man rather than a woman as its central character," I said. "*Mildred Pierce* is more of a *femme noir*."

"I *like* that!" she said. "If I use it, I'll always give you credit.

"I put some of myself into Mildred Pierce, but I'm an actress. I am *not* Mildred Pierce. She didn't rub off on me."

She patted Oscar on the top of his head. "I don't usually keep my Oscar out this way, but I thought you would enjoy seeing him.

"I've heard actors say they took their characters home with them at night. I've read that when some actresses play a bitch, they're afraid they might take that personality home with them. I've been very deep into my parts, but I've never been so deep into them that I couldn't separate the film from real life. I loved playing bitches, and you know, I think there's some bitch in *every* woman. And in every man, too.

"Mildred was one of the best parts I ever had. I won my Oscar for it." Proudly, she held up her Oscar. "I'm not one of those actors who sneers and says I keep my Oscar in the bathroom.

"I'd wanted an Oscar for a long time. I thought it would be wonderful to live with one. It is. Oscar is a wonderful man in my life, one who will never leave me. One day, I'll have to leave *him*.

"If you were telling the story of my life, you could say that I believe my greatest weakness was I needed love too much. I was love-deprived when I was a child, and my life has been a search for love the way a child craves it.

"I found love with Douglas, but only friendship lasted. I found great, true, romantic love a few other times, but the love that was lasting was with my audiences.

"When I was very young, I wanted to please every member of my public, every time. That was my goal, and I was willing to give everything I had. Only later, I learned that you can't please all of the people all of the time. I am happy I pleased so many.

"It's important to remember people. I pride myself on doing that. I remember hundreds of names, maybe more, not because it comes naturally to me, quite the opposite. I don't think I was naturally good at remembering names, but it seemed right to make the effort. I did, and I noticed how much it seemed to mean to the people at the studio, the crew, everyone, even regular fans. I saw how happy it made them, and that made me happy to know that I have been given such a gift to be able to do that.

"I like to remember people on special occasions. I'm sure there are people it doesn't mean much to, but if one lonely person was cheered, it was well worth the effort."

The phone rang and Joan answered, disguising her voice. "Hello. [*pause*] No, I'm only Miss Crawford's maid. She's away on a trip, and I don't know when she's coming back. [*pause*] Thank you for calling. 'Bye." She hung up and went on speaking with me.

"I was so fortunate to be given the opportunity to find what I wanted to do, and that it was what I *could* do. From the time I was a little girl, I dreamed of dancing, of being the best dancer. Dancing made me happy. Many little girls dream of dancing, but my dream came true.

"When I was a little girl and I hurt my foot and couldn't walk for a long time, I didn't think about not walking, only about not dancing again. I don't know just how to describe the way I felt when I danced, but when I was there in bed as a child, an invalid, feeling *in*-valid, I watched out of the window and saw the birds flying. They seemed to feel a freedom in flight that was the closest thing to the way I felt when I danced. *Transported!* One's dancing feet and flying with one's own feet or wings seemed much the same kind of thing.

"I danced where I wanted to go in life. I danced to Hollywood. I danced into the arms of M-G-M and into the arms of Douglas. Through dancing, I became a dramatic actress. It's so important to have the opportunity to explore the world and yourself, to have the chance to test yourself. I tested myself, and I passed.

"It's strange. As I've grown older, I've felt closer to little Billie Cassin, the child I was, and to my childhood. She is strongly within me, and I hear her voice in my voice, especially if something upsets me.

"I didn't get life right all of the time, but a lot of people would make more mistakes if they had as much opportunity to make mistakes as I did. If I had known everything I know now when I was very young, I guess I would have acted in smarter ways. But maybe I wouldn't have been so lucky as I was, and I wouldn't have succeeded at all. No, I wouldn't change anything for fear of changing it all.

"I believe you have to try to stay open to life. If you get angry and bitter, it only hurts you, not the other person. I can't say I'm so good at always doing this, but I am *pretty* good.

"Fortunately, I didn't know in the beginning that *being* the best didn't guarantee that you would be the one who made it. I'm glad I didn't know how terrible the odds were when I started out because it might have stopped me. But I had two things going for me.

"I believed I would be happy on the lowest rung of the ladder, if I could just make a living dancing, and it didn't have to be much of a living either as long as my feet were moving. I was lucky I didn't understand I couldn't last forever in that condition. You won't believe this, but I couldn't imagine not being young. The concept of not being young didn't even exist for me.

"The second thing was I didn't have any choice. I didn't have anyone to support me, so I had to do something, and I think maybe I was lucky I couldn't do too many things well. That gave me focus. If you have a lot of pulls and possibilities, having to decide depletes your energy."

"DO YOU PREFER New York City to Los Angeles?" I asked as I was leaving.

"I do now," she answered. "There are too many ghosts there."

Joan invited me to take some of her matchbooks. They were white, with her name elegantly engraved on the outside, as it was on her stationery. The matchbook had a special sheen. I took one.

"Don't take just one, " she said. "I have a lot of them."

I accepted the offer and took a few. As she said goodbye to me, she laughed. I didn't know why. In the elevator, I looked at the matchbooks. I realized that she had been laughing in anticipation of my reaction.

Inside the matchbooks was printed one word:
"Fuck!"

1

Dancing Daughter
(1908–1924)

W HEN I BECAME famous and had enough money to buy *any*thing," Joan Crawford told me, "do you know what I would have bought if I could have? My childhood.

"But I learned a valuable lesson from the childhood I had. It wasn't the way I wanted my life to be."

According to Joan, she was born Lucille Fay LeSueur in San Antonio, Texas, on March 23, 1908. Since Texas didn't register births until after 1908, there is no official record. Other birth years, a few years earlier, have been suggested, but this is the one Joan gave, and the one in the *New York Times* obituary.

Joan's mother, Anna Bell Johnson, had married Thomas LeSueur in 1902 and was happy to leave her job as a waitress. The twenty-one-year-old Anna was of Irish-Swedish descent, and Tom was French Canadian. Their first child, Daisy, was born in 1902 and probably died that same year. Their second, Hal Hayes, was probably born in 1904.

Shortly before Joan was born, Tom LeSueur abandoned his family, thus fulfilling Anna's parents' dire predictions of the unhappiness her choice of a husband would bring her.

When Lucille was still an infant, Anna moved with her two children to Lawton, Oklahoma, in the county of Comanche. Lawton is a relatively large town in southwestern Oklahoma, close to the Red River, which defines the border with Texas. Anna, a very attractive young lady, soon found another husband.

The man was Henry "Billy" Cassin, whom Joan described for me as "a vaudeville theater manager, producer, and entrepreneur." Since the Indian Territory, as Oklahoma had been known, had just become the 46th state, Cassin saw great opportunity there for a person with his energy, personality, and some capital.

He would lease or buy existing theaters and then book traveling acts to fill their bills. The acts were third-rate at best, but at the time there was not much public entertainment in rural America. Occasionally, when the theater business was slow, he would dabble in bail bonding, a business that required capital and a reasonably good reputation.

"I never knew how old Daddy Cassin was," Joan said. "He wasn't very young and he wasn't very old." Although eventually she did meet her birth father, Cassin was the only father she ever really knew. "I couldn't imagine anyone else being my daddy. For a long time, I didn't know that I *had* another father. When I heard that I had, it was sort of shocking to a little girl, but it didn't really matter."

Cassin was a caring, attentive father for little Lucille, whom he nicknamed Billie, after himself. Years afterward, she preferred Billie to Lucille and, at first, to Joan, the name selected for her in Hollywood.

Cassin owned two properties in Lawton, the Ramsey Opera House, where the celebrated Russian ballerina Anna Pavlova had once danced, and an "air dome." This kind of open-air theater was especially popular in Oklahoma and Texas, "before the days of air-conditioning and insecticides," Gummo Marx, the fifth Marx Brother, told me. "Only the most desperate acts would play there. The Nightingales qualified." This was one of the names the Marx Brothers used for their singing and dancing act when they were starting out in show business.

As a very young child, Billie loved to visit the opera house. "I can still feel Daddy Cassin's rings when he took me by the hand to watch from the wings. I would watch the dancers once or twice, and then I would do the steps they were doing. The dancers seemed very impressed, too, when they saw what I was doing. They applauded, patted me on the head, touched my curls, and said something encouraging when they came offstage. It was my first applause, kind of my first fan mail, you might say. I loved how it felt. I memorized the feeling."

When Cassin saw how quickly the little girl learned the dances, he was amazed and joined in the applause. It was his applause that meant the most to her.

He encouraged her to become a dancer. Billie didn't need much encouragement to do what she really wanted to do.

She remembered walking around their house for days on her toes. "My mother didn't notice, and I was very upset by that.

"Now, looking back, I suppose she *must* have noticed, but she didn't want to humor me and say anything because she thought if she did, it would encourage me. She probably figured I would get tired of it on my own, which I did.

"While I was still up on my toes, my brother, Hal, who usually didn't pay any attention to his little sister, me, said, 'Why are you walking around on your toes like that? Did you hurt your foot?'

"Hal was always *so* mundane.

"I announced, 'Because I'm going to be a toe dancer.' I thought that was pretty big news. I had made an important decision. I had decided on a career! But he wasn't impressed. He was on his way out the door, and I'm not sure he even heard my answer. He felt very superior because he was a boy. He had more confidence in himself than he had in anything else, and my mother encouraged that. He was her pet. All the mother love she had was for him. I think she felt closer to a son, and he'd been around longer.

"I remember when, after a few days, I got tired and came down from my toes, Hal said, 'So, you got tired of being on your toes.'

"'No,' I said. 'I've changed my plan. I'm going to be a tap dancer.'

"That produced a shrug. He didn't believe I was going to grow up to be a famous dancer. But *I* was sure. I knew I had to, because I felt I would die if I couldn't.

"My mother punished me frequently, not so much verbally, because she didn't really have much to say to me, but physically and, usually, wrongfully. I didn't like being hit, but what I minded most was I was always being blamed for something or other my brother had done. But Hal never got the blame, and he never *took* the blame. He would see me get punished for what he did, and he kept quiet.

"I could never have seen *him* punished for what I did. Of course, I tried not to do anything wrong and the situation never occurred. My mother was crazy about Hal, so he could get away with just about anything. I don't think she liked me at all. I had the idea that maybe Hal was only my half-brother, though he had the name LeSeuer, and my mother never said a word about us not having the same father. To the contrary. And my father never said anything, because he had already disappeared before I was born or when I was a baby.

"What I did wrong was never explained to me, and I decided I would never be that kind of parent. If I ever had to discipline my own children someday, I was going to be certain that they understood why, and that they agreed the punishment was appropriate.

"My mother never talked about the loss of a baby girl before I was born. Then, once when I was only maybe about four years old, my mother was speaking to me, and she called me 'Daisy.' I asked her why she called me that. She said, 'What?' I said, 'Daisy. You called me Daisy.'

"She looked shocked, like she didn't know what to say. Then, kind of angrily, she said, 'I never said that. You imagined it. You're hearing things.' Well, I know I didn't imagine it, and I wasn't hearing things.

"Since it had upset my mother that much, I certainly was never going to ask her again. But I didn't forget, and one day, I asked Hal. He knew everything, or so it seemed to me at that time. He did know a lot more about the world we lived in then than I did just because he'd been around longer than I had. Later, I understood he didn't know everything. He was a know-it-all personality. When we grew up, I found out he wasn't wise at all and hardly seemed to know how to take care of himself.

"I asked Hal if he knew who Daisy was.

"'Yeah, sure,' he answered, forcing me to ask him for an explanation.

"'Well, who *is* she?'

"'Our sister. But she died before you were born.'

"That should have made me more precious to my mother, but I never felt very precious to her. Maybe she had preferred Daisy and wished she had her instead of me. I was a tomboy, and my mother didn't approve. She said, 'A boy should be a boy and a girl should be a girl.'

"When my mother switched me across the legs, I didn't like that at all. It hurt, but it didn't hurt much. She didn't hit very hard. It was like she was doing her duty. She believed she was doing it for my own good, she said. If you'd asked me, I wouldn't have agreed. It wasn't that it was so painful, but it was humiliating, especially because I was usually being punished for something Hal had done.

"Hal was not just getting into trouble, but making it. He was a prime instigator of trouble. I wasn't in on any of the mischief. I was just a little sister, and he never wanted a little sister tagging along. He didn't need me. I needed him.

"I remember how my mother was to me when I was a little girl and I got hurt. I had an accident, which was my fault, and I thought she would scold me. But she didn't. She was very, very worried, and she was tender. I hardly recognized her that way. I was always dancing around, because that was what I loved best to do.

"Some people dance because they're feeling good. With me, if I danced, I felt good. In those days, nothing made me happier than dancing. It made me feel free, like birds flying high. And I always liked to walk around barefoot. My mother used to tell me not to walk barefoot outside. I heard her, but I didn't pay attention.

"I danced out of the house in my bare feet, right off the porch onto some broken glass. It hurt terribly, and my foot was bleeding badly. Someone came from across the street, and he picked me up and carried me into my house.

"The doctor came, and I could tell from the way he looked that it was more than just a little cut. The doctor looked very grave. Then, he took my mother into the hall, and they whispered. That wasn't a good sign. It also wasn't a good sign how much my foot hurt.

"I only had one question. It wasn't about walking. I wasn't thinking about when I would walk. I wanted to know when would I be able to dance again. The doctor said he didn't know.

"I hadn't thought my mother cared about me, but when I had my accident, she looked so worried and took good care of me."

Just as important as her mother's attention was the encouragement given her by Cassin, who filled her sickroom with dolls and fabulous descriptions of acrobats and dancers on the stage of his theater. He never stopped telling her she would dance again. His prediction proved accurate, earlier than expected, and Billie was soon dancing around her room.

ONE DAY IN 1913, Billie was playing in the cellar of the Cassin home, when she noticed a burlap bag. She tried to move it, but it was too heavy. Curious, she looked inside. It was full of beautiful gold coins, unlike anything she had ever seen before. Very excited, she rushed up the basement stairs to tell her mother.

She thought her mother would be pleased by what she had found, but she wasn't. Her mother became terribly upset, although she tried not to show it. What Joan remembered all her life was what her mother said to her, especially because of the somber tone in which she spoke. Billie was told to listen carefully to her: "'You must never tell anyone, not anyone, not even Hal, about what happened here today, about what you found.'

"Hal was the last person I would have told. I would never have shared a confidence with him, because if I had, the first thing he would've done was to tell everyone, screaming it like an extra edition of the newspaper.

"What really impressed me was that my mother spoke to me as if I were an adult. She had never done it before, not like that. For that one moment, we were very close. Circumstances had made me her confidante.

"I didn't know what it all meant. My first reaction when I found the heavy bag of gold coins was pure happiness. I thought it meant we were going to be rich.

"I never thought of us as poor, but I knew my mother was always worried about money. If we had more money, I thought it would make her happier, and then we would *all* be happier. I didn't ask her my questions because I saw she was very upset, and I didn't want to upset her more.

"My mother didn't have to caution me again not to say anything, and she didn't. You know, I would have *died* before I told our secret. I didn't realize that what I had found confirmed my mother's suspicions."

After that, Billie and Hal heard a lot of whispering at night, and then they were sent away to stay with Anna's parents in Phoenix, Arizona. Billie missed her daddy terribly.

On the train, Hal told Billie that Cassin wasn't her birth father. This made Billie very sad, and she didn't know if she should believe Hal or not. Sometimes he said terrible things to her that he knew would hurt her, and she tried to pretend they hadn't really hurt her because she knew if Hal saw how much his words had affected her, he would be sure to repeat them

She knew Hal was a liar. He lied so much, she thought maybe he didn't even know the difference anymore between the truth and a lie.

Other little girls said they wished they had an older brother to protect them and help them. When they mentioned their wish to Billie, she didn't say anything, but she thought, "You can have mine."

Henry Cassin had to stand trial. The bag of gold apparently belonged to one of his partners in bail bonding, and Cassin was keeping it for him. Billie's daddy was charged with complicity in embezzlement, "though it was all clouded," Joan said.

At the trial, he was found innocent, but his good reputation had been damaged. Some still questioned the verdict. "Why do so many people want to believe the worst?" the grown-up Joan asked.

Joan said that for the rest of her life she never escaped the guilt she felt because of finding that bag of coins. What if she hadn't played in the cellar that day? What if she hadn't told her mother about the bag of gold coins? What would have happened then? What part had she played in the disaster that befell her beloved Daddy Cassin and the terrible repercussions of that day? Then, why did they have to leave their home and Lawton? "Sometimes you wish you could tear the page out of a calendar so that day never happened."

When Billie and Hal rejoined their mother and Daddy Cassin in Lawton, it wasn't possible to ignore the difference in the family situation. People looked at Joan in a different way. The adult Joan was certain it hadn't been her imagination. The relationship between Henry and Anna, which had never been ideal, had deteriorated badly. Though Cassin had been found innocent, it was apparent that Anna, as well as Henry, had been disgraced. It was decided that the family would move to another place where Cassin could make a new start. He chose Kansas City. Joan never knew why.

They stayed in a transient hotel in the commercial section of the city while Cassin waited for what he hoped would be a large sum from the sale of his Lawton house.

Billie was enrolled at Scarritt Elementary School, where she was held back three grades when the school found she didn't have any education. Though she was small, it was still clear to her classmates that she was a few years older than they were. This did not make her popular. It was assumed there was something wrong with her.

She was ridiculed and occasionally pushed and hit by a few older girls who were bullies, but she didn't complain, at school or at home. She knew there was nothing to be done about it until she could manage to fit in, be accepted, and make friends. She had heard "sticks and stones will break your bones, but words will never hurt you," but more than half a century later, she recalled, "It *was* the words which hurt most. The bruises healed, but I replayed the words over and over in my head, especially at night, so that the punishment was ongoing."

Anna did not seem to notice her daughter's unhappiness, perhaps because she was so involved in her own and in the never-ending struggle for economic survival. If she did notice, she didn't know what to do about it. Cassin, being more aware of the little girl's troubles, enrolled her at St. Agnes Academy. The school had a good reputation, and since Cassin had been brought up Catholic, he had greater faith in it and felt that Billie would be better taken care of there. He managed to have her enter as a boarder, feeling that would mean she would have a better attendance record and more time for studies, and that there would be opportunity for her to make friends.

The families of most of the other girls could well afford to pay for their board as well as for tuition. Cassin intended paying the fees, but the sale of the house in Lawton brought much less than he had hoped. He had to find other means of support than a theater. When the operators of the transient hotel in which they were living left town, Cassin took over the lease and management of the establishment. Its clientele was chiefly men who often drifted on without paying their bills.

"Daddy Cassin was the eternal optimist," Joan told me. "I loved that about him. If you don't have optimism, there's no real happiness possible. You have to be able to enjoy the present and look forward to the future. It's a lot harder to be a success if you don't believe in yourself and in the future." When Cassin's fortunes failed, it was arranged with the nuns for Billie to do jobs around the school to earn her board. She waited on tables and washed dishes. This gave her less time for her studies, and the tasks often made her late for classes. She had even less opportunity to make friends. She had no free time, and the other girls looked down on her, since she was serving them. She was never able to earn the grades that would have qualified her for a scholarship.

Then, one weekend, Billie went home and was told Daddy had gone and that he wouldn't be coming back. "My heart was broken," she remembered. "I hoped it wasn't true."

Unable to continue managing the hotel and paying the lease by herself, Anna found work in a laundry. She then moved with Hal to some back rooms of the laundry building while Billie continued earning her board at St. Agnes. Hal had enrolled in a technical high school.

"The laundry had the most terrible smell. I didn't know exactly what it was, lye, disinfectant, some terrible soap, dirt and grease on the clothes. It made me feel sick and took away my appetite. That was its only advantage, since otherwise I would have gone to bed hungry most nights whenever I was at home. We weren't living at the bottom of the barrel, but close.

"We slept behind the laundry and our rooms had that smell. My mother said we'd get used to it right away and not even smell it anymore. Well, she couldn't have been more wrong, for me, anyway. I can *still* smell it. It was a long time before I got used to it enough to be able to sleep.

"Whenever I wasn't in school, where I had to do a lot of physical labor—scrubbing floors, serving food to the other girls, washing dishes, and making beds to pay my way—I worked with my mother in the laundry. I was always afraid that the smell of the laundry would stay with me, and that the children at school would be able to smell it.

"Later, when I was grown up and in another life, I had the choice, and I used to take a lot of showers, two, three, even four a day. Sometimes I was asked why, and I'd just smile and say, 'I enjoy it.' Well, that part was true. I *did* enjoy a shower.

"But so *many* of them?

"I've come to believe I was still washing off the smell and the dirt of that long-gone laundry. I guess part of us is made up of our memories; even the memories we don't remember we remember. That laundry had disappeared long ago, except in my mind."

IT WAS AT St. Agnes that Billie performed on a stage for the first time. She was January in a ballet-pantomime called *The Months of the Year*.

This was an important event for her. She had feared she might never walk again without a limp, if she could walk at all. Since her accident, a slight limp had persisted. At the time of the accident, no one, especially the doctor, had even considered the possibility of her dancing again, but *she* knew she would.

Despite some pain, Billie knew that she danced beautifully in the school production and that no one but she was aware that her foot still hurt. She had hoped for some acclaim, but the audience was composed of parents watching only their own daughters.

"The sisters never expected me to excel," Joan told me, "so they didn't notice. I shouldn't have cared, but I did. People see what they expect to see. I wonder how many of those parents and their dancing daughters recognized little Billie Cassin with a different name up on the screen in *Our Dancing Daughters* ten years later?"

Billie's mother couldn't be there because she had to work. "So, I didn't have the family support the other girls had. They had their families praising them, however they performed. I didn't need that. I might have been a very insecure girl who didn't have much confidence in herself, except for that one thing, my dancing, but that was a pretty big 'except.' Daddy Cassin had told me I had the best natural sense of rhythm of anyone he had ever seen, and he knew, because he was *in* show business. He couldn't be there, but for me, his spirit was there with me."

Cassin had left without saying goodbye to Billie. There was only one way she could interpret that. It meant his departure was only temporary, not for very long. If he had gone intending to be away for a long time, he certainly would have said goodbye to her, because she knew he loved her. She felt it, and he was, after all, her daddy, no matter what anyone said. Going as he did must have meant that for some reason she wasn't old enough to be told he had to move quickly, and it would have been too sentimental and sad for them to have to endure that last moment of parting. Later, she understood that he must have suffered a terrible loss of pride and probably found it difficult to face her. It wouldn't have made a difference to her, because "I would have loved him no matter what. He meant the world to me."

Joan's brother, Hal, would sometimes call her "Lucille" and hint that Thomas LeSueur had walked out because *he* wasn't really her father, either, and that she and Hal were only half-brother and sister. "Otherwise," he taunted her, "how could I be so handsome and you so ugly?" Little Billie knew her brother was handsome because her mother and everyone thought so, and she knew she wasn't very pretty because no one ever told her she was, except Daddy Cassin, and "he wore rose-colored glasses where I was concerned.

"After that, I was always watching for Daddy Cassin. I knew in my heart he would be back. He had to.

"I had my secret hope that when I saw him the next time, he would take me away with him. I wished he had taken me with him when he left.

"Daddy had very small, beautifully shaped feet, and he was very proud of them. He had many pairs of the most wonderful shoes, and he took very good care of them, every day shining the pair he was going to wear that day.

"Because I was small, small even for my age, I couldn't always see all the faces of people when there was a crowd. I would stand on my toes the way I had when I was going to be a toe dancer, but still, that wasn't enough, so I watched men's feet. I knew that I would recognize his feet instantly. And I did.

"One day, it happened. I saw his feet. I screamed, 'Daddy! Daddy!' and I jumped into his arms and he caught me. I knew he wouldn't let me fall. It was, up to then, the most wonderful, wonderful moment of my life.

"He was as happy to see me as I was to see him. He said, 'Let's have a soda, Billie.' He knew I loved sodas. He always understood me.

"He ordered two chocolate sodas with vanilla ice cream. He knew that was my favorite. He always remembered just what I liked. He liked best the same kind of soda I liked. It was that way. We couldn't have been more alike.

"We didn't talk very much. There wasn't really that much to say. It was all feeling. I drank my soda as slowly as possible to make it last, because I didn't want the moment to ever end. But finally there was the last gurgling sound, and Daddy Cassin said he would have to leave, but he said that he would be coming back.

"It wasn't a lie. He said he would be coming back because he didn't want to make me sad, but I think he hoped his promise to return would be the truth. Wishful thinking!

"He hugged me, and I didn't want him to let go.

"This time, I didn't feel in my heart that I would ever see him again.

"And I never did."

THE NEXT MAN in Anna's life was L. A. Hough, called Mr. Hough by Anna and her children. He owned a delivery truck and lived in a fine house. Anna said she had received word that Daddy Cassin had died.

If Anna married Hough, she could move from the cramped laundry quarters. The laundry had become too much for Anna to bear. She told her children that she needed help to get along in life.

Billie well understood her mother's desire to escape the laundry. "It was hard, unpleasant, and unrewarding, and my mother was always unhappy, with good reason. I wasn't so happy myself. When my mother married Mr. Hough, I was glad for her.

"I remember only one completely happy day with my mother. I was at St. Agnes, and we didn't see much of each other anymore. It was a Sunday and she'd saved up enough money to invite me to a ladies' tearoom in Kansas City. She picked me up at St. Agnes, and we took a streetcar downtown.

"I remember we had steak and kidney pie and ice cream sodas, and then we talked as we'd never talked before, or after. She told me about funny mistakes of laundry that was sent to the wrong people, and I described some childish pranks we'd played on the nuns at school. We laughed. I couldn't remember if I'd ever seen my mother laugh before. It was wonderful to hear her laugh.

"Afterwards, we went to a Mary Pickford movie, *Little Lord Fauntleroy*, and we cried.

"At that time, I didn't know that one day I would know Mary Pickford in her own home, Pickfair, with her husband, Douglas Fairbanks, and that I would be related to her by marriage. My mother wouldn't have believed me, and I wouldn't have believed it myself.

"I'd had a wonderful afternoon, and I saw how life could have been, *could* be. I promised myself I would give my mother some wonderful days.

"Then, my mother took me back to St. Agnes, where we hugged and kissed goodbye. It was one of those memories you play over and over again in your mind. I wonder why we had so few?"

WHEN HAL WAS old enough to leave home, he went to Phoenix and then California. Billie graduated from St. Agnes, and it was decided that she should go to a girls' boarding school for her high school degree.

She enrolled as Lucille LeSueur. Rockingham Academy was chosen because it had a respectable reputation and, most important, offered board in exchange for work, as had St. Agnes. "The school was," according to Joan, "a kind of dumping ground for teenage children from families that could afford the tuition and board, and didn't want their kids living at home." Billie's household tasks were unending and laborious, and she had little time to learn anything.

At Rockingham, Billie was so badly treated, even to the extent of being beaten by the headmistress for not having made a bed well enough or for stopping to look in a mirror, that one night she couldn't bear it anymore and ran away. She did it impulsively, without thinking about consequences. Since her mother was living with Hough, there was no place for her to go. She went back to Rockingham believing the headmistress's attitude toward her would only get worse. To her surprised disbelief, it got better.

"I was about fifteen," Joan told me, "and I began to notice there was a different reaction to me. I saw it in the eyes of people when they looked at me. Especially. I saw it first in the eyes of the boys.

"I took a good look in the mirror and I surprised myself. I never had time to study myself in the mirror, and besides, it seemed rather hopeless. I knew my mother was disappointed because I didn't look like her, and she didn't think I was going to grow up very attractive, the way she was. I looked more like a photograph Hal had shown me once of my [birth] father. He seemed to have eyes just like mine. He was a big man, and the only way I resembled my mother was I was small.

"I stayed by that mirror for a while. I could see the change myself. It wasn't just my figure, which had developed some shape, but it was my face. It wasn't regular like all of the other girls. It was different, interesting. I wasn't hard to look at.

"Boys from a nearby college began to ask me out, especially when they learned what a good dancer I was. At first, I attributed it largely to my dancing, but there was more to it than that. Boxes with corsages began to arrive for me ahead of going out on a date. I don't think any-one around there had ever seen an orchid before. I certainly hadn't."

The headmistress was impressed by the respectable young men from well-to-do Kansas City families who showed interest in Lucille, sometimes arriving in expensive new automobiles. Such attention not only reflected well on the institution and might lead to new and more affluent students, but also offered possibilities for soliciting charitable donations from their families.

One of those young men was Ray Thayer Sterling, who became Billie's admirer, best friend, and her constant companion in Kansas City. He took her to dances, where some of the girls made fun of what Joan described as "my rather pathetic frocks." Clearly, though, she was the outstanding dancer. "I would have been the best without even trying, but I always tried to do the best I could." Billie won her first amateur dance competition, the first one she entered, when she was fifteen.

Ray was a serious, intelligent young man who saw and believed in Joan's great potential, not only as a dancer, but as a person, and he encouraged her. Joan felt it was her first real encouragement from someone since Daddy Cassin's help in her childhood. "Just as I was going out to face the world, Ray offered me support when I needed it. Having him come into my life was a real blessing."

Joan graduated from Rockingham in 1923 and went to work as a department store clerk, earning $12 a week. Opportunities for a girl without higher education and without family connections were limited. Then, with Sterling's encouragement and that of Dr. James Wood, the former principal of Scarritt Elementary School, who had become the head of Stephens College, Billie was admitted to Stephens in nearby Columbia, Missouri. "He just happened to pass me on the street," Joan recalled. "It was so lucky. He had this new post, and he understood that I had merit and would try hard. What a wonderful coincidence!"

With a little help from Anna, who was pleased by her daughter going to college, and with a job at the college waiting on tables, Billie was able to afford Stephens.

Suddenly, she found out what it was like to be popular. "It was a different world," she said. Most exciting for her was being nominated for a sorority.

"I was indescribably happy," Joan remembered. "I had never considered such a possibility. Belonging to a sorority didn't seem anything I could aspire to. Then, a girl I knew slightly told me that she had nominated me for her sorority. I was ecstatic before I knew the meaning of the word.

"I didn't make it. She had to tell me that she hadn't known I was working my way through school. That made me ineligible for the sorority. I guess that it meant to them that I was different from them. I didn't belong.

"She told me that a lot of the girls liked me and were sorry I couldn't be in their sorority. I was indescribably unhappy. I was sorry that I had been asked at all. It wasn't something I was thinking about, but after I was rejected, at least for the moment, I was obsessed by it. When you are trying *not* to think about something, it makes it even more difficult not to think about it.

"Later, I remembered that feeling when I arrived at M-G-M, just a beginner. I hadn't really read the contract. I found out that what Metro had was an option, and that after six months, they didn't have to pick it up. They didn't have to pick *me* up. I could be thrown away. I saw it happen to many others. It was heartbreaking. They were destroyed. I knew the feeling would be like being rejected by the sorority, but so much more terrible."

Billie couldn't get over her sorority disappointment, nor did she manage to get good grades. She thought that maybe all of those people who had judged her as not very smart were right and that she just *wasn't* very smart.

One night, she decided to leave college and pursue a dancing career. She was stopped from acting rashly by Dr. Wood, who learned of her plan and urged her not to leave so abruptly. He told her that she was intelligent, but through no fault of her own had come to college unprepared. Someday, he predicted, she would become a fine teacher. He didn't discourage her from trying to become a dancer, but he did advise her not to break off her education. Joan had great respect for him, and his words, "Don't run away," stayed with her all of her life. She understood that running away from something was very different from running *to* something.

Back in Kansas City, Billie lived with her mother and Mr. Hough. She held various jobs, such as telephone operator and department store clerk, earning around $15 a week. She and Ray Sterling continued to go to nightclubs, by that time "speakeasies," where Billie often won the dancing contests. "Ray," she said, "was not a great dancer, but acceptable, and dancing as a couple, I could make him look good."

She still hoped she might dance professionally. Her ideal was Pavlova, whom she had never seen but remembered hearing about when she was a child. In reverent tones, people had talked about the great ballerina's appearance in Lawton. Someday, Billie hoped people would speak that way about her.

BILLIE'S FIRST professional opportunity arrived when Katherine Emerine's traveling revue arrived in Kansas City, auditioning for dancers. In the days before sound films and radio, entertainers could attain regional popularity without being known nationally, and Emerine was one of those in the Midwest. While her base was Chicago, she would take her show on the road all over the Midwest. To save money, dancers were recruited along the way, and then replaced at the next stop. Billie was among those who tried out as dancers for Emerine's Missouri stand. Sixteen chorus girls were chosen, among them Billie. She gave her name as Lucille LeSueur for the billing.

At the end of two weeks, in Springfield, Missouri, the show completed its run. As Billie prepared to return to Kansas City, Emerine invited her to get in touch with her if she ever came to Chicago. She told Billie that she liked her enthusiasm as much as her talent.

Life back in Kansas City meant finding another job in a department store while Billie lived with her mother and Hough. After two weeks of show business, Billie had more trouble than ever adjusting. She treasured the piece of paper Katherine Emerine had given her with her phone number and Chicago address.

"I was inspired by the life my mother lived, as a slave of circumstances, to live a completely different life. Life at the bottom of the barrel doesn't have anything redeeming about it, and it doesn't build character. It destroys character. My mother didn't have much chance to be a wonderful mother because she had to work so hard. The struggle was too hard for her.

"I never got to know the person she was when she was young, before life wore her down, the person she might have been if things had been easier for her."

Without announcing it to anyone, even Ray, and leaving only a note for her mother not to worry, Billie, using all of her small earnings, took the day coach to Chicago.

• • •

CHICAGO WASN'T ALL she had hoped it would be. Katherine Emerine was not a big star there. She wasn't even *there*. When Joan reached her address on the South Side, Emerine was on tour. Joan didn't even have a return ticket to Kansas City. She hadn't considered the possibility of failing and going back. Fortunately, she knew who Emerine's agent was, and found him in the phone directory. She didn't call, but went straight to his office.

He helped her, and she was immediately hired as Lucille LeSueur to dance at the Friar's Club for $25 a week. Next, she was sent to dance in a revue in Oklahoma City, and then to the Oriole Terrace in Detroit. There she attracted the attention of the powerful producer J. J. Shubert, who was at the club to hear Mistinguett, the legendary French singer.

Joan had heard a story that she "caught J. J. Shubert's eye" by spilling a drink on him as she was serving between the acts. She said it was not true. "I would never have deliberately done such a stupid, clumsy thing, and I was never a conniving person. If it *had* happened, an accident, I would have been so mortified, I certainly would have remembered it all my life. The drink part didn't happen, but Mr. Shubert seeing me was a turning point in my life."

Lucille was offered a part in the chorus of Shubert's new show, *Innocent Eyes,* which would feature Mistinguett singing music by Sigmund Romberg. The next night, she was on the train to Philadelphia, where the show would try out. "I was Lucille for this one," she said, "but Billie inside me was excited."

A quick study, Lucille learned all of the dance routines right away, and was even promoted from the back of the chorus to the front. The show opened in New York at the Winter Garden in March of 1924. It was not a big success, and sooner than expected, the bans were posted. Lucille declined an offer to go on the road with it, preferring to stay in New York, which she decided agreed with her. She was thrilled by the city.

"One of my happiest homes was when I got my place in the chorus in New York City," Joan told me. "I was invited to share an apartment with four of the girls in the chorus. It turned out to be only one room. I loved it."

Among Lucille's friends in New York was a young dancer named Lewis Offield, who chose to stay with the show as it toured. Like Lucille, he was from Missouri and desperately wanted to succeed as a dancer on Broadway. They met again some years later at a Hollywood premiere as Joan Crawford and Jack Oakie.

Throughout her life, Joan chose each of her friends individually for qualities she saw in them that she valued, "sincerity, honesty, intelligence, talent, good motives, knowing how to be a friend, understanding of pressures on a performer, humor, if possible, generosity, not being excessively judgmental, not being *too* temperamental, not liking to make scenes, and discipline."

Her friends were not from any single group, nor did they need to be people who knew each other. She ignored the Hollywood caste system. In her later years in New York, she said, "I consider several of the waiters at '21' to be my friends."

Lucille joined the chorus line of *The Passing Show of 1924* at the Winter Garden. Her weekly salary was now $35. She earned additional money by working at the popular Club Richman, a speakeasy, where she performed the new dances she had seen on visits to Harlem nightclubs. Harry Richman, who owned Club Richman and was himself a famous song-and-dance man, had been impressed by Lucille when he saw her dancing in the *Passing Show* chorus.

Also impressed was Harry Rapf, an important M-G-M executive who offered her a screen test. At first, Lucille was not enthusiastic, even indifferent. She was doing what she wanted to do, dance, and her goal was to go to the top of that profession. The Broadway stage seemed a better venue for a dancer than the silent screen. Besides, she hoped to go home for the Christmas vacation.

Lucille made a test along with some other girls, and then was asked to come back for another test. When she was asked by Rapf where she could be reached, she gave him her mother's Kansas City address. She had no idea at this point in her career how seldom opportunities like this came along or how important this one was.

"I learned a few things which I've passed on to younger aspiring actresses," she told me, "hoping to help them with what I had learned. Don't turn down parts, especially at the beginning when each part you turn down could be the last one you're ever offered. And I said that regret is the worst companion you can have. Looking back with regret is unhealthy. The frustration can make you ill.

"Later, if you become a big star, you can afford to pass up something because you feel taking it might mean a death knell to your career. But you'd better not make a habit of it no matter how brightly your star is shining.

"It's not just a matter of pleasing your bosses or not *dis*pleasing them, but it's your public, your audience. You always have to think about them. It's ideal to give your audience a picture a year, even more than one in a year, if you have the opportunity. Waiting two years is dangerous to a career. You have to be very well established to do that.

"Your audience has to see you, lest they forget. Always remember, you have to stay in view."

CHRISTMAS IN KANSAS City turned out to be disappointing. Lucille had hoped to see Ray, but he had gone home to visit his family. Instead, she stayed with Mr. Hough and her mother, who was critical of the work she was doing. Anna had heard lurid stories about the lives of chorus girls in New York City. "If chorus girls did all the things people *think* they do, they wouldn't have any time to dance," Joan said.

Just before Christmas 1924, a telegram arrived for Lucille. Her mother gave it to her. It was the first telegram she had ever received. It would be the most important telegram of her life.

It offered her a five-year M-G-M contract at $75 a week. There was something about an option. She was to pick up $400 for her traveling expenses at their Kansas City office and leave immediately for Culver City, California.

She had almost forgotten about those screen tests. The first one she felt wasn't too successful, but she thought the second one turned out much better. She received some direction, and when she was asked to "run the gamut of emotions," she thought she did rather well.

She had been asked to laugh, then to cry, which she did, using her own "method," remembering times her mother had hit her when she hadn't done anything. What really brought forth a flow of tears that actually rolled down her cheeks was remembering Daddy Cassin. She had difficulty when they told her to stop crying and she couldn't, but apparently they hadn't held that against her.

Then, she had an opportunity to move. She always moved well, and it was easier to act when she didn't feel "frozen." The first test had concentrated almost entirely on static close-ups of her face.

"Later, a girl at M-G-M told me," Joan recalled, "that Mr. Rapf really just chose the girl he personally liked best, not the one who *was* best. She said that I didn't win on merit, even though I knew my second screen test was so good. I didn't like to think I was chosen for something else. Her words hurt me because I always wanted to succeed on merit, not on the casting couch, and I thought I *had* succeeded on merit.

"I have never been able to get over that, cruel words hurting me, even if they *were* untrue, even if they *were* said in anger or jealousy by people who only meant to hurt me.

"Words can be such weapons, and once angry words are spoken between people, they can't ever really be taken back. I must say with my husbands, we were very careful, as best we could be, not to exchange angry words.

"I feel in my heart that my second screen test *was* good, but I also knew there was some truth in what she said about Mr. Rapf liking me. But if he liked me best, maybe it was because I *was* the best, and also I was happy because I had justified his recommendation of me."

Joan had no reason to want to extend her stay with her mother. She had looked forward to being home for the holidays, but the visit hadn't lived up to her hopes. She had forgotten how difficult it was for her to get along with her mother, whom she couldn't seem to please. They didn't have much to talk about and share because she felt whatever she shared with her mother "turned out to be ammunition to be used against me in the future."

She didn't feel her mother would be sorry to see her leaving a few days early, until the last hours at home, when suddenly her mother, who hadn't seemed happy at all to have her there, seemed so unhappy to see her going.

Joan showed the "glorious" telegram that she had received to her mother, but Anna scarcely looked at it and didn't appear impressed. She seemed to have no more interest in this confirmation that her daughter was moving forward than she had when she seemed not to notice that little Lucille had been walking on her toes.

M-G-M had provided enough money for her to travel in a Pullman sleeper, "but that wasn't how *I* wanted to spend their money," Joan told me. "I could travel coach. I had a much better use for the money. This was my opportunity of a lifetime, it seemed, to buy clothes. I love shopping for clothes, but I had never had much opportunity for it because everything cost too much."

She had very little to pack. Her wardrobe consisted mostly of homemade dresses and a few things she had bought with her discount during her brief jobs at department stores.

"I could go into stores where I'd worked, like Kline's and Emery, Bird & Thayer, where I'd been a sales clerk or had only just looked in their windows, and I could be a customer. It was lovely to be treated as a customer.

"I bought shoes first. I've always loved shoes. I could usually get a bargain because of my small feet, size four. I was able to get two pair for the price of one. So I got four pair.

"My next purchase was quite impractical, a summer coat. When you hear it, it doesn't make sense, because why would you need a coat for summer? Not for warmth. The one I got was real linen, white. It was the height of luxury. I'd seen rich girls when I was at school who had light coats for spring and summer when you didn't need one, but it made the outfit look very finished. Since it was winter in Kansas City, I bought what they called 'cruise clothes.'

"I bought a white purse and a black purse, and some lightweight billowy flowered print dresses because I was going to Hollywood, where it was always summer, or so they said. I would be happy to leave behind the puffed-sleeve dresses my mother had made, so everything

I'd bought would fit into one case. It was exciting. I was going to wear my new clothes in my new life."

Just in case she might be hungry, she bought a loaf of bread and some slices of cheese, and a few pieces of fruit. She didn't want to waste any of the money she had left on overpriced food in the dining car. "Besides, I realized I'd spent all my money on clothes. That last blouse meant I *couldn't* eat in the diner."

She hoped the train wouldn't be crowded, because she didn't like crowds. Crowds bothered Joan all her life. Crowds made it seem warmer than it was and they made her feel "small and lost." All of her life Joan preferred a temperature of 55 degrees. When she had the power as a star, she put into her contract that the set should never be over 55 degrees. Many people were cold on her sets.

On an unseasonably warm New Year's Day morning, Joan and her mother boarded the Country Club streetcar, which passed the Union Station entrance, where they got off. The *Sunset Limited*, coming from Chicago, was early. Joan and her mother exchanged only a few words, then as her daughter boarded, Anna, holding back tears, spoke: "Be sure and send some money home from your paycheck, honey."

Evidently, her mother was not totally convinced Joan would fail.

During the two-and-half-day journey to Los Angeles, Joan kept hoping M-G-M would be meeting her at the train station. "I'd spent so much that I didn't have enough money left to take a cab. If no one met me, I wondered how long a walk it would be to the hotel. Maybe there was a bus or a streetcar . . ."

2

Starlet by Starlight
(1925–1926)

WHEN I WAS sitting on the train to California," Joan said, "I remember after less than one day feeling a great wave of terrible homesickness. It was especially strange since I didn't really have a home to be homesick for."

Joan arrived in Los Angeles on January 3, 1925. It was an unusually hot January day in southern California, and Joan liked cold weather. She looked around, but there didn't seem to be anyone there to meet her.

She waited, however, because she didn't have enough money to go anywhere or any idea about how to get to her hotel. Happily, her arrival at the mission-style Union Station was expected by M-G-M, and a breathless junior publicist came running up to greet her.

She was taken by limousine to a hotel near the studio, the Washington, and to the room that had been reserved for her. It was the first time she had ever ridden in a limousine. Joan found it better than riding on a bus, "especially since I didn't have enough money for bus fare." The Washington looked good to her after two nights on the day coach, and she was excited about her present and future. She was bursting with more than her normal energy, and she didn't feel at all tired even after her long rail journey.

Sleeping on the train had been possible, in spite of having to sit up each night. It was actually a better sleeping accommodation, she thought, than what she had in the room behind the laundry.

She was anxious to hang up all of her new store-bought clothing and see how the outfits looked on her. The hotel, she hoped, would have an iron and ironing board she could use. If there was anything Joan had perfect confidence in besides her dancing, it was her ability to press clothes beautifully.

"I was happy at the Hotel Washington. I didn't really want to go to sleep at night, and I was anxious to wake up early every morning because every new day held promise. It wasn't until months later that I noticed that the Hotel Washington was, you might say, sort of a dump. It hadn't changed, so I guess *I* had."

AMONG JOAN'S EARLIEST friends at M-G-M was William Haines, one of the biggest stars of silent films. When Joan first met him, in 1925, he was filming *A Slave of Fashion* with Norma Shearer.

"I met him before I was anybody, in fact, when I was a *total* nobody, but he noticed me and treated me wonderfully, the same way he treated me after I was a big star.

"He gave me great advice and he escorted me to wonderful places. He enhanced everyone else's opinion of me, but the most important thing was he enhanced *my* opinion of me. A person who has a good opinion of herself conveys that to others, and they start to have a good opinion of *you*.

"He gave me what may have been the most important advice anyone ever gave me because of the moment when he gave it.

"'Look around you,' he said. "'Every pretty girl here under contract at M-G-M wants to do exactly what *you* want to do. It's the Big Lottery. The producers here don't know one pretty face from another. So, what you have to do is take yourself out of the lottery.'

"Then, he didn't just say that's what I should do, but he told me *how* to do it. He took me by the hand, literally and figuratively, and showed me. It was especially nice that the advice he gave me was exactly what I wanted to hear—to do what I *wanted* to do.

"He said, 'You have to go to everything you can go to, do everything that will get you seen, and you have to do it with a lot of energy.'

"Well, energy was never my problem. I had so much of it, I needed some outlet for it, and the most wonderful outlet possible for me was dancing. I was told that even if I only did what he suggested, it wouldn't be enough. I had to keep in mind that I would be doing it to catch the eye of the right person and that was chancy.

"'You must get a publicist,' he said. Then he recommended a publicist he knew, and he persuaded the publicist to take a very small amount of money as a fee from me. At the time, it seemed quite a bit of money because I'd had no experience with publicists before. I'd never heard the word. I didn't know what they did. I soon found out.

"Now, I suspect that the fabulous deal he made for me was probably because he gave part of the money to the publicist himself, to supplement my payment. He said to me, 'He's going to try to get you into newspapers, magazines, to get you noticed.'

"There were many young men who had been asking me out, but I thought I should only think about my work, even when I didn't have any. I wasn't very fond of spending so many nights alone in my hotel room, in this hotel that was looking less and less glamorous to me.

"I started saying yes instead of no. It was so much more fun, anyway. I forgot how to say no. I went to lunch dances, to tea dances, and to dances at night, and everywhere I went, as I'd agreed to do, I informed my publicist.

"If I went out with even a passable dancer, and I went out with many really fine ones, I usually came home with a loving cup or trophy. Sometimes the other dancers who were competing would just stop and watch. Sometimes there was a cash prize, ten, fifteen, twenty dollars, which my escort let me keep.

"Sometimes the prize was one of those long-legged French dolls. They were quite the rage, and I loved them. I always kept them, no matter how crowded my room got. You never see those dolls anymore.

"At night, it was often Billy Haines who took me dancing. He was quite right about my getting into the papers and magazines, and of course it helped a lot that William Haines was my escort. It was like being seen with Valentino.

"William Haines was one of the nicest friends of my life, and I hope I was one of his. But we were never lovers.

"He had never kept it a secret that he was a homosexual. It was never anything that mattered to me, but most people in Hollywood didn't like it. I can't imagine why they thought it was any of their business. What mattered to me was that for a long time he was my best friend. Right after I met him, he took me to his beautiful home—he had the most extraordinary taste and sense of decorating—and introduced me to his friend Jimmy Shields. They had the most beautiful relationship I've ever known.

"I've never known a greater relationship between a man and a woman, though I'll tell you about a wonderful one. It was Marion Davies and William Randolph Hearst, and they never could get married because he always had a wife, but Marion loved him. There were people who said she only loved his money and power and the wonderful gifts he gave her, real estate and jewels. But then, when he got into trouble and was going to lose everything, she sold the real estate and jewels and gave him the money so he could save himself.

"I happened to think of them because they were often at dinner at the William Haines house. They had great taste and admired him.

"Later, my first husband, Douglas Fairbanks, Jr., liked Billy, too. He admired his taste, and he thought Billy was a fine friend for me. He was especially happy when he learned Billy was homosexual. He said otherwise he would have been 'damn jealous' of our being such good friends.

"There were people who gossiped about Billy's lifestyle. Mr. Mayer [Louis B. Mayer, head of M-G-M] knew perfectly well about Billy, because Billy had never made any effort to hide it. He'd been discreet, not blatant. Well, Mr. Mayer believed it would be difficult for audiences to watch William Haines if they knew that he was a man who liked men. Women wouldn't fall in love with him, men wouldn't identify with him.

"Suddenly, things went wrong for him at M-G-M. I always confided in Billy, but he didn't always confide in me. It might have been because he had a disagreement with Mr. Mayer.

"I heard that Mr. Mayer wanted him to appear romantically involved with me to hush any gossip by creating some different gossip with me. It wouldn't have been too difficult, because we not only danced together, but he went shopping with me. He helped me choose clothes. He helped me choose a bed. I learned how close a man and a woman can be without having anything romantic or physical between them. Billy wouldn't agree to Mr. Mayer's idea."

Haines and Shields found themselves unwelcome at many Hollywood parties, though never at Joan's home. "William Haines was *always* invited to my parties. *I* chose my guests. And I was a frequent visitor at his home."

When Joan rented her first house, Haines decorated it, as he did the first home she bought, and then her final California house. When Fairbanks left, Haines redid the house, as he redid her homes when she parted from husbands Franchot Tone and Phillip Terry.

When Haines died in 1973, he left his fortune to his two sisters and Shields. Immediately, Joan flew from New York to California to try to help Shields, but he was inconsolable. Less than a year after Haines's death, Shields committed suicide, leaving a note that said, "It's no good without Billy."

JOAN MADE SIX films in 1925 as Lucille LeSueur, mostly uncredited. In *Lady of the Night*, she was a double for Norma Shearer, and in *Proud Flesh*, directed by King Vidor, she played a party guest. Vidor told me that even though she only had a small part, he noticed her. Partly, he remembered her because she had such a funny name, but mostly he remembered her striking looks, personality, and presence, and the grace with which she moved. He remembered wishing he had a part for her in something he might be doing because he felt she would be "a real discovery," and the idea of discovering unknowns and giving them their chance appealed to him. He had selected James Murray from a group of extras to star in *The Crowd*.

Joan appeared briefly in Jack Conway's *The Only Thing*. Uncredited, she played Lady Catherine, a member of the royal court.

Lucille was an extra in Frank Borzage's *The Circle* and in Erich von Stroheim's *The Merry Widow*. Her first substantial role was as Bobby in Monta Bell's *Pretty Ladies*.

Pretty Ladies was the fifth picture during Joan's six-month M-G-M probationary period. If the studio liked her work, she would receive a five-year contract. Far from the indifference she had displayed in New York when she said "a Hollywood career seemed as distant as a California sunset," she realized that now it meant everything to her. Her starting salary was $75 a week, a high salary, especially for a woman in 1925. Money, however, was not of the greatest concern to Joan. Her needs were modest, and she had found what she loved to do.

Pretty Ladies was inspired by the *Ziegfeld Follies*, the popular Broadway revue of the 1920s, which featured such stars as Will Rogers and Eddie Cantor, supported by beautiful chorus girls in elaborate costumes performing spectacular musical numbers. Joan received credit as Lucille LeSueur for her small part, the only time she received screen credit with her real name. Some of the film was shot in an early two-color process that preceded Technicolor.

Pretty Ladies (1925)

Comedienne Maggie Keenan (ZaSu Pitts) is the most popular girl in the *Follies* cast. Everyone loves her, but she can't find a man to fall in love with her. While handsome, wealthy men court the beautiful chorus girls (among them, Joan and Myrna Loy), Maggie has only a fantasy man (Conrad Nagel) to keep her company in her waking dreams.

Al Cassidy (Tom Moore), a drummer in the orchestra, tries to cheer her up. Maggie, not realizing that Al is only offering friendship, falls in love with him. Al is inspired to write a song about her, and it becomes a big hit.

Al marries Maggie, but is soon captivated by Selma Larson (Lilyan Tashman). Their affair devastates Maggie.

Selma turns out to be false and scheming. Realizing how precious his relationship with Maggie is, Al asks her to forgive him. She does, gratefully, and they are reunited.

About sixty years after *Pretty Ladies*, Myrna Loy talked with me about working on that film with Joan. They were both chorus girls, beginning starlets. Loy's strongest memory was of "hanging on to something like a chandelier and going around with our toes pointed out."

She recalled that Joan seemed to be living on nothing but black coffee. "It wasn't just not being able to afford much, but Joan wanted to lose weight. Actually, I should say *Lucille* wanted to lose weight. I'm one of the few people around now who knew Lucille LeSueur. That was before Joan changed her name. It was after *Pretty Ladies* that they had this contest to find her just the right name. I guess they did!

"She didn't think much of the name Joan Crawford. She didn't think it suited her at all, but it must have been the right name because she went a long way with it. It served her very well, and she served *it* very well.

"She had more willpower than anyone I ever knew. I don't know if it was because she didn't care that much about food, or because her drive for success was so great.

"She had a splendid figure and the most beautiful legs, but she discovered, as we all did, that the camera added weight, and she felt that being lighter would help her as a dancer. She thought of herself as a dancer. At that time, she hadn't begun hoping for anything else.

"She was so thrilled when she learned a new dance, and she learned them all. She just watched them being done, and she did the steps. She had won a Charleston contest, which was important in her career and which had led her to Hollywood. I remember she came in one day, all excited about a new dance she'd learned, and she wanted to teach me how to do the Black Bottom.

"I said I wasn't interested in learning it. Probably what that meant was I didn't think I *could* learn it, and I never liked doing things I couldn't do well. I also had airs and thought myself rather above a dance called the Black Bottom.

"The thing that I don't think people knew about Joan, unless they knew her early in life before she put her guard up, was that she was a terrible fretter. She worried a lot. She was the opposite of carefree. She was care-filled, I suppose you would say.

"I remember this time, her eyes were filled with tears. I believe it's the only time I ever saw Lucille cry, or Joan, either, after she changed her name. I never saw Crawford's tears. Joan just never complained, not about her difficult childhood or about her difficult children—her Christina and Christopher made me glad I didn't have children. Not even when she was dying and in pain did she let anyone know.

"The reason she was upset was she was having so much trouble fighting off the executives at M-G-M. Some of them were very powerful, and they were grabbing her and touching her, and she didn't know what to do. She didn't want them doing it, but she was afraid because of the power they held over her career. Joan was a girl of principle, even back when she was Lucille."

TALKING WITH THE other new girls, all of whom had read their contracts more carefully than she, or who had help from their families and even family lawyers, Joan learned that they were all troubled by the fact that the five-year contract didn't actually mean five years unless M-G-M's six-month option was picked up. "Five years seemed almost unimaginably long to me at that moment in my life," Joan remembered, "but I could imagine the end of six months. That didn't seem so far away at all.

"I truly believed that most of us, nearly all of us, would have our options picked up. But for the ones who didn't, I feel the thought of being rejected was unbearable, the end of all of one's dreams, the end of one's life. What if they picked up twenty-nine options and there was one they didn't pick up, and that one was mine?

"I was a fearful girl. I wanted it so much I couldn't face losing it. I loved what I did, dancing. I hadn't even given a thought to being a dramatic actress. I just wanted to go on. What I had was so precious.

"I was very selfish. I wished the other girls well, but in my heart, the option that really mattered to me was *mine*. It wasn't in my nightmares, but it was constantly in my waking dreams.

"I tried to stay busy every minute so I could shut out the nagging thought and be exhausted by night, so I wouldn't torture myself. The perfect escape was right there at the studio. I always felt good there. I was there early, and I never left until everyone was gone. When I wasn't working on a film, I watched and watched.

"All these years later, I can't say specifically what I learned in those months, and what I learned later, but I know those months made a difference in how well-prepared I was for the life I had chosen and which, hopefully, had chosen me. All my life I've felt better when I was prepared.

"I learned about the camera. I made friends among the technicians. They were all glad to help me learn. I began to feel very comfortable on the set. It was where I belonged.

"Strangely, the joy of getting word that my option had been picked up wasn't equal to the agony I had endured fearing it might not get picked up. I had what I wanted, and that was that. It was sort of taken for granted, and all I could think about then was doing my best, so that M-G-M would never regret having chosen me.

"I was lucky that I started low where I was pretty well qualified or even overqualified where dancing was concerned. That way, I got accepted and not rejected and kept moving along. I don't know how much rejection I could have handled. When I saw those poor girls whose options weren't picked up, the pain seemed unbearable.

"When I knew I would be staying, and my salary was increased, I quickly went house hunting. Of course, it wasn't to buy, but to rent. No matter. It was going to be my first home of my own."

AFTER HER OPTION was renewed, Joan was cast for a featured role in *Old Clothes*, and her name, Lucille LeSueur, was noticed by the head of publicity at M-G-M. He said that Lucille LeSueur was a terrible name. He called it "too stagey," she remembered.

"No one believed my real name was Lucille LeSueur. They would say, usually laughing, something like, 'Can't you do better than that? That's the phoniest-sounding, most made-up stage name I ever heard.'

"Someone said to me, 'Lucille LeSueur sounds like a burlesque queen who made up her name.'

"At first, I would say, 'But it's my real name. Really . . .'

"That usually brought on more laughter, so I stopped defending my choice of a name which wasn't *my* choice of a name, but the name of my father and the given name my mother chose. She liked 'Lucille.' Then, behind my back, there were the 'sewer' jokes.

"I heard that Mr. Mayer said, although he never said it directly to me, that my name sounded like 'a sewer.' If he'd said it to me, that would have been enough for me to change it. I wanted so to please Mr. Mayer.

"I preferred being Billie Cassin, but they didn't like that name either. They said, 'Billie sounds made-up, too, and it's also stagey.' Cassin, they said nobody would know how to pronounce it and nobody would remember it, and it had no glamour.

"I wasn't dead-set against changing my name, having already been Billie Cassin, and I felt more like Billie, but I thought a new name might change the way I felt about myself. I never wanted to be anyone else, just the best of myself that I could be. They had a contest in a movie magazine to choose my new name.

"Joan Crawford was the second-choice name in the contest. I don't remember the name anymore that came in first. I know I didn't like it, and besides, it already belonged to another actress at M-G-M. I remember. I think it was Arden, Joan Arden. The name, Joan Crawford, well, I hated it. Willie Haines used to call me 'Cranberry.' Later, I would come to love it."

The first time she appeared as Joan Crawford was also her first substantial featured role. It was in *Old Clothes*, a picture produced by Jack Coogan, Sr., to star his ten-year-old son, Jackie. A decade later, twenty-one-year-old Jackie would be in court suing his parents, whom he alleged had cheated him out of $4 million.

Old Clothes (1925)

Junk dealers, precocious ten-year-old Timothy Kelly (Jackie Coogan) and grown-up Max Ginsburg (Max Davidson), make a bad stock market choice and end up with a lot of worthless stock certificates, which they use to paper the walls of an upstairs bedroom in their house. Then, to make ends meet, they rent the bedroom to young, out-of-work Mary Riley (Joan Crawford). Clever Timothy gets her work as a secretary for young Wall Street broker Nathan Burke (Allan Forrest).

> Mary and Nathan fall in love, but his family blocks their marriage. Nathan then makes some bad investments and finds himself desperately in need of a certain stock. It happens to be the stock that is now serving as wallpaper in Mary's bedroom. Timothy and Max are saved, and Mary can now marry Nathan.

Hollywood gossip columnist Louella Parsons noticed Joan Crawford in *Old Clothes* and wrote of her, "She is very attractive and shows promise." Joan saved the clipping.

The campaign that followed Joan's rechristening exploited fully the enormous potential of the M-G-M publicity machine. "Of course, it was flattering to be noticed, and it was reassuring because it meant that I wouldn't get dropped. The fear of not having my option picked up had been terrible, even worse than I dared admit to myself. But even after my option was picked up, I knew there was no absolute security in the career I wanted so desperately." Her M-G-M option was picked up in mid-1925.

"I have never been one for business, but I noticed that Mr. Mayer was, and there was a lot of business involved in show business. I learned what it meant having the studio invest the maximum possible in me. The more money they put into promoting me, the more certain it would be that they would want to get their investment back. The way to do that would be to keep me working all the time—just what *I* had in mind.

"It had been noticed that I was photogenic. It surprised no one more than me. Every feature that I had been told was 'too much,' especially my eyes and lips, even my 'too-broad shoulders and big head,' suddenly were just right because the sum total of my parts photographed so well. They began taking countless photographs of me. I loved it! I was only sorry that the girls who looked down on me as Lucille LeSeuer and Billie Cassin probably wouldn't recognize me as Joan Crawford.

"A cameraman told me my head was perfectly proportioned for pictures, but only if I lost weight. Since I was already on a diet, I had to go on an even stricter diet. I even stopped eating in my dreams.

"It was heaven being under contract, especially to M-G-M. Heaven and a haven. You were nurtured. They took a big interest in you, and you were part of the family. You weren't allowed to bite your fingernails, but who would?

"My outward manner, the confidence, was important, but luck is nearly everything. I don't like to think about it, because one can influence that so little, if at all. You have to put yourself out there and hope for a good roll of the dice.

"Narrow escapes terrify me. The thought, 'What if I had missed some moment, doing this or that? What could have happened?' Or worse, 'What might *not* have happened?'

"I know how lucky I was to have the long and wonderful career I have had. I am always aware of it and grateful.

"But knowing you're lucky is accompanied by a fear, since you don't really know why you have been so lucky, what to do to keep trying, and what to do if it goes away."

Joan's next film was directed by Edmund Goulding, who later directed Joan in *Grand Hotel*. One of her co-stars was William Haines.

Sally, Irene and Mary (1925)

The careers of three Broadway chorus girls are influenced by their preferences in men. Sally (Constance Bennett) seeks security, Irene (Joan Crawford) yearns for lasting romantic love, and Mary (Sally O'Neil) wants excitement and glamour. Sally gets her security with an older sugar daddy (Henry Kolker). Mary, after a disappointing fling with a philandering playboy (Douglas Gilmore), settles for a faithful plumber (William Haines). Irene, disillusioned in her quest for true love with the same philandering playboy, runs off with her unexciting longtime suitor (Ray Howard), but they are killed in a railway accident.

William A. Wellman, who would make cinema history in 1927 with *Wings*, directed Joan in *The Boob*.

The Boob (1926)

Peter (George K. Arthur), an idealistic Wyoming farm boy, woos his beloved Amy (Gertrude Olmstead) in the chivalric manner of Don

Quixote, but his Dulcinea is more attracted to glib city slicker Harry (Antonio D'Algy). Suspecting Harry is a bootlegger, Peter joins forces with federal prohibition agents, among them sympathetic Jane (Joan Crawford), to trap his rival, become a real hero, and win Amy.

Joan was loaned out to First National to be Harry Langdon's girlfriend in *Tramp, Tramp, Tramp*. During her eighteen years at M-G-M, she was loaned out only three times. The other occasions were *Rain* to United Artists in 1932 and *They All Kissed the Bride* to Columbia in 1942.

Tramp, Tramp, Tramp (1926)

Loser Harry (Harry Langdon) enters a cross-country hiking contest, hoping to win first prize, $25,000, so he can afford to marry his girlfriend, Betty (Joan Crawford), and pay off the mortgage on the property of his father (Alec B. Francis). Harry is victorious, but only after surviving a cyclone and breaking out of jail, among other misadventures. After he marries Betty, the adult Harry appears in a crib playing the part of their baby.

This was Harry Langdon's first feature-length comedy. During the later silent era, Langdon was as popular as Charlie Chaplin, Buster Keaton, or Harold Lloyd.

Edmund Goulding wrote the story for *Paris* and then directed the film. Joan credited him with giving her an important piece of advice. "Eddie Goulding told me, 'Hold something back, Joan. Control all that wild energy or you'll wear out your audience right away.' I listened and learned."

Paris (1926)

Jerry (Charles Ray), a young American millionaire in Paris, flirts with an Apache dancer called The Girl (Joan Crawford). When he is stabbed by her jealous dancing partner, The Cat (Douglas Gilmore), The Girl nurses Jerry back to health while trying to shield The Cat from the police. The Cat is finally apprehended and sent to jail. Jerry stays with The Girl, falling in love with her, though she remains faithful to The Cat. After his release, The Cat returns to kill The Girl, but she is saved by Jerry. Although she is grateful to Jerry, she welcomes The Cat back as her lover.

Joan's continued presence in mediocre films, even when she was the star, depressed her; but it did at least serve to showcase her talents while she waited for a breakthrough role in a worthy picture. *The Taxi Dancer* was not that film.

The Taxi Dancer (1927)

Unable to find work in New York, aspiring dancer Joslyn Poe (Joan Crawford) tearfully prepares to go back to Virginia when a sympathetic friend, gambler Lee Rogers (Owen Moore), finds her a temporary job as a taxi dancer.

At the dance hall, she is introduced to wealthy men looking for girls to accompany them to Park Avenue parties. At a party, Joslyn meets Jim Kelvin (Douglas Gilmore), a handsome ballroom dancer with underworld connections, and Henry Brierhalter (Marc McDermott), a womanizing millionaire involved in politics. They are both attracted to her.

Lee, realizing he has fallen in love with Joslyn, feels responsible for having introduced her into a dangerous world. While he is desperate to rescue her from what he foresees as her fate, first, he must rescue himself. He vows to give up gambling. Meanwhile, Joslyn has fallen in love with the charming but unscrupulous Kelvin.

In a fight, Kelvin kills an influential Park Avenue party host. Joslyn, willing to do anything to save Kelvin, offers herself to Brierhalter if he will use his influence to help Kelvin.

Kelvin does not appreciate Joslyn's willingness to sacrifice herself to save him. Disillusioned, she turns to Lee, who takes her back to Virginia and a new start—together.

Critics dismissed everything about *The Taxi Dancer* except Joan. The director on Joan's next film was W. S. Van Dyke. "I know many people didn't like Woody Van Dyke," Joan said. They called him 'One-Take Woody,' which was an exaggeration, but he did like to work fast. I didn't mind that, because I like to work fast, too. I don't get better with a lot of takes. Just the opposite. I don't even like to rehearse.

"But Van Dyke really outdid himself on a Tim McCoy picture I did. I should say 'pictures,' because he was directing McCoy in our film, *Winners of the Wilderness*, and another film, whose name I've forgotten—at the same time!"

Winners of the Wilderness (1927)

During the French and Indian Wars of the mid-eighteenth century, the English were temporarily allied with the Indians. Soldiers of fortune like Colonel O'Hara (Tim McCoy) fought with the Indians against the French, though he could never be certain who was friend or foe. When Pontiac (Chief Big Tree) has René Contrecoeur (Joan Crawford) kidnapped, O'Hara knows his foe is the Ottawa Indians, and his ally, the French. She is not only the daughter of French General Contrecoeur (Edward Connelly), but also the woman O'Hara loves. He cannot court her because her family is on the other side.

O'Hara leads his English forces to victory against the Ottawas and René is rescued. He also defeats an old personal foe, French Captain Dumas (Roy D'Arcy). He wins not only the respect of General Washington (Edward Hearn), but of General Contrecoeur, who accepts O'Hara as his daughter's suitor.

From her early days in the studio, Joan felt secure at M-G-M, according to Douglas Fairbanks, Jr., "because she so believed in Louis B. Mayer and that he was watching over her personally and professionally. She saw him as all-powerful because he was the Mayer in Metro-Goldwyn-Mayer and she believed that this meant he owned the studio, rather than being an employee, as was she. She wasn't alone in that incorrect belief. Most people believed that, until Mayer lost his place."

Unlike many Hollywood stars of her time, Joan enjoyed cordial relationships with her bosses, especially Mayer.

"I have only wonderful things to say about Louis B. Mayer," Joan said. "He was a fine man and I admired him. I still do. I regarded him as my protector. He was like my daddy Cassin and Dr. James Wood at Stephens College had been before for me.

"Norma Shearer had [Irving] Thalberg as her protector. He married her, and you couldn't compete for parts with her, not for any part she wanted. Thalberg was mad about her personally, and professionally, and she was good. She was a little aloof, but not bad, considering she was royalty, the queen of the lot.

"My relationship wasn't personal like what Norma Shearer had, but Mr. Mayer was very important in my life, and I felt he watched over my career. I always had access and could call him or arrange to see him if I needed to."

3

Douglas and Pickfair
(1927–1929)

I N THE EARLY days," Joan told me, "I made some films in which the male star was everything. I *was* one of the leads, but I knew I was only there to build up the hero. Someone had to do it. But I didn't mind. I felt pretty lucky to be getting those parts with stars like Billy Haines and Lon Chaney and John Gilbert. Still, I knew I couldn't keep on being a pretty young thing for too long.

"Sometimes, I couldn't tell whether the picture was a step up or a step down, and there was no such thing as a step sideways. A starlet didn't have time. I saw too many faded starlets all around me. They were like white dandelions in their last moments of bloom."

The Understanding Heart (1927)

Monica Dale (Joan Crawford) is a fire lookout for the forest rangers, stationed at the top of a high hill. She is in love with ranger Tony Garland (Francis X. Bushman, Jr.).

Bob Mason (Rockcliffe Fellowes), a rejected lover of Monica's coquettish sister-in-law, Kelcey Dale (Carmel Myers), is falsely accused of murdering another suitor when he was only acting in self-defense. He is sent to prison.

He escapes and makes his way to Monica's observation station, where she gives the fugitive sanctuary. He falls in love with her.

A forest fire surrounds the station, and rescue efforts led by Tony are unable to reach Monica. Then, a rainstorm puts out the fire. Bob, knowing how Monica feels about Tony, surrenders to the police. Later, he is cleared of the charges against him.

Just after Joan finished *The Understanding Heart* and was about to begin *The Unknown* in mid-1927, her brother, Hal, arrived in Hollywood, not a visitor she was hoping to see. She would have been even less thrilled if she had known that he intended staying for the rest of his life—at her expense.

She noticed that he hadn't changed. He may or may not have said, "Hello," but Joan only remembered his first sentence of greeting to her: "If *you* can do it, *any*one can."

Then, he added for good measure, or "bad measure" as she remembered it, "And with your funny face!"

Dutifully, Joan tried as hard as she could, using what influence she had at the studio, talking with everyone she knew, asking favors. With considerable effort, she was able to get him some work as an extra in crowd scenes and even a few bits.

Hal blamed her for not trying hard enough. For Hal, "somebody else" was always to blame for his failures. "It was never *his* fault in his own mind," Joan said.

His solution was alcohol. He drank, and then drank more. "Maybe he did more than drink," Joan speculated, but if he did, she didn't want to know about it.

"Hal was very good-looking," Joan said, "though he didn't have any talent, except for women, who seemed to me to overappreciate him. He believed his looks and a natural charm, which I didn't understand, entitled him to a free ride through life. He was lazy, spoiled, an arrogant egomaniac, with no respect except self-respect, and even that I wondered about. He spoke in a contemptuous tone to everyone about everything, but he reserved his most contemptuous words for me, his little sister. He acted as though he knew everything, and I think he was his own first believer.

"He was used to being served and serviced by women. My hardworking mother had started his spoiling in the time before I was born, not only because he was a boy, but because my sister, Daisy, had died and my father had left, all this by the time I was born.

"My father may have been a lot like Hal, certainly in terms of irresponsibility."

The Unknown not only starred Lon Chaney, but was directed by Tod Browning, who would become an outstanding director of horror films, two of them masterpieces, *Dracula* (1931) and *Freaks* (1932). Joan remembered this film as being an important learning experience for her, especially because of working with Lon Chaney.

"Mr. Chaney was known as a generous man to young actors," Joan said. "He certainly was to me.

"The first time I met him, he greeted me like a long-lost daughter. Then, he treated me like *I* was the star of the picture—me, a little contract player.

"Once, at the end of the day, he was being driven off the lot in his limousine. He saw me and motioned for me to get in, and then he had his chauffeur drive me home. He told me when I became a big star, I could do the same for him. Unfortunately, he died too soon.

"He had such a friendly, charming manner, except when he was putting on his makeup and getting into his character. He did this in his dressing room for a couple of hours before we started shooting. Then, he *became* Alonzo. That was when you had to be careful.

"I learned from him to be so well prepared you can forget you're in a film studio and lose yourself in the story."

The Unknown (1927)

Nanon (Estrellita in some versions) Zanzi (Joan Crawford) is the assistant and target of Alonzo (Lon Chaney), the armless knife-thrower of her father's circus in Madrid. Alonzo is passionately in love with her, but she is only mildly fond of him, chiefly because of his deformity. Yet she has a phobia against men with arms and hands. She dreads being touched by a man. No one, not even Nanon, knows that Alonzo *does* have arms, which he keeps strapped close to his body to hide his real deformity, double thumbs on each hand. He has become so adroit with his feet that he can throw knives that outline Nanon's body without touching her.

During a violent argument with Nanon's father, Zanzi (Nick de Ruiz), Alonzo frees his arms and kills him. The only witness is Nanon, who does not recognize Alonzo with his arms. All she recalls is that her father was killed by a man with four thumbs.

Hoping that Nanon will accept him, Alonzo goes to the hospital to have his arms amputated. On his return, he finds that she has taken up with Malabar (Norman Kerry), the strongman, who apparently has cured her of her phobia against being touched.

Alonzo plots to murder Malabar by sabotaging his act, which involves horses running on a treadmill, but Nanon risks her life to save the strongman, and Alonzo is trampled to death by the horses.

M-G-M executive Paul Bern, a friend and associate of the young but already legendary Irving Thalberg, invited Joan to the opening night of the John Van Druten play *Young Woodley*, at the Vine Street Theater in Los Angeles. Joan knew if Paul suggested the play, it was something she should see and probably would enjoy. She liked live theater very much as long as she was seated in the audience and wasn't on the stage. She loved being in films and had no desire whatsoever to appear live onstage.

Well placed at M-G-M, Bern was a young Austrian, refined and cultured, and was considered one of the most desirable escorts an actress could have. "They knew," Douglas Fairbanks, Jr., said, "they were going out with a gentleman." Later Bern married Jean Harlow and then, shortly afterward, committed suicide. The rumor circulated that he killed himself because he was sexually impotent with one of the most desirable women in Hollywood.

Joan enjoyed *Young Woodley*, as it seemed the entire audience did. There was a warm feeling in the theater as the curtain went down and the audience applauded appreciatively. Much as Joan had been impressed by the play, she was far more impressed by the young actor who played the title role—Douglas Fairbanks, Jr.

The actor had a name known to all because of his father, Douglas Fairbanks, Sr., who was married to the much-loved and admired Mary Pickford. Fairbanks, Sr. and "little Mary" resided at America's palace, as famous as England's Buckingham Palace, Pickfair. Young Douglas, Jr., however, was on his own that night, and his performance predicted a fine acting future.

"I thought he was really swell," Joan remembered. "He had the most wonderful voice. He moved with such grace. At that time, I preferred men who were good dancers, and I assumed young Mr. Fairbanks would be a good dancer. He had wonderful long legs. He was very tall and slim. But if he wasn't a good dancer, I would be very happy to teach him.

"Paul asked me if I would like to go backstage, and I was eager to. I knew that he, as my refined and sophisticated escort, would be the perfect introduction, and he mentioned that he already knew the young leading man. But when we saw the dressing room bursting with people and more waiting outside, I felt that was not for me. I was never at my best in a crowd, and I always tried to avoid them. It certainly wasn't the setting I'd envisioned for a first meeting. I didn't want it to be our last one.

"I asked Paul to deliver my message as soon as he could to Mr. Fairbanks, to say that I had been in the opening night audience and had so enjoyed the play and particularly his performance. I instructed Paul to give my telephone number to Mr. Fairbanks, if he asked—and even if he didn't.

"When I fell asleep that night, I dreamed about the handsome young man who was such a wonderful actor and, I was certain, a sensitive person. When I awoke, I didn't remember exactly what I dreamed, but I do remember that I woke up smiling.

"I went to my writing desk and I took out some of my blue note paper monogrammed with my name. I hand-wrote with my favorite fountain pen and with my heart. I told him how wonderful I thought he was in the play. And I was certain to include my phone number.

"I got up early and called Paul for the address, and then I had my note hand-delivered."

Joan did not know how that opening night of *Young Woodley* ended for Fairbanks, Jr. The crowd in the dressing room stayed for a long time, and everyone offered praise for the actor's performance. They said that the play could not have been what it was without him, that he gave his role life. In the group, there were family, friends, acquaintances, and strangers. Douglas Fairbanks, Sr., and Mary Pickford were there. Fairbanks's mother rushed in, but left quickly so as not to meet her ex-husband and his second wife. One other person remained behind as well, Charlie Chaplin.

Chaplin understood that after all of the clamor and acclaim Fairbanks, Jr. might feel let down. "Charlie also had a few subtle suggestions for my improvement," Fairbanks remembered. "I was deeply appreciative."

Fairbanks slept well and awakened to be greeted by congratulatory telegrams and notes. One of the notes stood out among all of the others. It was the first envelope he opened, and it contained a very feminine-looking note on blue stationery. The envelope paper was thin, and the sheet inside was even thinner. The note was charmingly handwritten and extravagantly complimentary. At the top of the paper was printed "Joan Crawford." At the bottom was her signature.

"Besides some gracious compliments for my performance," Fairbanks told me, "she asked me—and this really surprised me, quite pleasantly, I must say—she asked me if she could possibly have a signed photograph of me. How naive. In the most wonderful way. Of course she could have a signed photograph of me. Actually, she could have *me*."

JOHN GILBERT WAS going through an emotional trauma when he made *Twelve Miles Out*. He had just divorced his wife, Leatrice Joy, during the filming of *Flesh and the Devil*, with his fiancée, Greta Garbo. Garbo, however, had stood him up in front of Louis B. Mayer, William Randolph Hearst, Marion Davies, King Vidor, and Eleanor Boardman at a San Simeon double wedding. Gilbert and Garbo were supposed to share a ceremony with Vidor and Boardman. Not until Joan made a second picture with Gilbert did she find out why he had seemed so aloof and distracted during the filming of *Twelve Miles Out*.

Twelve Miles Out (1927)

Soldiers-of-fortune Jerry Fay (John Gilbert) and Red McCue (Ernest Torrence) battle each other all over the world in the pursuit of quick profits and fast women. McCue, increasingly resentful of Fay's successes with both, vows revenge after he has been imprisoned because of Fay.

Independently, they embark on rum-running operations in Prohibition-era America. Fay expropriates the seashore home of June (Joan Crawford), planning to use it as a repository for his bootleg bounty. June is at first hostile to her captor, but gradually becomes fond of his swaggering manner, as he does of her strong spirit.

During a bootlegging operation at sea, Fay and McCue confront each other in a gun battle. Both are mortally wounded. As Fay dies in June's arms, she realizes that she loves him.

Spring Fever and *West Point* were shot together in New York. The pictures were primarily vehicles for William Haines.

Spring Fever (1927)

Allie Monte (Joan Crawford), a golf enthusiast, falls in love with handsome Jack Kelly (William Haines), the new member of an exclusive country club. Jack is not only potentially a professional golfer but apparently a millionaire. When he proposes to Allie, she pretends that she really isn't rich. He doesn't care, and they get married.

Then she finds out that *he* isn't really rich, just a shipping clerk in a factory owned by another member of the country club. When Mr. Walters (George Fawcett) found out what a good golfer his shipping clerk was, he introduced him to the country club as his nephew, hoping to improve his own game with tips from Jack. Allie is infuriated to have been fooled like that and leaves Jack.

Jack turns pro and wins $10,000 in his first tournament. In the crowd cheering him along is Allie. She admits that *she* is the one who really isn't rich, and they are happily, and wealthily, reunited.

Between *Spring Fever* and *West Point*, a momentous event took place: sound. Warner Brothers' *The Jazz Singer* changed movies for-ever, although M-G-M continued making only silent films for two years more.

West Point (1928)

Spoiled, overconfident Bruce Wayne (William Haines) enrolls at West Point. Though he is very unpopular with his classmates, he proves himself a fine athlete and they have to accept his arrogant behavior. When the press touts him as a great fullback, he becomes so impossible to get along with, the coach benches him. Even his girlfriend, Betty Channing (Joan Crawford), finds him unbearable.

Angrily, Bruce gives an unfavorable interview to the press just before the Army–Navy game. For his insubordination, he faces a student committee and possible expulsion from West Point, but is saved by the testimony of his roommate, Tex McNeil (William Bakewell). Tex has found Bruce to be a fine person.

"Joan didn't believe in being either coy or excessively shy," Douglas Fairbanks, Jr., said. "She saw that as a kind of pretending, a falseness."

Joan told me that though it's assumed the man should make the first move, "What can a girl do if the man doesn't make it, and you want him to? Well, I thought with someone as special as Douglas Fairbanks, Jr., I'd better make the first move.

"I'd learned that men are shy, even ones who don't seem like they are. It may not be obvious, but especially when men are young, they may be very shy."

"In her note to me," Fairbanks said, "she had included her phone number, and she asked me to call her if I might be free to have tea with her.

"She mentioned that she had attended the performance the night before with Paul Bern. I knew very well who Joan Crawford was. She had been the subject of a tremendous publicity campaign by M-G-M. She was in films, and recently she had become a star not only of these films, but of the movie magazines. I confess I had seen some of those magazines, looking for photos of my father and even on a rare occasion, very rare, of myself."

For a time before she met Fairbanks, Joan had gone steady with a handsome nineteen-year-old man named Mike Cudahy, heir to the

Chicago meatpacking fortune. Cudahy was a friend of Douglas Fairbanks, Jr. He was a fine dancer, and he and Joan had won many prizes and trophies together. Cudahy already had a drinking problem, but it didn't impair his dancing. Joan knew that his family did not approve of her as anything but a dancing partner.

Douglas continued. "I'd also seen her at some dance contests. She was with Mike Cudahy. Mike was a superb dancer, and she was even more superb. They were rather an item for a while, but his mother strongly disapproved of Joan Crawford as a person in her son's life, probably without ever having met her. Mike was about my age, a few years younger than she. She was a few years older than I was, I guessed, but I planned to lie about my age, if she asked me.

"Joan Crawford was stunningly beautiful, and I have to admit I was quite nervous as I rang her up. She answered her own phone, and she suggested that I come to tea that very afternoon. I did."

ROSE-MARIE WAS A "silent musical," which meant that the melodies from the Rudolf Friml operetta were played by the theater accompanist, with no singing. This worked well with audiences for *The Student Prince*, but not for *Rose-Marie*. Ten years later M-G-M would redo the film successfully in sound, with Jeanette MacDonald and Nelson Eddy.

Rose-Marie (1928)

Rose-Marie (Joan Crawford), a French-Canadian mountain girl, is the belle of the trading post. Her most ardent admirers are Sergeant Malone (House Peters), a Canadian Mountie, and Etienne Doray (Creighton Hale), son of the post's most prominent family. But she chooses a mysterious trapper named Jim Kenyon (James Murray).

Kenyon is accused of murder and imprisoned. He escapes, along with the real murderer, Black Bastien (Gibson Gowland), and they both take the river route out of town.

To save Jim, Rose-Marie agrees to marry Etienne if he will

use his influence to help Kenyon. Sergeant Malone pursues the fugitives with a posse and is killed by Black Bastien, who also wounds Kenyon in the gun battle.

Black Bastien is finally apprehended, and Kenyon is cleared of the murder charge. He and Rose-Marie are happily reunited.

Rose-Marie is of interest not only because of Joan Crawford's appearance in it, but also because it was the next film James Murray made after his overnight success in King Vidor's *The Crowd*. While casting for the perfect "everyman" for *The Crowd*, Vidor spotted Murray in a group of extras. After such a wonderful beginning, Murray's career went downhill. Ten years later he drowned in New York's East River while performing drunken stunts for some coins.

"JOAN'S HOUSE ON Roxbury Drive in Beverly Hills was tiny and overdecorated," Fairbanks said, "with a kind of yard-sale elegance, but nicely put together, beautifully kept, and she was so proud of it. I liked the way she felt about her home."

The meeting was uneasy for each of them, both trying to at least appear, if not *be*, sophisticates. Before Fairbanks left, having given Joan the photograph he had brought with him, signed to her, he asked if he might have a photograph of her. While his was a small photograph, practically a snapshot, the photo Joan gave to him was one of the elegant 11" x 14" portraits, with a great deal of handwork, provided by M-G-M. He remembered what she wrote, long after he had lost both Joan and the photograph. It said:

> To Douglas,
>   May this be the start of a beautiful friendship.
>
>   Joan

"And it really *was* a beautiful friendship," Fairbanks told me.

Douglas and Joan began a very special relationship crammed into the time they had. She had to rise at five in the morning, and he didn't leave the theater until eleven at night, but Sunday was theirs, and sometimes she didn't have a call to be at the studio during the week. From the first, Fairbanks was fascinated by her.

When *Young Woodley* finished its limited run in Los Angeles, it was booked in San Francisco. That meant separation for Fairbanks and Joan. Fairbanks knew he didn't want to be involved, even though he already was. Joan was shooting *Across to Singapore*.

Across to Singapore (1928)

The seafaring Shore brothers, Joel (Ramon Novarro) and Mark (Ernest Torrence), are in love with the same girl, Priscilla Crown inshield (Joan Crawford). Although Priscilla loves Joel, his older brother takes the liberty of announcing his own engagement to her without even asking her to marry him. He does this just before the brothers set sail for Singapore on their clipper ship.

During the long voyage, Mark comes to regret his arbitrary behavior and takes refuge in rum, leaving the duties of the captain largely to the inexperienced Joel. In Singapore, the first mate, Finch (James Mason), takes charge of the ship and leaves the drunken Mark ashore. When Joel objects, he is put in irons and accused of mutiny.

Back in New England, Joel is set free, but his claim that Finch led a mutiny against Mark is not believed. Instead, it is assumed that Mark abandoned ship in a drunken stupor, as Finch claims.

To save Mark and prove his innocence, Joel sets sail back to Singapore, where he finds his brother in a pitiful condition. When Joel attempts to bring Mark aboard and reinstate him as captain, a mutiny ensues. Seeing his younger brother being overpowered, Mark pulls himself together and leads a victorious counterattack against the mutineers, but not before he is mortally wounded.

Joel sets sail for New England and Priscilla, who anxiously awaits his return.

After *Rose-Marie* and *Across to Singapore*, Joan complained to Thalberg about the parts she was being offered. He told her to be patient. She needed more experience before she could take on the kind of dramatic roles she wanted. Her next film, a Tim McCoy western, was not the kind of experience she was hoping for, but she plunged into the project with her usual enthusiasm and energy, always determined to do her best.

The Law of the Range (1928)

Ranger Jim Lockhart (Tim McCoy) relentlessly pursues the Solitaire Kid (Rex Lease), a notorious outlaw. When the Kid holds up a stagecoach, he falls in love with one of the passengers, Betty Dallas (Joan Crawford), who is already Lockhart's sweetheart. Betty notices a striking similarity between the two men: They have similar tattoos. She finds herself attracted to both men.

After subduing a raging prairie fire, the two enemies face each other in a shoot-out in which the Kid is mortally wounded. As he dies, his mother (Bodil Rosing) appears to tell Lockhart that he and the Kid are brothers, separated when very young.

Because *The Law of the Range* was unexpectedly successful, Joan got more of what she wanted in her next film, *Four Walls*, a crime drama with John Gilbert. This time, she was not disappointed in Gilbert. His daughter, Leatrice Fountain, talked with me many years later about her father and Joan.

"When my father made *Twelve Miles Out* with Joan Crawford, she was pretty disappointed in the John Gilbert she encountered.

"Not only did my father not pay any attention to her, but he didn't seem to be paying any attention to the film they were making. He hated making *Twelve Miles Out*, which was a bootlegging picture. He thought the subject was good, but the script bad. Crawford was, of course, enthusiastic about working with John Gilbert, who was the studio's biggest star, but he didn't seem enthusiastic about working with her. She attributed it to his involvement with Greta Garbo, with whom he was still madly in love. He was obsessed with her and their romance.

"Well, that was understandable to Joan. It was obvious to her that the relationship between Garbo and my father wasn't going well, and he was only sending his body to the set. Every break, he would rush to the phone. Crawford noticed that every time my father came back from making a phone call, he was unhappy. Joan could imagine that either he couldn't reach Garbo, or if he did, it wasn't the conversation he was hoping for. It didn't make it any easier for Crawford, who was just starting out. I don't think my father ever bothered to see the finished picture.

"Then, when it came to acting with him in *Four Walls*, Joan found a completely different John Gilbert. What she learned from him then was the importance of keeping up your energy. She saw the way he was able to do this, and she became fully aware of the importance of never flagging. Jack Gilbert was the man she had heard so much about, and this time, he lived up to everything she expected.

"My father reached out a helping hand to Joan, and he had his heart in what he did."

Four Walls (1928)

Frieda (Joan Crawford) is the girlfriend of East Side gang leader Benny Horowitz (John Gilbert). When he is sent to prison for killing a rival gang leader, his next-in-command, Monk (Louis Natheaux), takes over the gang and Frieda, as well.

In prison, Benny is visited by his young neighbor, Bertha (Carmel Myers), who inspires him to change his ways. Released, he returns to his mother's flat, where he renounces the life of a gangster.

When he proposes marriage to Bertha, however, she rejects him, not because she doesn't love him, but because she believes he is still in love with Frieda. Unsettled by Bertha's rejection, Benny considers rejoining the gang.

Frieda tries to make him jealous by announcing her engagement to Monk. During a party, a rival gang attacks, and Benny returns to leadership. Afterward, he and Frieda escape by way of the rooftops, pursued by the jealous Monk.

When Monk falls to his death, Benny is accused of a second murder. Cleared, Benny finds a new life with Bertha.

Joan's next film firmly established her as a dramatic actress. Its shock value for the time made it a big hit in 1928, testing the limits of what the Hays Office censors could tolerate and control. This censorship organization, established by the studios to govern themselves (and to ward off stricter government censorship), would not prove really effective until 1935.

Our Dancing Daughters (1928)

Diana (Joan Crawford) and Anne (Anita Page) are wealthy young socialites whose uninhibited behavior symbolizes the "jazz baby" flapper during the Roaring Twenties. The film opens with "Dangerous Diana," as she is known, dancing in front of a full-length bedroom mirror as she puts on her dress over her panties and slip. Then, she is seen at a wild Prohibition-era party, dancing seductively, as she takes off that dress to reveal those same panties and slip while Anne looks demurely on.

The two friends, however, are not what they seem to be. Diana is privately demure, and Anne privately lustful. Both girls are interested in wealthy young Ben Blaine (Johnny Mack Brown). He likes Diana, but her outwardly immoral behavior offends him. Instead, he is won by Anne's apparently moral demeanor, and the two get married.

Soon, it becomes apparent to Ben he has made a mistake, and he confides in Diana, whom he realizes he really loves. At a party, the drunken Anne confronts the two, accusing them of having an affair. Then she stumbles down a stairway and falls to her death.

Diana and Ben are left free to pursue their lives together.

King Vidor, who was an M-G-M director at the time, thought that *Our Dancing Daughters* was just like its main character, "Dangerous Diana. She was a good girl," he told me, "pretending to be a bad girl. The picture itself is a morality tale disguised as a lurid romance. And audiences loved feeling purified after they'd just vicariously sinned."

"This was the perfect role for me," Joan said. "That's what I was, a dancing daughter." *Our Dancing Daughters* was the first of five films that were significant turning points in Joan's career and defined her as an actress. The others were *Grand Hotel, The Women, Mildred Pierce,* and *What Ever Happened to Baby Jane?*

• • •

"IF THERE IS one thing I knew," Fairbanks told me, "it was that I wanted to marry late, and not just marry late, but I didn't want any deep emotional involvements until that time. I knew several young women I liked, but I couldn't imagine spending the rest of my life with any of them.

"I hoped my career in films would go forward. If it moved at all, that was the only direction in which it *could* go. I was also very interested in the stage. I loved the reaction of the live audience. And I was interested in living real life, not just playing characters in films and plays. I wanted to see the world. I had traveled as a boy with my mother and lived in Paris, but it would be a different experience, grown and without one's rather overprotective mother. I looked forward to enjoying a life of freedom.

"As I said, I knew immediately that I liked Billie. At first, I called her 'Miss Crawford.' That didn't last long. It was Joan I met, but soon after she wanted me to call her 'Billie.' She said she didn't really feel like a Joan, but she had changed her name because M-G-M, and especially Mr. Mayer, wanted her to. Her real name, I understood, was Lucille LeSueur. She explained that Billie was reserved for only the closest old friends, and I was glad to be admitted to that circle. So, for the rest of her life, I mostly called her Billie.

"Personally, I couldn't imagine changing *my* name, and no one ever asked me to. In fact, it may have been one of the reasons they wanted me, to cash in on my father's great name. Maybe they had hopes that some tickets would be sold to people who didn't read carefully and thought Jr. was Sr. Well, they would quickly discover their error, but perhaps they wouldn't ask for a refund.

"The only person who would probably have relished my name change would have been my father. I know that he was less than overjoyed to have a son as tall as I was, a grown-up, turn up with *his* name when he hoped that people would think he was only a few years older than I. My appearance gave the lie to that. He would have preferred people think that we were brothers, rather close in age. He hoped people didn't think about his age at all. I know, for that reason, he regretted having given his baby son, me, his name.

"Well, I didn't care what Billie's name was because she was a terrific girl. I was pleased that, even though she was so young, she seemed to know her way around and know what she wanted. And what she wanted most was her film career. But she also wanted me.

"It was perfect! We could share wonderful times and with no emotional involvement. Well, that didn't last long."

"I WOULD WISH every girl the great romantic experience I had with Doug when I was very young. I think mine was unique. I am certain it has to happen when you are *very* young. We were both in our late teens. It was spontaneous combustion. Is that a trite thing to say? Well, I don't have words. I don't now. I didn't then.

"We couldn't get enough of each other in any way. We tried to keep our passion private. But we didn't do a very good job of it. He was the most attractive man I'd ever met, and he still is the most attractive man I've ever met.

"He was tall and thin, with a firm body, muscular, but not those obvious clumpy muscles that never particularly attracted me. I could understand muscles developed by dancers, but the idea of wasting time building muscles just for posing didn't seem to be something a man I would find interesting would be doing.

"Young Doug was even more handsome than his father and just as good an athlete, but his mind was very lovable, too. He was funny in a witty way, a way he had of seeing things. He was extremely well educated, not formal education, but he was so sophisticated. He had lived in France. He was very attracted to England.

"Douglas was a great fun-raiser.

"I held nothing back. I felt I had found the one and only love of my life, for a lifetime. I belonged totally to him. It was what I had dreamed life and love and marriage could be since I was a child. Though I had not seen great loves or a great marriage, I knew there were those so fortunate that they had found it.

"I hadn't wanted to leave the set before I was with Doug, but then I found myself feeling anxious to go home to the arms of Doug. I learned to laugh out loud with him."

"WE FELT WE had a lot in common," Fairbanks told me, "if not everything. Our backgrounds are not the same.

"In real estate, they say—location, location, location. In our relationship it was—Sex! Sex! Sex! *That* was what *we* had in common.

"It was wondrous, I thought. Of course, I hadn't had much experience at that point. I still lived at home. And my mother kept as watchful an eye on me as possible. I hadn't yet made my break from home.

"I think that one of the things that worked against our ongoing sexual relationship was that we had so much sex that we used up all our sexual energy, at least for each other. That, besides work, keeping us apart and always tired."

JOAN'S TWENTY-FOURTH FILM was based on the play *Adrienne Lecouvreur*, by Eugène Scribe and Ernest Legouve. The director of the film, Fred Niblo, had directed Valentino.

Dream of Love (1928)

Prince Maurice de Saxe (Nils Asther) is having affairs with a countess (Carmel Myers) and a duchess (Aileen Pringle), who is the wife of the duke (Warner Oland). He has usurped power from his father, the king, in a little Balkan kingdom. The duchess is part of a plot to depose the duke and put Maurice on the throne, with her as his queen.

Maurice meets a ravishingly beautiful Gypsy girl (Joan Crawford) in a traveling circus and has a one-night love affair with her. Afterward, he makes the mistake of leaving her money, and she is furious, though she remains in love with him.

A few years later, the Gypsy girl visits the kingdom as Adrienne Lecouvreur, having become a world-famous actress. She is touring in a play that closely parallels her relationship with Prince Maurice. After the play, he breaks a dinner engagement with the duchess to meet with Adrienne. Their love is renewed, but at the price of incurring the duchess's vengeful anger.

The duke fears that Maurice threatens his dictatorship and sentences him to die by firing squad. As he is about to be executed, there is a revolution, and the soldiers joyfully shoot into the air.

Maurice and Adrienne are happily reunited.

Dream of Love was a disappointment to the studio after the smashing success of *Our Dancing Daughters*. Joan's next film, *The Duke Steps Out*, co-starring her with William Haines, was much more successful, possibly because it also featured synchronized sound. As with *The Jazz Singer*, a few scenes were shot with spoken dialogue, though none of Joan's. M-G-M was entering the sound field relatively late because of Irving Thalberg's aversion to the new technology and the vast changes in the motion picture medium it would bring about. Like many other Hollywood people, Thalberg was perfectly happy with silent films and said, "They are here to stay," Joan reported.

The Duke Steps Out (1929)

In a diner, some bullies insult pretty young Susie (Joan Crawford). Duke (William Haines) comes to her rescue with his fists. Although Duke is a millionaire's pampered son, he is also a skilled boxer. His ambition is to become a world champion.

Learning that Susie is a college student, he enrolls in the same school. His arrogant behavior soon antagonizes the other students, and his chauffeur-driven limousine sets him apart. In spite of this, Susie remembers his brave defense of her in the diner, and she admires his ambition to win the boxing championship of the world.

Duke has not been training since he entered college, so when he is beaten badly by a fraternity loudmouth, Susie believes he has been lying all along and loses faith in him. Realizing he is neglecting his dream, he goes back into training.

In a broadcast of a championship bout from San Francisco, Susie and her friends hear Duke win. She now knows he was telling the truth, and Susie and Duke are happily reunited.

"I had such fun working with William Haines. I loved him dearly as a person. He was one of the very first people I met when I arrived as green as salad at M-G-M. He had so encouraged me, helped me, brightened my social life, and I was proving him right in his great predictions for me. His own loving fandom helped make *The Duke* successful."

Delmer Daves, who in 1944 directed Joan in *Hollywood Canteen*, recalled a memorable scene he played as a young actor with Joan in *The Duke Steps Out*.

"I had a small part in the picture. My one big scene is at a train station where Joan faints on the platform. I catch her and then carry her to the station, the camera following me all the way.

"When she fell, I caught her in such a way that I had one hand cupped over her left breast. I didn't want to spoil the long tracking shot, so I left it there and went on, and so did she. It was a long take, and I had my hand on her breast the whole time I was carrying her.

"Finally, we got to the station and [director James] Cruze yelled, 'Cut.' Only then did I let go of her breast.

"She turned to me and said, 'Well, you got a pretty good feel there, didn't you?'"

"ONE OF THE first things I noticed about Billie," Fairbanks told me, "was she had the flattest stomach I'd ever seen. It was flatter than mine. She had *no* stomach!

"I can't say it was a feature I especially cared about, but I did regard it as amazing. I was quite athletic, but Billie was a greater natural dancer than anyone I have ever known. Compared to her, I was a really good dancer, but I was lazy. I danced for pleasure. For Billie, her work and her pleasure were one and the same.

"She had such a wonderful body, a dancer's body, the greatest legs.

Marlene Dietrich and I were very close, but not even Miss Dietrich had greater legs.

"Besides being the best dancer I ever danced with, she had a lovely singing voice. It was really good, but you didn't notice it so much because her dancing was unique. The voice wasn't the equal of her legs, but it was damned good.

"Oh, something else that was very striking about her. She had the tiniest feet, size four, she said. I just know they were very small. She enjoyed shoes, wonderful high heels with all kinds of straps, dancer's shoes. She said they gave support, and I suppose it helped them stay on. They looked especially wonderful on those tiny feet. My step-mother, Mary Pickford, had tiny feet, too. I don't know which lady had the tinier feet, but if they had been any smaller, I don't think Mary and Billie could have walked, let alone danced.

"Billie was a very small person, but the way she dressed and carried herself gave her stature. Especially when she was sitting and you only saw her head, which was larger than you would have expected, and her broad shoulders. You were surprised when she stood up. You expected her to be much taller than she was.

"I think some of what enthralled me about Billie was the reflection of myself I saw in her eyes. She was so impressed by me. Everything I said pleased her. Everything that I did pleased her. What man wouldn't enjoy having such a desirable woman make him feel irresistible!"

Joan would call Fairbanks "Prince Charming." As the son of Douglas Fairbanks, Sr., he had been referred to as Prince Charming in the press, he said, "by gossiping tongues who believed my name meant I was already wealthy and the heir apparent, none of which was true.

"My mother had received about $400,000 when my parents divorced. I was about ten. My father said that's all my mother and I were *ever* going to get. He did put me into his will for a trust fund, I was told, but when I went into acting at an early age, thus displeasing him, he disinherited me totally. So, I wasn't quite the rich heir people thought I was.

"Billie would say to me, seductively, 'You're *my* Prince Charming.'

I felt more like a frog, and I kept hoping that I wouldn't *turn* into a frog and embarrass us both."

"I loved sunbathing," Joan said, "the most foolish practice imaginable for anyone, especially for anyone with skin as fair as mine. It wasn't as generally well-known then as it is now that too much sun isn't good for the skin. I especially liked it in southern California, where there was hot, dry sun with a cool ocean breeze.

"Douglas loved the sun as much as I did. His skin was as fair as mine, but he never burned and he always developed a wonderfully healthy-looking glow. If he kept sunning, it developed into a nice even tan, which was very sexy.

"It was certainly a foolish practice for someone with as many freckles as I had. I could not afford to keep up with him because I became one big freckle on occasion.

"I suppose it's trivial, but Douglas was one of those blessed persons who could stay thin while eating whatever and whenever he wanted, and worse yet, he took it for granted. I'd been starving ever since I arrived in Hollywood and saw how the camera adds weight. In a year, I could count my ice cream indulgences on one finger. Lucky Douglas."

"As we got to know each other better," Fairbanks said, "our romance grew. She told me the story of her life. It seemed a hard and sad life, but she told it all without any trace of self-pity. I admired her bravery.

"Myself, I'd had quite a privileged life. She knew a lot about me because she had read about me in movie magazines. I couldn't imagine what she might have read. I rarely read any, but I believed they printed any old thing with no concern for accuracy. Occasionally, I did rather like to look at the pictures, though.

"Obviously Billie didn't have much education, though at first I thought she was sophisticated, especially for her years. But knowing her better, I understood that she was really naïve. That naïveté was a part of her charm, for me anyway. I was kind of naïve myself.

"Billie was rather an easygoing person when it came to judging people. She always wanted to see the best in people, and she did. She was even more open than I, friendly and prepared to like people. I also tend to be that way myself.

"She had the greatest respect for the printed word. Somehow, when it was printed, she felt it was true. I told her lies got printed just as easily as the truth, but I don't think she was ever convinced of that.

"She had this great desire to learn. She was always striving for self-improvement. I felt reading seemed to be like doing her exercises. She wanted a lithe body, so why not a live mind? Anyway, she had a lithe body, and a live mind, too.

"It seemed to me an obvious good beginning for her library, which she didn't yet have, would be Shakespeare. Shakespeare seemed a perfect beginning. I told Billie that there were valuable lessons to be learned and unimaginable entertainment. I didn't think she would understand everything. I wasn't certain Shakespeare would entertain her, not the way it did me. I loved the stories and the words, as did my father. People didn't know 'Pete' [Fairbanks, Sr.] as a Shakespearean scholar, but he was.

"I needn't have concerned myself. I don't think she ever opened the books, but I know she appreciated the gift. She always appreciated *every* gift, and in this case, she appreciated the giver. And I think she was flattered by my choice of Shakespeare for her."

AFTER JOAN AND young Douglas began seeing each other, she felt Douglas Fairbanks, Sr., didn't like her because, as she told me, "he was cool, aloof, and ignored me no matter how hard I tried."

Fairbanks said, "She didn't understand that it wasn't personal. It had nothing to do with her. My father found her cute, attractive, but he was unhappy because all he cared about was he didn't like the public, his audience, learning that he had a son, me, old enough to get married, even if I was only nineteen, to Joan Crawford.

"Mary [Pickford] was in love with my father. My father was in love with Mary's character on the screen. He liked her girlish innocence.

"She was tiny, but her brain wasn't. She was always thinking. It would be too extreme to say my father never thought, but he wouldn't have minded if anyone said that to him. He was a physical person, a great athlete, and he never feared anything. Well, yes, he did fear one thing—getting old.

"He tried to talk me out of getting married, largely on the grounds of my being too young, which was true, but I didn't think so at the time.

"Billie hoped that we could marry at Pickfair. As far as I know, it was never considered by anyone except Billie. I think it would have been fine with Mary—if it had been fine with her husband. But it wouldn't ever have been fine with my father. Our wedding at Pickfair would have been the very last thing, the very last, my father would have wanted.

"Mary had wanted children, and she was my great friend. She didn't call herself my stepmother, but I think she felt that way and liked it. She was wonderful to me, and she was important in my father's increasing acceptance of me. Yes, she was tiny, but she was not tiny in her influence with my father."

"BILLIE WAS ABSOLUTELY terrified," Fairbanks told me, "that I would find out about a film she had made when she was in a financially desperate moment. When she told me about it, as we began to be *very* involved, she said, 'I have to tell you in case it makes a difference . . .'

"I tried to get as many details from her as possible, especially as to what she wore or didn't wear in the film, and specifically what she *did* in the film, but I only got tears. I've always found a woman's tears a powerful weapon. I could more easily face a duel in a film or a real-life naval battle in World War II. Before a woman's tears, I've always felt helpless and frustrated.

"Billie threw herself on my mercy, which wasn't necessary. She only had to throw herself on *me*.

"She said a blackmailer claimed to have a print of the film. She hadn't ever seen the film, and she didn't remember it well, but she thought it would be embarrassing, not anything she did in the film, but just her being there in it. I told her she was to stop paying the blackmailer immediately, and to tell him that her husband would be meeting him the next time. The next time he called, I took the phone and told him it would be thrash instead of cash.

"That did it. She was never bothered again. She felt I was her hero, and the man was afraid of the beating I would give him. I was happy to be her hero, but my own personal theory is that this was someone who didn't have any film and maybe didn't know for certain that there was a film until he called her. There had been rumors about such a film's existence. It was her reaction that let him know there had been a film, which gave him his power over her.

"She was not just afraid about how I would feel, but she was certain it would finish her relationship with my parents. She was wrong. She couldn't finish her relationship with my father and Mary because she had no relationship with them. I scarcely had one with my father, myself.

"Billie thought that my father looked down on her. Actually, he wasn't paying that much attention to her. If he had been paying attention, he would have found her adorable, but what he would have wished for would be for my marriage to attract as little attention as possible. He liked for me to call him 'Pete.' I never knew why. I just knew that he didn't want me calling him 'Father' or 'Dad.' He'd never liked the name 'Douglas,' and I guess he must have liked the name 'Pete.'

"Billie asked me if there was anything more I wanted to do about the blackmailer. I said, 'Yes. I want to know where can we get a print of the film.'"

JOAN SELECTED A house she wanted to buy. At $40,000, it seemed a little expensive for her, but for Fairbanks it was *much* too expensive. "I was very anxious to carry my full weight," he told me. "And I was very slim. She arranged to buy the house with the help of M-G-M and an advance on her salary.

"The only debt she considered a good debt was owing money to M-G-M when they advanced her money against her future salary to buy her house. She said, 'As long as I owe them money, they can't very well let me go.'

"She said it was the house of her dreams, and it was, and she went forward. She loved the house and stayed with it much longer than she stayed with me. Much longer. The house rose tremendously in value, and at some point, she might not have been able to afford it. I've never had a good sense for money or given it a lot of thought, unless I ran short, but Joan just knew what she wanted. For a while, what she wanted was me. The house had a better resale value.

"I wasn't really *that* happy she'd bought the house without my agreeing or being a part of it, though I didn't tell her that. It made it seem it was *her* house. I liked to think of it as *half* her house." Betty Barker, Joan's secretary for many years, told me that Joan was earning almost $150,000 a year, and her husband about half that. When Barker learned that, she thought, "That kind of thing could mean trouble along the way."

JOAN AND DOUGLAS Fairbanks, Jr., appeared together in *Our Modern Maidens*. The film was released about the time they were married. It followed in the footsteps of *Our Dancing Daughters*, and it also co-starred Anita Page. Again she plays the bad girl and Joan the good girl. In subject matter, the film is even more daring than *Our Dancing Daughters*. Fairbanks had been very pleased to make a film at M-G-M with Billie or, in this case, Joan. She was also pleased.

Our Modern Maidens (1929)

Automotive heiress Billie Brown (Joan Crawford) plans to marry her childhood sweetheart, Gil Jordan (Douglas Fairbanks, Jr.), as soon as he receives his first assignment in the diplomatic corps. To help Gil get the best assignment possible, Billie goes to senior diplomat Glenn Abbot (Rod La Rocque), who is also waiting for an assignment. They are immediately attracted to each other, and in a short time, Billie realizes that while she will always love Gil, she is *in* love with Glenn.

Gil makes a similar discovery when he drunkenly seduces a girl named Kentucky (Anita Page), and she becomes pregnant. Although Gil would now like to marry Kentucky, he feels obligated to marry Billie.

Glenn is assigned to a diplomatic post in South America, and Billie and Gil are married, as planned. Gil decides to be honest and tell Billie about Kentucky. Amicably, Billie suggests an annulment, and then leaves for South America and Glenn.

"She did her makeup beautifully," Fairbanks said. "No one could have done it better. Her eyes, lips, and cheekbones were exaggerated, and she knew how to exaggerate them even more.

"How the camera loved her! How she loved the camera! I could well have been jealous."

FAIRBANKS TOLD ME, "It's difficult to step back into your eighteen-year-old self when you're eighty-ish, back into the beginning of a teen-age romance with a beautiful, talented girl. We danced wonderfully together. We did everything together, wonderfully.

"We were two youngsters over their heads in love. We lived happily ever after—for a while.

"In order to be a star, I think an actress has to be unforgettable, her looks and the way she appears on-screen. Joan Crawford was unforgettable in *every* way. Certainly *I* have never forgotten her."

"I'll tell you something I loved about Douglas," Joan said. "I liked a man who made the earth move. I don't mean only sexually, but in every way. He didn't have to make the earth move for everyone but he had to be able to do it for me. Passion without love isn't really possible, and romance is nice, too. Perhaps I hoped for too much, and then, I expected it to last. It didn't last forever, as I had hoped it would, but while Douglas and I were together, he definitely made the earth move for me.

"I think the greatness of our romance was the heat of our passion, the unbearableness of any separation, be it minutes, hours, or days. It was so thrilling. A part of me searched for that feeling again when it was gone, but I never found it again, or anything close to it. Perhaps an intense love like that has to be experienced when you are very, very young. We both were. You are open to desire. There is nothing like youthful passion. It's something new, you aren't afraid, and you don't hold back.

"Love and passion aside, some people said I was marrying Mary Pickford, Douglas Fairbanks, Sr., and above all, Pickfair.

"It wasn't true.

"It seemed to me that some people might think I was the last person in the world Douglas would know and certainly the last person in the world he might marry.

"I wasn't what Douglas Sr. and Mary had in mind. I worked very hard, but you could tell I wasn't to-the-manor-born."

"One of the memories most painfully seared into my mind," Fairbanks told me, "was one jolly evening at Pickfair when Joan and I noticed an invitingly comfy chaise lounge, quite wide. Since neither of us was wide at all, we decided to save a chair by sharing the chaise lounge during the showing of a film. We thought we were being publicly discreet and privately indiscreet when we used the chair as a love seat, for a good cuddle. Joan called it 'having an oogly-woogly.'

"When the lights came up at the end of the film, neither one of us knew much what it was about nor did we much care. We were in our own world, all rosy glow, and we thought no one had noticed our naughty behavior. We certainly hadn't noticed them, so intent were we on each other and our feelings.

"My father, probably not the only one, had observed the goings-on in which his son was engaged. He was very gracious to everyone at the end of the film and during refreshments. But then, as the guests were leaving, he said he would like to have a word with me *alone* when everyone had gone.

"He had quite a few words with me, in fact. He said that I had disgraced him and myself, the name of Fairbanks, and the reputation of Miss Crawford, whom I had dishonored.

"I refrained from mentioning that I believed Joan had enjoyed the film (we hadn't seen) as much as I had. I was very quiet.

"He let me know that if I behaved like that again, I would not be invited to Pickfair anymore. I was more than properly admonished, and I heeded his hint and never behaved like that again. At his home, that is.

• • •

THE HOLLYWOOD REVUE of 1929 was made very quickly to show-case on sound film M-G-M's stars of that moment, including Norma Shearer, John Gilbert, Jack Benny, Laurel and Hardy, Conrad Nagel, Marie Dressler, Lionel Barrymore, Buster Keaton, William Haines, Cliff Edwards, and Joan.

The Hollywood Revue of 1929

There is no plot, only a stagelike revue. Joan is introduced by Conrad Nagel, and then she does the opener, singing "I've Got a Feeling for You," the first time audiences heard her voice. She follows this with a short, vigorous dance while still singing. She finishes her song, sitting on the piano, not out of breath, while a five-man chorus pushes her and the piano offstage. At the end of the film, she joins the chorus in a slicker for a "Singin' in the Rain" reprise in color.

In 1929, there was no pre-dubbing to allow Joan to lip-sync her song while she danced with such exuberance. She apparently *is* singing while she dances.

The film is best remembered for having introduced "Singin' in the Rain." Betty Comden and Adolph Green told me that this was the picture that inspired their 1952 *Singin' in the Rain*, a satire about Hollywood's transition from silent to sound pictures.

"When I saw that movie as a kid," Green said, "I had no idea that someday Gene [Kelly], Stanley [Donen], Betty [Comden], and I were going to be 'Singin' in the Rain.' I'm sure glad I went to the movies that day."

The silent film made a virtue of necessity by perfecting its own visual language, in the process creating a new art form that was accessible to a worldwide audience. The silent film spoke a universal language. Because the silent film seemed perfect as it was, images accompanied by music without dialogue except for supertitles, many people didn't believe sound would ever replace it.

"Everyone at Metro panicked when it looked like sound was coming," Joan said. "A lot of actors had been living in wishful-thinking-land, saying it was only a whim, a passing fancy, and audiences wouldn't want it and the studios would find it too costly to invest in, and it probably wouldn't work.

"But finally, it was becoming clear that the tide couldn't be held back. The powers-that-be said, 'We have to do talkies.' So, that was it. No discussion. We all had to speak into a microphone.

"The actors who had been on Broadway, or who were British, had more confidence, but I don't think there was anyone who wasn't a little worried, no matter how brave a face they put on. Executives, actors, actresses, I guess everyone was scared about the changes. Everyone except starlets—which is what I still was, at heart—didn't know enough to be afraid. I was a starlet, though maybe a super-starlet, so I didn't know to be afraid.

"I was aware of the atmosphere around me. Pretty tense. There was Wally Beery, and the Barrymores, and John Gilbert. They brought in a man to teach us how to articulate and to speak in a very unnatural way, like we were on the British stage in Victorian times.

"We were told to mod-u-late our pear-shaped tones, and the big thing was not to get too far away from the microphone, which was hidden in a flower vase or a lamp in those days and couldn't move. They told us not to shout at the microphone because it was very sensitive and that would cause distortion, but to talk loud enough because it wasn't *that* sensitive. I started to get frightened. I did something with Bob Montgomery, who was one of the most confident actors, and that helped me to feel less shaky, and I hoped to *sound* less shaky.

"They let me hear my voice, and I said, 'When do I hear *my* voice?' I truly didn't even recognize it. They said, 'That's you.' And I didn't believe them. I thought they were playing a joke on me. I said, 'That's a man.'

"I couldn't believe that was the way I sounded to other people. It was not the way I sounded to myself. I assumed that was what the microphone did to your voice. And certainly sound wasn't the same in that primitive stage as it would later be. But fortunately, they liked the way I sounded. They seemed to like it *very* much. They said I sounded the way I looked, and that was what audiences would want."

• • •

FAIRBANKS TOLD ME that despite a mutual passion for their work, when he and Billie had time together, away from acting, it was spent indulging *different* passions.

"We never gave each other acting advice," he said. "We were just full of mutual admiration. It made it very cozy to have your cheer-leader at home. We each had a pair of rose-colored glasses we wore for the other. We didn't give each other film advice or acting advice, but I did tell her something my father told me, which had very much impressed me and I never forgot. He'd said, 'Feelings are for the silent films, thoughts are for the sound films.' Billie agreed with me that the idea was profound, and she told me later that she was able to apply it in her acting. From this, she said she learned, 'Less can be more,' and she held back. Holding back is very important, because then you have someplace to go."

4

M-G-M Star
(1930–1933)

I LL TELL YOU the way I remember Billie," Fairbanks said.
"Whenever we were in crowds, she would cling to me.

"It made me feel very good. I suppose it made me feel that
she depended on me as her gallant protector. It was the role my father
played in films.

"She was so tiny and clinging to me, she seemed very much in need
of my strength. She had this frightened, worshipful look in her eyes,
and when I held her tightly, she stopped trembling. That's the way I
remember her, clinging to me."

DOUGLAS AND JOAN were married on June 3, 1929, in the chapel of
St. Malachy's Church in New York City. There was difficulty in finding
a church because she had been brought up Catholic and he, Episco-
palian. "St. Malachy's was known as an actor's church because it was
close to the Broadway theaters and attended by many actors and people involved in the theater." Fairbanks's mother, Beth Fairbanks, who
was living in New York, was there with Jack Whiting, whom she would
soon marry. They were the witnesses. A few close friends attended.

Though Fairbanks said it wasn't Joan's dream of an elaborate wedding, he found it "very beautiful, serious," and he enjoyed "the intimate nature of it and the privacy."

"It was a day full of promise, of hopes, of dreams," he said. "I was very impressed and it has remained a beautiful memory all my life, even though it did not all turn out as I believed it would.

"Billie received a telegram from her mother and Hal, and while she had told me that what they said didn't matter to her, I felt that was bravado on her part and that she *did* care. Their good wishes made her quite happy.

"Billie didn't have a birth certificate for some reason. I don't remember exactly why. I thought maybe she didn't want me to see it. She admitted to being born in 1908, so if she had one and didn't want me to see it, it could have been because it would have shown she was born a few years earlier. There was some story about birth certificates not being issued in Texas until 1908. I accepted that. Her mother obligingly wrote a letter for her swearing that she had been born on March 23, 1908. I really didn't care at all. Whatever made her happy. But, of course, she wanted to have it appear there was as little age difference as possible between us.

"I had been born in 1909, but my mother wrote a letter saying it was 1908, which made Billie even happier. Her March 23 birthday and my December 9 birthday meant she was only a few months older than I.

"We thought we had kept our marriage a perfect secret because we had been so careful, but somehow the press got wind of it. Right after the ceremony, my father sent us a marvelous telegram. I was unsure as to what he might say, but there was not a word of rebuke, only happy blessings. I felt a sense of great relief and then of joy. I knew dear Mary was an instigator, but all Mary could do was encourage. Dad was his own man. He would, *could* only do what he, himself, felt. He was an utterly sincere person. I think after that telegram, my relationship with my father improved, or at least I felt it did, which meant I acted on that, and he did, and it was or became true that it was a new relationship. I hope that's clear. For me, that telegram added a rosy note to the occasion.

"Dad was someone I greatly admired as an artist, and as a man, and I wanted to emulate him as much as I could. I knew that we had a physical resemblance. Some people told me we sounded quite a bit alike, which seemed strange, because I hadn't known him well, and even his films were silent. I'd wanted him to be proud of me. I certainly was extraordinarily proud of him. I wanted to have a genuine friendship with him.

"My young bride's dream was to wear the most elaborate Hollywood fairy-tale white gown with a twenty-foot train, and the place she wanted to wear it was Pickfair.

"This was her hope, but not because I ever encouraged her. She *hinted* it to me, and I knew she would have liked to have me pass on those hints to my father. She never asked the direct question, but her hints were increasingly less subtle.

"Unfortunately, her dream would have been my father's worst nightmare, not because of Billie, but because of me. The idea of my being old enough to marry—a sexy movie star, at that . . . Unacceptable.

"Our New York wedding suited him more."

"WE HAD OUR honeymoon before the wedding," Fairbanks told me, many years later, looking back.

"I was really wildly excited on our honeymoon in New York when I took my bride to the hotel, after our marriage. I'd never made love to a bride before. The idea of that sounded very stimulating to me. I imagined hours of glorious passion.

"My first stop was the bedroom. I couldn't get my clothes off fast enough.

"I was down to my shorts and socks. Billie had just entered the room, and she was disrobing. She always had the most wonderful silk underwear, and she looked beautiful in it—and even more beautiful out of it.

"I tore off my socks and tossed them onto the floor.

"Then, I was startled by Billie's voice, which was usually well modulated. I was jarred by the sharp tone of her command:

"PICK UP YOUR SOCKS!'

"The mood of our honeymoon night was changed. I could not get back to the way I felt a moment before.

"I think the earlier mood of our entire courtship actually never returned to our marriage. Our marriage lasted only a few years.

"Maybe the beginning of the end of our marriage began with a pair of socks."

"BILLIE AND I were something alike," Fairbanks told me. "We both were show-offs. But we both had a deep shyness and insecurity which we didn't want anyone to know about, even each other, especially each other. We each got to know only a part of the other person, because we were so shy. Except in bed.

"We wanted to show only our best selves. Actually, they *weren't* our best selves, but they were our interpretations of our best selves.

"I know that for me it was something of a strain trying to be perfect all the time. Billie was more adjusted to it. I don't know how she felt about it, but when we spoke about it years later, it seemed that we both had been trying too hard when what was natural between us was the best part.

"She was always telling stories about everything she did, and she would tell them in an animated way that was reserved for private life, not the screen. She had a lovely speaking voice, especially off-screen in our private world.

"For intimate things, Billie was shy about using words related to sex, and she made up her own language. Making love was 'going to heaven.' I didn't care what we called it.

"In the beginning, I thought it was just funny, but after a few years, it seemed we knew each other well enough for her to be able to say 'breasts,' for example.

"When Joan first referred to her breasts as 'ninny pies,' I *almost* giggled. Fortunately, it was *almost* or our whole romance might have disappeared right then.

"To tell the truth, I've never cared what they were called. What interested me was that hers were beautiful and very sensitive. She was proud of them, and that in itself was stimulating.

"She seemed a bit grown-up for baby talk, but it pleased her. It wasn't as if she was shy about sex, which she wasn't, but I think she found the language of sex embarrassing. Not the act, but the talk of it."

JOAN AND HER new husband were not invited to a formal occasion at Pickfair until after they were married. According to Fairbanks, they were invited because Lord Mountbatten expressed an interest to Sr. in meeting his "ravishing new daughter-in-law." Joan, however, was worried that she wouldn't measure up to Mary Pickford's standards.

"I had the greatest respect for Mary Pickford," Joan told me. "When I first met her, it was difficult for me to accept that she was just a person. I was surprised to find her so small, even smaller than I. I'd always seemed taller than I was. Mary always seemed smaller than she was. I looked older than I was, even as a girl, even as a child. She looked younger than she was, and she emphasized that look because it appealed to her audiences and I think her husband liked her little-girl look.

"Looking back, I think she tried hard to be very nice to me. Friendly, well, maybe that would be too strong. It seemed to me she was uncomfortable with me. She was in her own home and was completely at ease with the greats, of whom she was certainly one. But with me, I felt she was nervous. At the time, I thought it was because she didn't like me, didn't think I was good enough for Douglas, 'the apple of her eye.'

"I told Douglas, who adored her, but he said I was being foolish. It wasn't until years later that I thought about it and decided that *she* was so nervous because *I* was so nervous. When I was with her or in the company of her legendary husband, who awed me, either I wouldn't speak and was tongue-tied, or I talked too much and bored everyone, especially myself.

"Douglas would always tell me I behaved very well and I was lovely, so I felt better. At dinner, I always watched Mary, and I used whichever fork she used. I knew about what silver to use for normal occasions, but they had more forks, knives, and spoons than I had ever seen before, and I'd never used asparagus tongs, and I not only didn't know how to use a marrow knife, I didn't even know what it was *for*. I'm proud to say I learned my dinner party etiquette from Mary Pickford, and I couldn't have had a better role model."

"WHEN DOUGLAS AND I were first in love," Joan said, "my pet name for him was 'Dodo.' Of course, I only said it in private, very private. At the time, he didn't seem to mind. At least, he never registered any objection.

"I don't know how it came to me. I suppose he just looked to me like 'Dodo.' It seemed persons in love should have special, private names for each other.

"Occasionally, it slipped out and I called him that in front of friends. In the beginning of our love affair, I thought he enjoyed my name of endearment for him. I may have been wrong. Looking back, I think he just didn't notice it, or didn't seem to. He was so in love, as was I.

"Later, I remember he asked me not to call him 'Dodo' in front of his father or Mary Pickford. His father called him "J.R." for junior, and he didn't seem to mind that. Larry Olivier called Douglas 'Douggie.'

"He had a sort of an irritated tone when he asked me not to use 'baby talk' in front of other people. I was quite hurt, though I tried not to show it, and I made up my mind *never* under any circumstances to call him 'Dodo,' not even in the confines of our most private world. I have to admit I slipped a few times, but not many.

"Later, it seemed more correct to call him 'Douglas.' I just slipped into it, and he never commented. And then, gradually, I didn't even think of him that way. He didn't seem anymore like *my* 'Dodo.'

"Perhaps it signaled some kind of downhill in at least a certain aspect of our relationship."

Fairbanks told me that her affectionate "Dodo" in reference to him jarred and embarrassed him from the first time she said it to him, but he thought it was "just a passing phrase" and hoped it would go away. It didn't. It made him "cringe" if she said it in front of anyone.

"Even when we were alone," he said, "it made me cringe in front of myself."

● ● ●

Untamed WAS JOAN'S first real sound feature. In it, she not only spoke, but she sang. For the role, she took singing lessons. Fairbanks remembered her having "a lovely singing voice." Critics found her voice and diction "clear and unaffected."

It was her first picture with Robert Montgomery, with whom she would make five more.

Untamed (1929)

Wild, untamed Bingo (Joan Crawford) inherits her father's South American oil wells. She is a millionairess who grew up in the Amazon jungle and is not prepared for modern urban society. Her oil-rigging guardians, Ben (Ernest Torrence) and Howard (Holmes Herbert), decide that her rough edges need some polishing if she is to fit into polite society. They take her from Caracas to New York for a quick course in refined social behavior.

On board the ship, she meets Andy (Robert Montgomery), a young man with all of the polish she seeks, but none of the money. She has no trouble asking him to marry her, but he does not accept, and her lack of social graces is not a factor. He does not want to be a kept husband. Ben and Howard agree that she shouldn't marry him.

In New York, Bingo acts as if she is still in the jungle. Only her great wealth makes her boisterous, uncouth behavior passably acceptable.

Though he is in love with Bingo, Andy continues to resist her advances. Finally, he decides to settle the matter by marrying someone else. This enrages Bingo so much that, before he can marry another woman, she takes a revolver and shoots him. Fortunately for both of them, she is a very bad shot, and the wound is only superficial. Andy understands her jealousy, and he forgives her.

Ben and Howard agree that this passion signifies *true* love. They offer Andy a good job in the oil company so that he can maintain both a wife and his pride, and he accepts.

"When she had to sing a couple of songs for a film," Fairbanks said, "she hit the road, driving a tremendous distance a few times a week to visit a great voice teacher, and she practiced at home. 'Preparation.'

That was a key word in our house. I didn't find it an unpleasant word. The other word she liked was 'discipline.' I can't say I ever fancied that word.

"My own philosophy, if you could call what was unthought-out but came naturally to me a philosophy, was to try only what I knew I could do well, or if I *thought* I might do it well; to give it a chance, but to drop it if it didn't seem to come rather naturally."

FAIRBANKS REMEMBERED ONE day when he was away from Los Angeles for a week and called Joan.

"She was very excited, in a wonderful mood, which came right through the phone. She giggled, and Billie was not a giggly type. On the right occasion, at that time, I might have been more likely, myself, to giggle.

"She told me she had news for me when I came home—*wonderful* news. I was curious, but I couldn't get a word more from her.

"Well, I wondered what it might be. I must say, I did have an idea. I hoped it would be a son, a third Douglas.

"I was very thrilled at first. Then, I thought about it a little more, and I felt some panic. We were really too young. Our life together was just beginning, and it meant a lot of responsibility.

"Well, maybe the news was about a new part she had. I wasn't certain whether she would be more excited about a baby or a good part. My own feelings, I have to admit, were mixed."

When Fairbanks arrived home a bit breathlessly, he expected to hear some news. Joan greeted him, but she didn't say anything special. She didn't say anything about the news.

Finally, he felt compelled to ask her. "'What is your news?'

"She looked puzzled. 'What news?' She went on arranging some papers.

"From time to time, I referred back to her mention of good news, but she never wanted to speak about it.

"I had my own theory, though I would never know for sure. I think she *was* going to tell me that we were going to have a baby. She had sounded so delighted.

"Then, before I got back, I think she lost the baby, a miscarriage, and that's why there was nothing to tell. Or maybe it was a mistake. Or something else. I never knew, but I experienced all the emotions. I know I rather missed that baby who never was. It was sixty years ago, so emotions I had then are hard to describe now. I can only remember the feelings as belonging to someone else, and I was there observing.

"I don't know how we would have felt after the initial happiness, if there had been a baby. I didn't have enough money. She cared so much about her figure, and her career. She said she *would* like children— someday.

"It would have been nice, though, and I think with that bond, we could have made our marriage work.

"I never knew the answer.

"Baby? Maybe."

IN 1930, MUCH of a film based on Vincent Youmans's Broadway musical, *Great Day*, starring Joan, was shot before M-G-M abandoned the project. Joan had been unhappy with her part.

"I had this character with a very strong southern accent. So I went to Mr. Mayer, and I told him in that accent, the worst I could manage, 'Ah jus' cain't talk like this any mo', Mistah May-uh, you-all. And Ah ain't nev-ah gonna be an ingenue. Ah nev-ah was one, and Ah jus' cain't talk this heah kinda dialogue.'

"Then I said, 'I've been shooting for ten days and nobody, not even the director [Harry Pollard], has told me what I'm doing. Mr. Thalberg hasn't seen the rushes. Won't you *please* look at them?'

"That night, I received a call from Miss Kay, Mr. Mayer's secretary. She said, 'Mr. Mayer says stay home. You're right.' So, they put it on the shelf after already spending $280,000, which was quite an expensive film in those days."

Great Day co-starred Joan with Johnny Mack Brown. Adrian was the costume designer. She had worked with him before when she made *Our Modern Maidens*. Some of the footage from *Great Day* was used later in Pollard's *The Prodigal* (1931).

• • •

JOAN'S SUCCESS IN *The Hollywood Revue* and *Untamed* qualified her for better films than *Montana Moon*, but she had already been committed to it before those films opened. The *New York Times* reviewer found Joan's camel's hair coat one of the highlights of the film.

Montana Moon (1930)

Joan Prescott (Joan Crawford), the hedonistic, profligate daughter of a wealthy Montana cattle rancher, spends most of her time in the company of Manhattan's social elite. On one of those rare occasions when she returns home to see her father (Lloyd Ingraham), she becomes restless near the end of the journey and gets off the train at the Montana border, intending to return to New York.

Bored during her wait for the next express train back east, she wanders away from the station and encounters a group of cowboys. One of them, Larry (Johnny Mack Brown), immediately catches Joan's fancy. He is a tall, handsome Texan who has come to Montana in search of work. They fall in love, and Joan stays in Montana.

Her father is overjoyed that his unmanageable daughter has found a down-to-earth man who seems able to tame her wild and willful spirit, and he blesses their marriage. They plan a big party before the wedding.

At the party, Joan dances the tango with Jeff (Ricardo Cortez), a suave Latin type whose appearance alone is enough to offend Larry. As the dance becomes more sensual and suggestive, Larry is infuriated. At the end, when the dancing couple kiss passionately in front of everyone, Larry explodes and hits Jeff, knocking him down.

Joan is humiliated. She cancels the wedding and leaves town. Larry makes no attempt to stop her.

As her train speeds toward New York, Joan has misgivings. She misses Larry, and he misses her, too. He regrets letting her go so easily.

Incredibly, the train is held up by a band of masked cowboys who want only one thing: Joan. As she is carried away on a horse, she recognizes her masked abductor as Larry.

The third *Dancing Daughters*–type film was not about wealthy socialites but struggling department store employees. It struck a responsive chord with sympathetic audiences, and it was a box office success. As in the original film, Harry Beaumont was the director, and Anita Page was a fallen woman.

Our Blushing Brides (1930)

Three shopgirls who work in the same department store dream of escaping the dull monotony of the drab apartment they share. Gerry (Joan Crawford) is a practical girl who rejects what she considers the improper attentions of Tony (Robert Montgomery), one of the store owner's sons, even though she is in love with him. Connie (Anita Page) agrees to an affair with Tony's younger brother, David (Raymond Hackett), but when he leaves her for a debutante, she is so heartbroken that she commits suicide. Franky (Dorothy Sebastian) becomes involved with a con man (John Miljan), who implicates her in a crime. With Gerry's help, however, Franky is able to prove herself innocent and return to her small hometown. That leaves Gerry alone in the flat, but not for long. Tony, realizing that he really loves Gerry, convinces her of his sincerity, and they plan a life together.

Within the Law was a vehicle intended for Norma Shearer, but she announced she was having a baby, and the part was given to Joan. The screenplay was rewritten for her and retitled *Paid*. Playing an inmate in a women's prison, Joan insisted on appropriate makeup, or lack of it, and a hairstyle appropriate to her character.

Paid (1930)

Mary Turner (Joan Crawford) is released from prison after serving a three-year sentence for a crime she did not commit. Prison has only strengthened her belief that those who uphold the law are just as dishonest and corrupt as those who break it.

Unable to find a job, Mary turns to one of her fellow ex-convicts, Agnes (Marie Prevost), who introduces her to Joe Garson (Robert Armstrong), a successful con man always looking for new scams. At the moment, he is considering blackmail, but Mary has a better idea, one that is within the law.

She and Agnes, who are attractive young women, will lure older men with money into infatuations that inspire them to write passionate love letters that can later be used as evidence in breach-of-promise or "heart balm" suits. To avoid public embarrassment, the men will probably choose to settle out of court, and if they don't, no laws have been broken. The scam is successful, though Mary suspects that Garson is cheating her.

She meets Bob Gilder (Kent Douglass), the son of Edward Gilder, the man who was responsible for sending her to prison. When he falls in love with her, she coldly plots a scheme combining her desire for revenge against both Gilder *and* Garson.

She marries Bob and then tells Garson that Bob's father has a famous painting in his possession that is worth hundreds of thousands of dollars. As Garson plots the theft of the painting, Mary alerts the police, who capture the gang in the act of attempting to steal a painting that is non-existent.

Mary recognizes that she is too intelligent to waste her life trying to avenge real or imagined wrongs, or to risk going to prison again in get-rich-quick schemes. She accepts her life as it is, finding satisfaction and happiness she didn't realize was there all the time.

"Every day" Fairbanks told me, "Billie would massage her whole body, especially her face, with ice cubes. Sometimes my masseur would come in and massage her with ice cubes. To tell the truth, it seemed a little foolish to me at the time, but she claimed it was her beauty secret. She said it was great for circulation, and she felt good circulation was the greatest beauty secret. When I knew her, she didn't drink, though she smoked, believing it would help keep her thin. But the ice cubes, those were indispensable.

"She weighed herself at least once a day, which I suppose was not inordinate since her career depended on the maintenance of her magnificent figure. She was the only person I've ever known who did her push-ups, more than I wanted to do, joyfully. I always got bored immediately with exercise for the sake of exercise. I got bored even before I did it. Just the thought of it bored me.

"I could enjoy athletic pursuits, but only for the fun of doing them—tennis, golf, running, walking, dancing. Billie enjoyed the same ones I did, but she was more disciplined. Sometimes I used to wonder if, when we played tennis or went swimming together, she was enjoying it as much as I was, or if it was something of a discipline for her. I even wondered if she ever thought of our sex as good exercise."

DANCE, FOOLS, DANCE is not a musical, though Joan dances. The title refers to the passion for dancing that prevailed during the Roaring Twenties, just before the 1929 stock market crash and the worldwide depression that followed. This was Clark Gable's first important role and his first appearance with Joan, although he isn't the romantic lead. They were to appear together in seven more pictures. In this film, Gable's voice is not yet as distinctive as it would be by the time he played Rhett Butler, and he doesn't yet have his mustache.

"To know Clark," Joan said, "you had to know him B.M., not just A.M. That's 'Before Mustache,' not just 'After Mustache.'"

Dance, Fools, Dance (1931)

Fearing her brother, Roddy (William Bakewell), has become part of a bootleg gang, cub reporter Bonnie Jordan (Joan Crawford) volunteers to cover the follow-up story to the murder of the paper's star reporter, Bert Scranton (Cliff Edwards), while he is investigating a Prohibition-era massacre. Bonnie is a former socialite who, after her father lost all his money in the stock market crash, had to find work.

Posing as a professional dancer, she infiltrates the gang of Jake Luva (Clark Gable), working in one of his speakeasies. Flirting with Luva, she finds out to her horror that her brother was not only involved in the gangland massacre, but was the one who murdered Scranton. Luva finds out who she really is, and he orders her killed. Luva, however, is killed after he shoots her brother.

Bonnie, rather than hiding her brother's guilt in the newspaper story she writes, tells the whole truth. In so doing, she wins the respect, admiration, and love of Bob (Lester Vail), the man who previously rejected her as a silly flapper in the days when she was wealthy and didn't make any contribution to life.

"Imagine being paid for what you love to do," Joan told me. "I was thrilled to be paid to dance, and in a picure with Clark Gable!"

"When I married Douglas," Joan told me, "I married his life. It was very upper-crust.

"We went to all of the best parties. We were invited to parties of studio heads.

"The parties we gave were very social. I didn't want that. It was expected that I not invite the crew people I liked. I had to have separate parties for them because there was a kind of caste system at the top of Hollywood. So, at the A-plus parties, we saw all of the same people over and over." Fairbanks said that they received all of the top party invitations because people wanted to have Joan Crawford at their parties.

"I wondered if some of the people had a very good time," Joan continued. "I know one person who didn't. Me.

"I think Douglas was such a people person," Joan told me, "because he was totally comfortable in himself, so confident, always at ease with any group of friends, no matter how famous they were: stars, royalty, the richest people in the world. He never felt superior to others. Never. And he certainly never felt inferior to anyone.

"I suffered a great deal, not from feelings of inferiority, but from feelings of inadequacy because of lack of experience, education, and association with people who had more sophisticated childhoods. Learning for me meant learning something specific, specifically how to dance.

"We were like children, Douglas and I, although we didn't consider ourselves children, not at all. Our emotions and passions were not those of children, but our brains were younger."

LAUGHING SINNERS WAS originally titled *Complete Surrender* and co-starred Johnny Mack Brown with Joan. Midway during production, Brown was replaced by Clark Gable. Much of the film was reshot, and the title was changed.

Talking about the film, Joan said, "I'm not ashamed. I think it was a step forward in career-building, not exactly a giant step, more of a baby step, but in high heels. One of the great things about this film for me, professionally and personally, was Clark Gable. He wasn't the really famous Gable then, but he had it, 'it' being what makes a star on the screen, and in life, too."

Laughing Sinners (1931)

Ivy Stevens (Joan Crawford), a café singer, is abandoned by her lover, Howard Palmer (Neil Hamilton). Distraught, she contemplates committing suicide by jumping off a bridge but is dissuaded by Carl (Clark Gable), a Salvation Army officer. Carl offers her salvation at the Salvation Army, and soon she becomes an officer herself.

Howard returns to town, and she resumes her affair with him. Carl finds out and breaks into their hotel room, knocking out Howard. He forgives Ivy, and they realize they love each other.

Laughing Sinners was scarcely noticed by the public, but *Billy the Kid*, starring the replaced Johnny Mack Brown, was a huge success.

During this period, both Joan's and Douglas's careers advanced, though not as rapidly as either would have liked. "It was even more true for me than for Billie," Fairbanks said, "but we both observed that a successful play or film did not necessarily produce the breakthrough success of which we eagerly dreamed, which we anticipated.

"You might do something people, critics, everyone proclaimed as brilliant, with which even you were satisfied, and then, after the applause, nothingness. It didn't lead anywhere. Only a postcard in the mailbox, from your maiden great-aunt. No constantly-ringing telephone.

"One of the hardest things an actor has to do is wait. And wait. Especially when you've had a rousing success, you have to enjoy it for itself and in its moment, just in case it isn't the happening that leads anywhere. You never know which will be the stepping-stone."

Joan said, "Douglas didn't really know it, I think, before we married, but he realized—we both did, after we married—that though he hadn't thought about it, he didn't really like his wife working. He absolutely never asked me to *stop* working. If I had told him I was thinking of giving up my career, which I certainly wasn't, I'm sure he would have stopped me. He knew what being in films meant to me. He admired the marriage of his father and Mary, and she worked, but *my* working and his working meant our separation.

"After Douglas and I were together, I cared even more about my career because I had someone I cared so much about that it would be a supreme pleasure to be a shining star for him, and part of his being proud of me, I thought, was having Douglas, Sr., and Mary take note of my advancing career. But sometimes my career, rather than helping our union, got in the way.

"Douglas's energy was very even and steady," Joan recalled. "It made it seem he didn't have so much, but I think he had more than I had because, when needed, he always had more to draw on."

Fairbanks said, "Both Billie and I had tremendous energy in those days, but we each had a different kind. Hers showed all the time. Mine was more held in reserve, more even. I had never before met anyone with more physical energy than she, unless it was my father.

"Personally, I never saw him tired until near the end of his life, when he started getting tired. I never saw Billie tired because I always collapsed first. Maybe she got tired after that. I needed more sleep than she did.

"When she worked, her part and the film had to be the entire focus of her attention. I was expected to be a between-films husband. I have to say, it took me a while to adjust to that. Then, I admit, I adjusted too well.

"I had many interests, mostly with male friends, but after a while, I did have a few dalliances. It was unfair, I know, but I had grown up in a double-standard world. And there's no doubt that the double standard was an advantage, if unfair, for a man.

"This was a problem that I think grew out of marrying so young, having had such limited experience with the opposite sex. I was suffering from a slight case of male curiosity.

"If she had asked me, I would have told her I was faithful in my heart, and that would have been true. I could never have lied to her."

Fairbanks said that he *was* perfectly faithful *before* their marriage, but afterward, he found it more difficult. "I had tried to be discreet, secretive, that is," but her attitude toward him cooled, and only years later did she tell him she knew.

"I had married so young, my wife and I were often separated, and I was in a world where temptation was everywhere. I was in my very early twenties and, I'm ashamed to admit, longing for a bit of experience.

"Apparently Billie got wind of this and was quite ruffled. I don't know if she wanted to get even, or if she was just curious, too. Mine were not relationships, but what is referred to as one-night stands. I don't know why. We certainly weren't standing up.

"She never said a word to me, so I didn't know what she suspected. We both hated negative confrontations, as did my father. We tended to do anything to avoid them, if at all possible—to avoid those words that couldn't ever be taken back.

"There was a young man we both knew from dinner parties, but Billie knew him better than I did. Clark Gable. They had worked together.

"My wife informed me that she needed rest after working on a film. She rented a cottage in Malibu, and she did *not* offer me her address or phone number. So, I *asked* her for her phone number, and she said she preferred to keep it private. I could not understand that by 'private,' she meant private from me.

"When other people heard about her Malibu cottage, I never

admitted I didn't have her telephone number and address. I would have been too embarrassed, mortified. This private Malibu cottage was not the end of our marriage, but it certainly represented a downhill trend."

CLARA BOW WAS scheduled to appear as the lead in *This Modern Age*, but she was replaced by Joan. Unfortunately for Bow, who was only twenty-five, her nasal Brooklyn accent seemed comical, not appropriate to her glamorous "It Girl" silent film image.

This Modern Age (1931)

Wealthy Valentine Winters (Joan Crawford) travels from New York to Paris to visit her mother, Diane (Pauline Frederick), whom she has not seen in years. Since divorcing Valentine's father, Diane has been living in France with André de Graignon (Albert Conti).

In Paris, Valentine meets Tony (Monroe Owsley), a playboy who likes sloe gin and fast cars. One day when he is not suffering from a hangover, he takes her driving. Showing off, he drives too fast, and the car overturns. Unhurt, but stranded, they are picked up by an American driver. His name is Bob (Neil Hamilton), and he is a Harvard varsity football player on vacation in France.

Valentine falls in love with Bob, making Tony jealous. When Valentine is introduced to Bob's ultraconservative parents (Hobart Bosworth and Emma Dunn), Tony appears. They are horrified when he tells them about Valentine's mother and her French lover.

Diane, putting her daughter's happiness ahead of her own, and being tired of Graignon anyway, leaves him. Family respectability restored, Valentine and Bob are free to live happily ever after.

"In *Possessed*," Joan said, "Clark and I were brought together again, and our parts weren't bad either. We had Clarence Brown as our director. He was first-rate, and so were our reviews." The title was also used for a 1947 picture made at Warner's, but the two films have nothing in common except Joan Crawford.

Possessed (1931)

Small-town girl Marian Martin (Joan Crawford), tired of working in a cardboard box factory and seeing no future in her life there with a dull suitor (Wallace Ford), leaves for what she hopes will be a better life in New York City. There she becomes the mistress of Mark Whitney (Clark Gable), a successful lawyer with political aspirations.

He has been unhappily married and has no intention of marrying again. "Losing a sweetheart is a private misfortune," he says. "Losing a wife is a public scandal." Posing as a wealthy widow, Marian is escorted to social functions by Mark, and they travel to Europe together.

When Whitney announces his ambition to run for governor, his true relationship with Marian becomes known. In the scandal that ensues, only Marian stands by him, and he finally realizes his deep love for her.

"In those days," Joan said, "we were able to suggest a lot of sex without showing people actually doing it on-screen. I don't think blatant sex is sexy. It can be funny. A bit of gauze allows you to wonder. I prefer some chiffon to cover female nudity. A nude woman covered by chiffon, that teases, that is *really* sexy.

"I think one of the sexiest scenes I ever did was with Clark Gable. I have to admit it's easier to do an effectively sexy scene with an actor you are attracted to. Clark was the co-star on-screen I was most attracted to in all my years as an actress. I have to admit that I was even more attracted to him off-screen.

"In *Possessed*, we had a scene in which he came up behind me and undid a string of pearls I was wearing. The string of pearls dropped to the floor. Fade to black, and use your imagination.

"Clark was all man. I've been asked many times about him and what it was that was so attractive about him. I can tell you, and I can tell you in one word, if you won't be too shocked:

"Balls!

"Clark Gable had balls.

"There were people who said we were having an affair. Well, they could say what they wanted, but the source of their information wasn't me, and it wasn't Clark. We weren't that kind of people. Our relationship was private, between us, and I never saw any witnesses in the bedroom."

Fairbanks told me, "I learned about Billie's purported affair with Clark from some male friends of mine. They came to me and said, 'We have something to tell you which is for your own good.'

"At the time, I believed them, since they were, I thought, good friends. I believed what they had to tell me really *would* be for my own good, and I listened to them and believed them.

"Whenever people approach me now with, 'This is for your own good,' I run in the opposite direction, as fast as I can.

"These so-called friends asked me if I knew that my wife was having an affair with Clark Gable. No, I didn't. I wasn't her confidant in matters like that. They said everyone knew. I hadn't. I totally believed them.

"I was informed by those very friends that my wife and Gable had begun their affair in *her* dressing room, which was famous at the studio for the privacy and luxury it provided for Joan Crawford.

"It had been my wedding gift to her, which made it worse, and then, as they say, to add insult to injury, I wasn't quite finished paying for it yet.

"It wasn't very long after that we were divorced. Her idea.

"I was quite hurt. It was only many years later that I wondered, how did they know? Maybe they were wrong. . . . Too late now.

"Later, I came to know Clark much better. I liked him. I could see what my wife had seen in him. We were men together—masculine, adult. We enjoyed each other's company without talking a lot. We never, *never* mentioned Billie.

"We certainly were not going to compare notes. I don't even know if he called her Joan or Billie. I would guess Joan. I thought at the time that our behavior was adult, sophisticated, discreet. Well, so it was, if anything really transpired between them.

"I never asked him any questions, and he never volunteered any answers.

"I've wondered in recent years if maybe it was because there was nothing to talk about. Clark and Billie are both gone, and I'm going all too fast toward ninety."

"*GRAND HOTEL* WAS a grand film, a grand experience in my life," Joan told me. "I'm so proud. I was thrilled when I heard I was going to be doing it. I only wanted to be worthy.

"I never made a greater film in all the rest of my career, which was a very long time, even including *Mildred Pierce*.

"That part of Flaemmchen was what I was dreaming of.

"Garbo. I would be in a film with Garbo. With the Barrymores. With Wallace Beery. What actors! And me.

"I have remembered it all my life.

"It was perfect. A great script. Our director, Eddy Goulding, was perfect. And Adrian. Dear Adrian. He was the greatest costume designer of them all. There will never be a greater one. Adrian dressed Garbo and me, and he made sure we were dressed fabulously, but always perfectly in character.

"This is one of the first films, maybe the first, I would choose, if they ever do a retrospective of my work."

Irving Thalberg bought the rights to Vicki Baum's novel, *Menschen im Hotel*, for $13,000 in 1930 and then had it adapted into a stage play that was performed in New York for a short run. Satisfied with the results, he had it adapted for the screen and produced as a film for $700,000, a very high budget for that time. Its enormous success justified the expense. There were glowing reviews, and this was the picture that firmly established Joan as a star.

Grand Hotel (1932)

At the opening, a doctor (Lewis Stone), whose face has been disfigured in the Great War and is a permanent resident of Berlin's Grand Hotel, chants, "People coming, people going. Nothing ever happens."

The Baron von Geigern (John Barrymore) befriends another guest, Kringelein (Lionel Barrymore), a lonely accountant who is dying and wants to spend what remains of his life enjoying luxuries he has never known. The Baron has squandered his own inheritance and survives as a card player and occasional jewel thief.

Available for dictation at the hotel is the young but experienced Flaemmchen (Joan Crawford). She is now working for Kringelein's ex-employer, Preysing (Wallace Beery), a ruthless industrialist who is there to close an important deal.

Another guest is Mme. Grusinskaya (Greta Garbo), a Russian ballet dancer whose career is waning. She has been dancing to half-filled halls and unresponsive audiences, and each night she has to be convinced the theater is sold-out to get her to the performance.

The Baron is interested in Flaemmchen. He would like to take her dancing that evening, but he has other plans—stealing Grusinskaya's jewels. He invites Flaemmchen to an afternoon tea dance the next day, and she accepts.

Flaemmchen returns to her duties with Preysing, and they talk about her wish to become a movie star. She has already posed for some magazine photos, which she shows him, implying that for help in her career, he can expect something more than good typing.

Meanwhile, the Baron is in Grusinskaya's room stealing her jewels when she unexpectedly returns from the theater. As she changes, the Baron watches unobserved from the shadows. Audaciously, he announces his presence.

At first startled, she then intones, "I vant to be alone." The Baron does not leave, but talks to her. She falls in love.

The next morning, the Baron apologetically returns the stolen jewels, but she decides she doesn't really want them. They have brought only bad luck. He may keep them. What she really wants is for him to come to Vienna with her. He agrees to meet her at the train station.

The Baron joins Flaemmchen and Kringelein in the tea salon. She insists on dancing with Kringelein, even though he has never danced before.

Preysing appears in the tea salon, ordering Flaemmchen to

his suite. His deal has fallen through, and he requires her services urgently. Kringelein doesn't like his arrogant, imperious tone, and for the first time in his life, he acts boldly, telling Preysing what he thinks of him. As his bookkeeper for years, he knows all about Preysing's dishonest dealings. Preyshing is about to hit Kringelein when the Baron intercedes.

Kringelein offers the Baron all of his money, but he proudly declines the money. Instead, the Baron hopes to win at cards, and he invites Kringelein to join him and some others in a game.

Kringelein wins everything, and then gets drunk, dropping his wallet. The Baron picks it up, but even though he desperately needs the money, he has become too fond of Kringelein to steal from him.

Preysing must now go to London to seek new backers. He invites Flaemmchen to accompany him, asking her to name her price, and she agrees.

Preysing discovers the Baron in his suite attempting to steal money. In a fight, Preysing kills the Baron, using the telephone as a weapon. Flaemmchen, who is a witness, rushes to Kringelein for help, and he confronts Preysing.

Preysing claims that Flaemmchen and the Baron planned to rob him, and that he only acted in self-defense. Kringelein summons the police, and Preysing is arrested.

Grusinskaya leaves for the station, expecting to meet the Baron. Flaemmchen is left with Kringelein, who wants to take care of her. She cries tears of joy as she realizes she has found her knight-in-shining armor in an unlikely figure. Together, they plan to go to Paris, where, with her help, they hope to find a cure.

Only the disfigured doctor remains, chanting, "Grand Hotel, always the same. People coming, people going. Nothing ever happens."

During the filming of Grand Hotel, Joan noticed that Douglas was visiting the set rather often. She was quite pleased. It made her a little nervous, but that was more than balanced by the pleasure it brought her that he was taking such an interest in her career.

Then she noticed that he was coming at the wrong times, even though she had carefully written down her schedule and given it to him.

It didn't take Joan long to understand that what Douglas wanted was to see Greta Garbo, not easy because Garbo required a closed set.

Even if she and Garbo had no scenes together, Joan was ecstatic to be working with the legendary Swedish actress. She was also nervous.

"At M-G-M," Joan said, "we had to go up a big staircase to get to our dressing rooms, and when we did *Grand Hotel*, I thought, 'Oh, my God! Miss Garbo will have a dressing room near mine!' *Miss* Garbo. That shows you how much I respected her.

"Every morning, I passed her dressing room, and I said, 'Good morning, Miss Garbo,' and she never answered back. I could have gone a shorter way, but I just wanted to say, 'Hello, Miss Garbo,' and curtsy, because of the respect I had for her. Whether she ever looked out the window or not, I'll never know. But one day, I was late on the set, and I ran past her dressing room, and I *didn't* say, 'Good morning, Miss Garbo.' That time, she came out, and she said, 'Allo.'

"Then, late one afternoon, I was standing outside my dressing room, about to go down the stairs, when I saw her coming up. I tried to make myself small because I knew she didn't like to see anybody.

"She came up, and she paused. She was below me. I was on the top step, and I didn't know what to do. I said, 'Excuse me, Miss Garbo.' She reached up and took my face in her hands, and she said, in her Swedish accent, 'Oh, I am so sorry. We have no scenes together. I am so sorry.'

"I looked at this beautiful face, back-lighted by the sun in the west—it was five-thirty in the afternoon at the time—and I was thinking she was the most beautiful thing I had ever seen in my life. Then she screwed up all her features to make a funny face and said something I couldn't understand in Swedish. I think it was Swedish. It was more like a sound than a word. I loved it!"

For *Letty Lynton*, Joan would again be working with one of her favorite directors, Clarence Brown. After this film, he would direct her three more times.

Letty Lynton (1932)

In search of romance and adventure, wealthy New York socialite Letty Lynton (Joan Crawford) takes a cruise to South America, where she has a passionate, but temporary, affair with handsome international playboy Emile Renaul (Nils Asther). Renaul however, feels differently. He wants her to stay with him permanently, so when she breaks off the affair to return to New York, he confronts her with her love letters to him, threatening to make them public if she leaves him. Letty is not intimidated by this threat.

On the return voyage, Letty meets another man, Hale Darrow (Robert Montgomery), with whom she falls in love. Her happiness is short-lived, however. Renaul meets her at the New York pier, having arrived earlier by plane. He remains just as insistent about renewing their affair, and she fears her romance with Hale will end.

Renaul continues to threaten Letty, alarming her mother (May Robson), who dreads a scandal more than she wishes for her daughter's happiness. Throughout all of this, Hale remains understanding.

Half out of her mind with anxiety, Letty accedes to Renaul's demand that she come to his place. She takes with her a vial of poison, intending to take it herself if matters become any worse. The wineglasses get mixed up, and Renaul dies.

Letty is accused of murder, but her mother, finally understanding her daughter's plight, and Hale, continuing to love her, make up an alibi that clears her of all guilt.

Joan's shoulders were much broader than average, and Adrian had the idea not to try to make them smaller but larger. He made extra-large shoulder pads, and the style caught the fancy of women all over. An important new style was born. *Letty Lynton* was one of the most influential films in fashion history.

JOAN APPROACHED *RAIN* with trepidation. For the first time since 1926 she was being loaned out to another studio to work with seasoned stage actors in a part, Sadie Thompson, that had already become closely identified with two other actresses on the screen, Gloria Swanson and Jeanne Eagels.

While Joan struggled with *Rain*, Douglas went yachting with Robert Montgomery and Laurence Olivier. Joan had again told Douglas that she needed to be alone to concentrate on her work.

Rain shot for a month on Catalina Island. When Fairbanks made a surprise visit, Joan was not pleased. She considered his visit "distracting."

Rain (1932)

Passengers aboard a British ship traveling through Samoa find themselves quarantined on the island of Pago Pago because of a cholera epidemic. Because this happens during the monsoon season, the rain beats down relentlessly on the roof of the general store where they have taken shelter.

One of the passengers, Miss Sadie Thompson (Joan Crawford), is a prostitute who doesn't care *where* she is. Pago Pago, with its garrison of American marines, is as good a place as any. She dresses like a trollop and plays suggestive popular songs on her phonograph. One of the marines, Sergeant Tim O'Hara (William Gargan), called "Handsome" by Sadie, falls in love with her and wants to take her to Sydney, Australia.

Two of the other passengers, the Davidsons, are missionaries dedicated to saving the souls of the heathen one of whom is Sadie. Mr. Davidson (Walter Huston) is especially concerned and involves himself in Sadie's case. He not only implores her to renounce Satan and embrace God, but also to return to San Francisco and surrender to the authorities, who want to imprison her for three years on a felony conviction. She insists she was "framed" and wasn't guilty.

In his zeal to "save" her, Davidson has already used the influence of his powerful religious foundation to have her deported to San Francisco. Sadie begs him to let her go with O'Hara to Sydney, but Davidson is as unrelenting as the continuous rain. His distorted logic dictates that she must suffer an unjust punishment by man in order to be redeemed by God.

Finally, his stern, unfeeling refusal and the monotonous incantation of the Lord's Prayer, not to mention the incessant downpour of rain, wears Sadie down to where she will say or accept anything, and she appears to be converted. She dresses more modestly and stops playing her phonograph.

When O'Hara escapes from the brig to take her with him to Australia, she seems a different woman. She declines because Davidson has become her savior.

In the evening, Davidson comes to her, more conciliatory. He says he is satisfied with the sincerity of her conversion but wants to give her the choice of leaving for jail or not. Clearly, *he* has changed, too. For the first time, he looks at Sadie as an attractive woman, a temptation of the devil.

As if in a trance, Sadie declines his offer of clemency, making her even more irresistible. He realizes she is *truly* converted. Smiling in a depraved manner, he follows her into the darkness.

The next morning, the natives find his body in the surf, his throat cut, a suicide, the authorities conclude. From Sadie's quarters comes the sound of the phonograph playing "The St. Louis Blues."

Sadie appears as she had before her "conversion." She is dressed like a trollop again and ready to leave with O'Hara on the ship for Sydney. By her demeanor, it is clear she has been betrayed by the man she believed had "saved" her.

As she passes his covered body on the beach, Sadie encounters Mrs. Davidson (Beulah Bondi), who says she is sorry both for her husband and for Sadie. Sadie replies:

"I feel sorry for everybody—the world, I guess."

"*Rain* was an ordeal for me," Joan said. "At the time, I thought it was my worst performance yet, but now I think I was wrong. Because of my motion picture background, all of those Broadway actors treated me like I really *was* Sadie Thompson. And being in a strange studio where I didn't know anyone made me feel quarantined, just like her. But looking back, I'm proud of my Sadie Thompson."

• • •

"WE COMPLETED OUR cruise," Douglas told me. "I wished it could have been longer. When I got home, Billie had finished *Rain*, and then she had taken a week 'to rest.'

"I asked where she had gone. She didn't answer, then or ever. She may have been annoyed about the yacht trip, though she didn't say anything about it. Our marriage seemed to be continuing on a down-hill course. I thought it could be ending. That wasn't what I wanted.

"One day, she had casually asked me about our having an amicable separation. I was stunned. I was driving her to the studio at the time, and she just said, 'I can't be late,' and got out.

"So I was happily surprised when Billie said, 'There's something I want to ask you about,' and despite my dire premonition, it turned out to be a cheerful question about our delayed honeymoon in Europe. She was always full of surprises.

"I was ecstatic. I had six weeks before my next film assignment, and I instantly began to plan every second, beginning with theater tickets. I probably had friends who could get us tickets for just about anything, and I was anxious to see everything that was happening in the London theater. My interest was professional, looking for parts and studying acting techniques, as well as for personal enjoyment, and I was certain Billie would love the chance to see all of those plays.

"I was exhilarated by the task, and I enjoyed paying the greatest attention to every detail. Billie was exactly the opposite. Whenever I asked her opinion about something, she said, 'Oh, do what you like. Surprise me.'

"I thought that was good-natured of her and that it was because she realized that I knew London and Europe, and it was going to be her first trip abroad. I suppose I should have understood that her lack of response was not really a good sign. I suppose our long-delayed honeymoon had been delayed too long.

"Billie did not like to lie. She preferred not to answer. Usually I accepted her silence as negative and didn't pursue it further. I never liked to argue. It seemed a waste to spend one's energy that way, especially since nothing good ever seemed to come out of it. Usually, it led to people saying things they didn't mean, or worse, that they *did* mean.

"Her interest in seeing the world was less than mine because she was afraid of going away and missing something at M-G-M. I think she feared they might forget her if a good part came along. I think she had found the place of her heart on the M-G-M set and didn't really enjoy going far away from the M-G-M lot. It was as if she thought it might disappear in her absence. Or worse yet, her place there might disappear.

"We had talked many times before about taking a *real* honeymoon, but it had remained only conversation. I had suggested going to England and some cities in Europe. Billie suggested Italy as the country she would most like to visit.

"I asked her why she had chosen Italy. She said she had no reason except that from pictures she had seen, it looked like the most beautiful place in the world, paradise. She said it was her intuition.

"I said, 'But we don't know anyone there.'

"She said, 'That's another reason it sounds so wonderful. We'll be alone together, in a new place, which we can discover together and share. And I wouldn't have to be Joan Crawford all the time.'

"She pointed out that I knew London and Paris, and I would be sharing *my* places, and we would be reliving *my* memories.

"She said, 'Italy would be *our* place. Our *private* place.'

"I heard her, but I didn't pay any attention to her wishes. I was so carried away by my own desire to go back to London and introduce my beautiful bride to all of my friends. I suppose I wanted to show off. I suppose I also wanted to dazzle my wife with my wonderful friends.

"Later, when I went to Italy, I understood how right Billie was to want to go there. It was as beautiful as she imagined it would be. We would have discovered it alone, together. It might have been just what our marriage needed. Joan loved Italy when she went there much later without me. An important part of it for her was not knowing anyone. She loved living life in her parts on the screen, and when she wasn't on the screen, she liked to escape. For me, acting on the screen wasn't real. I wanted to escape into life.

"As I came to know her better, I became aware that wondrous confidence was the part she played, but that she was really a bundle of insecurities. I think I could have done a great deal to reassure her and protect her if I had understood that she needed and wanted reassurance. I wanted and needed reassurance myself. I was young and terribly self-centered. I was so self-centered, I didn't even know I was self-centered.

"My great friend Larry Olivier and his wife, Jill Esmond, were planning a trip to London, and it seemed an inspired idea for us to all go together. Two couples with love in bloom.

"There were a few rough edges showing in our young marriage, but I thought Billie and I would easily smooth them out. I learned, though, that it isn't so easy to smooth out rough edges. If they don't get repaired, they can easily get rougher.

"We had six weeks before Billie started work again, just like me, and six weeks seemed forever. That was enough to refresh our relationship and get the adrenaline going, I was certain, and to top it off, the limelight was going to be all paid for. A little limelight is quite glamorous.

"We were both pleased when we learned that M-G-M would pay for our trip because they saw it as good publicity. It was not only the cost of the trip, which was quite a lot, and everything luxe, but it was also the convenience of having everything arranged.

"Some of the publicity people for M-G-M let it be known that our honeymoon trip was Louis B. Mayer's idea, which couldn't have been further from the facts. Our honeymoon was an idea that belonged entirely to us. Where we were going, London and Paris, the decision of the particular ship, everything was entirely our idea; but when the powers-that-be at M-G-M learned of our trip, Mayer offered to pay for everything, telling Joan it was 'a delayed wedding gift.' It was actually handled by publicity. I must say, they did a perfect job, and the gift needed no explanation. No, indeed.

"We were going by ship, there and back, so six weeks wasn't a lot of time, after all. We ended up going back a little early. Billie had tired of the trip."

"I BELIEVE IF we had gone alone to Europe for a month," Joan told me, "it could have been all different. I was very thrilled. It was my first time out of America. On the ship, we spent just about all our waking time with another couple, Larry and his wife, Jill Esmond. Jill wouldn't have been my choice for a companion. She seemed unfriendly to me. Maybe I seemed unfriendly to her.

"Something we had in common was husbands we had romantic, passionate relationships with. They were two gorgeous men, and to use a phrase I learned from Douglas, they had *savoir faire.*

"Douglas and Larry always knew instinctively exactly the right thing to say and do. They were quite a duo. You could see Jill was in love. I felt she wanted to be alone with her husband. Larry seemed pleased with the way it was.

"The idea that we should travel together was hatched by Douglas and Larry. Looking back, I think they were both men who loved women, but the full-time company of just women didn't seem to satisfy them. They enjoyed the friendship of other men and the physical activity of the deck games on the ship."

"In London," Fairbanks told me, "my wife and I were entertained at parties given by Ivor Novello and Noël Coward, and in Paris, we went to a party in our honor attended by Maurice Chevalier and the fighter Carpentier. It was so different in London. Paris was a mixed bag of people, and you never knew whom you would meet.

"In Hollywood, the guests at any party were so predictable. It depended on whether you were A-list, B-list, C-list, or no-list. The list was determined by your position in the hierarchy—studio head, star, stunt man, grips, and no exceptions, so you always knew who would be there, and if you gave a party, as film people, you were expected to adhere to the code. The higher you were in the order, the more you were expected to conform. It could get rather boring.

"Everything about our trip to London and Paris was perfect. I hoped Billie shared my enthusiasm. I thought she might have found it a little tiring, our own dazzling whirlwind. One day, I asked her if she was enjoying it as much as I was.

"She didn't say anything. That was a bad sign, but this time, I pursued it. I said, 'Aren't you having a good time? Don't you love our trip?'

"She looked directly at me as she answered. 'No, I don't love it.' She paused.

"Then, she said, 'I *hate* it.'

"I couldn't believe it. I knew the word 'hate' was exaggerated, but it was a word I'd never heard her use before. It became clear she really didn't like an experience that I loved. It brought home to me how different we were. I thought that whatever difference there was was exciting, and that with a little time, we would grow closer. But it seemed, rather, we were growing further apart."

"DOUGLAS WAS IN love with me, the real me, underneath the layers of frosting," Joan told me. "He was in love with Billie. He's the only one who really got to know Billie. He knew me before I learned to hide my inner self, Billie, and not to throw my head back when I laughed or to laugh too loudly. He knew me when I was totally open, before I felt on guard, before I had my defenses. We had a relationship of trust. It came to an end, as a marriage, but our friendship could only end with the death of one of us.

"They say sex isn't so important because you can't stay in bed twenty-four hours a day. Well, of course, they're right, but when Douglas and I met, we were at an age when sex was our most persistent thought.

"With Douglas, sex, passion was really a strong point before we married. At that age, sex is a pretty powerful drive. And we loved our careers, which were both on the upswing. I was more dedicated to my career than he was to his, but he had a lot of drive, too. I think if he'd had my kind of drive, he would have been one of the biggest stars of all time, bigger than his father, bigger than me.

"Then, you know, he spent a long time in military service during World War II, giving up what would have been the best years of his career. He was very patriotic.

"When I met his British world of people during our postponed honeymoon, they were very nice to me. There was no one who didn't try to make me feel comfortable, but I didn't feel comfortable. I wish we could have been alone in London, not always with people.

I couldn't ever be Billie. I always had to be Joan Crawford. My husband didn't have that problem because his public person and his private person were the same."

"PERHAPS WE DELAYED our honeymoon too long," Fairbanks said. "It was the only practical thing we did. We put our careers over taking a honeymoon, she more than I, but I, too. We thought we could choose a good time for both of us, if we waited for it. I guess romance isn't like that.

"The impulsive, the foolish, that has a place in life, whatever the price.

"One of the striking changes I noticed in Billie, during the years after we first met and enjoyed our torrid affair and then married, was her laugh.

"When I first knew her, she laughed out loud, freely. She loved to laugh, and she found numerous occasions for laughter.

"As I knew her, her laugh changed more than any other thing about her. It grew softer, more modulated, less spontaneous. It became a finishing-school laugh.

"She was trying for self-improvement in those early days. She didn't want her background to show, and she observed how ladies in society behaved. During our delayed honeymoon in London, she observed the titled ladies. I think she left her boisterous laugh behind her there in London. It may not have been what my mother would have called ladylike, but I missed it.

"I didn't marry Billie because she was a lady, but because she was a woman."

When Douglas Fairbanks and Joan Crawford separated it was her idea.

Joan filed for divorce on May 13, 1933. Fairbanks believed they would get back together again, but they did not.

The divorce became final a year later.

In the years that followed, Mary Pickford occasionally sent a note to Joan. She always signed the note or card, "Love, Mary Pickford."

One Saturday afternoon while they were still together, Joan looked out the front window and saw a teenage girl sitting on the front steps. She was Betty Barker.

"I was just a fan, and I was crazy about Douglas Fairbanks, Jr.," Barker told me recently. "I used to go over to his home when he was married to Joan. I was almost fourteen years old. I went over there and sat on the front steps.

"The first time I went there, I was waiting for Douglas to come home. Since he was married to Joan, I thought Joan was out, too. But she was at home, and she invited me in and talked with me.

"Joan was very, very, very nice to me, and here I was, a fourteen-year-old girl who was so crazy about her husband. She would talk to me. She was actually friendlier to me than Douglas. She was a lady, you know, and she just thought it was funny I was so crazy about Douglas. He didn't want to sit around talking to a little fan, but he was very polite. Joan would be very, very nice to me.

"Then they separated, got a divorce. I was very sorry about that. They were both wonderful people, and they seemed so perfect together. Douglas and Joan were divorced in 1934. I was then fifteen. But Joan was so nice to me that I still went over to the house, maybe like on Saturdays, and just got to know her quite well that way. When I was fifteen or sixteen, and I was in school, I would go over there on Saturday or Sunday. She put me to work. I loved that.

"By that I mean maybe I would address photo mailers for her, little tiny things like that. Or I would rake the lawn for her. Or I would cut roses and do little things around the house. Then, I graduated from high school and went on to junior college, and I would still go over there, though not *every* Saturday, but at least two Saturdays in a month. Maybe I would type envelopes for her. She would put me to work on tiny things, and she paid me. Almost from the very beginning she insisted on paying me. I didn't want to accept money for what I did because I enjoyed it so much.

"It just happened. I would just do anything there was around to do. She was knitting at that time. I'd help her work with the yarn."

• • •

When Joan's marriage to Fairbanks ended, Joan was optimistic, hopeful that her next marriage would be "the perfect meeting of souls," which she had hoped to find with young Fairbanks. The marriage to Douglas did not discourage her. "Quite the contrary," she said. "In fact, it encouraged me. So much of it was so wonderful, ecstatic. It didn't turn me against marriage. Far from it, it made me more certain that marriage could be the ideal state."

Their days of courtship had been everything of which she had ever dreamed. She had "a great deal of happiness to remember, ecstasy." She told me she attributed the failure of the marriage to their extreme youth and that "we were just finding ourselves, so it was difficult to find each other."

She had believed that if everything was "right" between two people, "there would be no adjusting, no compromise."

She believed that if she had met Fairbanks later, she would have been "a grown-up," and their marriage would have lasted. "When we divorced, I thought he was a great person, but that we weren't going to make each other happy over a lifetime. It might have been. I really didn't know much about life yet.

"Douglas was very understanding about my fierce drive and ambition for my career. He gave me free rein. He didn't make any demands at all.

"I admit now that I was less understanding when it came to his spending time with his men friends doing things men do. I was worried that the things men *do* is look at other women—and more. I was quite possessive. If the price of ecstasy was agony, I was more in search of peace.

"I was extremely confident of my own attractiveness, so I didn't feel it would be easy for Douglas to find another Joan Crawford. Of course, there was the chance he might not be looking for another Joan Crawford, that he might be looking for some variety. I knew that men were more that way than women were, liking variety.

"I've wondered all these years, what was it that went wrong for Douglas and me? We were so in love. I don't think I ever really stopped loving him. He was really the first man in my life who counted, not just because he was my first husband. Not that I hadn't known other men and liked them, but Douglas was a high I'd never known. I couldn't have imagined that anyone like that existed.

"Perhaps it actually was because the highs in our relationship were so high that if they weren't *always* that high, it seemed that something had gone wrong.

"When Douglas married me," Joan told me, "he married a chorus girl, and I tried as hard as I could to make him proud of me by doing everything I could to become a lady. I felt I was a lady on the inside, but I lacked the outside polish and finish of the women in Douglas's world. I wanted Douglas to be proud of me. I never wanted him to feel ashamed of me.

"I read boring books I didn't understand. I toned down my private wardrobe. I stopped wearing some of my favorite clothes. I studied French. I learned which forks and knives to use by watching Mary at Pickfair. I minded my Ps and Qs, and I became a 'high etiquette' specialist.

"Douglas never said he wanted me to change, and he never commented on my efforts. I thought he didn't notice, but I guess he did. He never liked to express negative criticism, but I think now he really didn't want me to change. He married a chorus girl, and I think that's what he liked.

"I think he'd seen enough of the other kind, and didn't think it would make him as happy as we were in our early days.

"I think he missed his chorus girl."

"I WAS QUIET when she studied lines," Fairbanks recalled. "She was quiet when I studied lines. We understood each other's work and needs, and we loved our work. In the early days, that seemed like something very important.

"Every man who met Joan Crawford fell in love with her. Couldn't help it. She seemed oblivious to it, but now I realize she was well aware of it.

"I've had time, decades, to give some thought to why our marriage failed. I suppose if I were to say why our marriage failed, I'd have to say, it just wasn't meant to be.

"I've had a lot of experience, but I still can't say I've ever known anyone like her. She was what might be called tempestuous. I called it artistic temperament."

"WHILE I WAS married to Doug," Joan remembered, "I was married to the most socially graceful man who ever lived, whether he was with men or women. There never was a man more graceful and at ease. He had a reserved and refined manner, but he was the most genuinely social person I've ever known. He loved people and being with them. He was a social athlete. Tireless. He was a wonderful dancer. His lead was gentle, but firm, and I felt I never danced better than when I danced with him. He made me feel I was the most graceful woman in the world.

"He had so many friends. They weren't people I would have known or who would have known me, I thought, but they accepted me in their circles. I was pleased to feel that acceptance.

"It was a great shock after our divorce when I found out that all of his friends had also divorced me. Not a phone call.

"Early, I liked to be called Billie by my closest friends. Later, I understood that the part of my life I loved the most was lived by Joan Crawford.

"When I was very young, I thought my life was about finding love and happiness in my personal life. I found love and happiness, but it didn't last. My first marriage produced everything anyone could want, but it didn't last long enough. It had been so great, I couldn't bear living in the shambles of it.

"My friendship with Douglas survived our marriage. We have never lost touch, and I know if I ever needed a friend in life, I could turn to him. Many years have passed, and I have never met a more generous spirit.

"There were people who, behind our backs, whispered that I 'married up.' Our marriage, Douglas and me, was a marriage of equals, born of true love. I know it shouldn't have mattered to me what other people thought, but it did. What people think of me has always mattered to me, perhaps too much.

"I know now what I didn't completely understand then. I loved my career more than I ever loved any man, even dear Douglas. Maybe Douglas sensed that, and it came between us, even though I hadn't yet articulated that thought, even in my own mind."

5

M-G-M Superstar
(1934–1944)

URING HER RELATIONSHIP with Fairbanks, Joan had advanced from promising starlet to established dramatic actress. She had become one of the biggest stars in Hollywood, whose status now demanded the best parts in the best movies M-G-M could make. The problem was scripts. M-G-M couldn't find any that were suitable for her. Without success, they had even assigned F. Scott Fitzgerald to write a film for her. Soon, the studio simply had to put her to work or lose money. That was why director Howard Hawks cast her in *Today We Live*.

"I had to use Crawford in a picture I was making," he said, "even though there was no part in it for her. It was based on one of [William] Faulkner's World War I short stories. Nothing about the Deep South, or anything like that. He was a pilot in that war, you know.

"Well, anyway, Metro said we've got to put Crawford to work or it's going to cost us a pretty penny, and I said, but not with this Faulkner story. There aren't any women in it. 'Well, put one in,' they said. 'You've got Faulkner working on the script, don't you?'

"So, I called Faulkner, and he thought it was all pretty funny, but he said, 'Okay, we'll give them an ambulance driver or nurse or something.' Metro wanted Joan Crawford. They didn't even care that much about Gary Cooper, because at that time, he and the other guys, Bob Young and Franchot Tone, were relative newcomers. But Crawford, she was like Garbo.

"When I told Joan about the picture, she was pretty unhappy. She said it was the English accent that terrified her. I told her not to worry. All she had to do was sound as English as her ex-husband, Douglas Fairbanks, Jr., and that made her laugh.

"She was a smart gal. She was a personality actress, you know, which you only get to be if you're lucky."

Today We Live (1933)

In England during World War I, wealthy Diana Boyce-Smith (Joan Crawford) believes herself to be in love with Claude (Robert Young), a British naval officer. Her feelings, however, quickly change when she meets Bogard (Gary Cooper), an American fighter pilot, and falls in love with him.

Bogard is reported killed in action, and Diana goes back to Claude. Ronnie (Franchot Tone), a fellow naval officer and Diana's brother, tells her she is being unfair to his best friend by not being honest with him about her real feelings toward Bogard.

When Bogard returns unhurt, a rivalry springs up between the two men for Diana's affections. At first, it takes shape as a friendly dispute over which branch of the service is the more daring, the navy or the air force. Bogard takes Claude and Ronnie on a flight full of dangerous stunts. Then they take Bogard on a perilous ride in their motor launch equipped with a single torpedo. The men agree that both branches of the service are equally dangerous.

When Claude returns from a naval battle blinded, Diana faces a dilemma. She feels an obligation toward Claude, but loves Bogard. Bogard solves her dilemma by volunteering for a virtual suicide mission, bombing a nearby enemy ship. Claude and Ronnie take their motor launch and beat him to the German vessel, destroying it with their single torpedo, but they are killed in the explosion.

Diana and Bogard are now free to follow their love, but with lingering sadness.

"Today We Live," Joan quipped, "became 'Today We Love' and 'Tonight We Love,' too. The picture itself wasn't a highlight of my

career, but it was a highlight in my life, for a while, because of Franchot."

Joan was impressed by the way Franchot Tone looked and the way he was. She thought his looks "sensitive" and "aristocratic," and that "he knew about everything."

Tone found her different from what he expected. He was quite taken with her looks, but what surprised him was her intelligence.

"She was more ladylike, sophisticated, and cultured than he expected," publicist John Springer, who knew Tone, told me.

Joan invited Tone to her home to have tea. The teapot was highly ornate Victorian English silver. It was as close as Joan could find in a local antiques shop to the one that Mary Pickford had used at Pickfair. She had practiced alone, so that she would know how to use the heavy pot gracefully, and she poured the cold milk from the matching silver milk pitcher into the cups before pouring the tea, just as Mary had done.

FRANCHOT TONE WAS born in Niagara Falls, New York, on February 27, 1905. His full name was Stanislas Pascal Franchot Tone. His father was the president of the Carborundum Corporation, and the family was prosperous and socially prominent in the community.

After primary and secondary education in private schools, Tone entered Cornell University in 1923. Active in the university theater, he was elected president of the Dramatics Club in his junior year. Graduating in 1927, he sailed for France and lived in Paris for a few months in order to practice his French. He then enrolled for courses at the University of Rennes.

Returning to the United States in 1928, he went to work as the stage manager and stand-in for a stock company theater in Buffalo, New York. One of his stand-in performances was seen by a Broadway director, who arranged for an audition with the New Playwrights Theatre in New York City, where he was offered a three-year contract to do small parts. He was certain the opportunities to do bigger parts would come his way, and that he would be up to it. His first major part was in a stage adaptation of Edith Wharton's novel *The Age of Innocence*, directed by Guthrie McClintic and starring McClintic's wife, Katharine Cornell.

It was at the Group Theatre, which Tone helped found, that he was approached by an M-G-M talent scout, who offered him a screen test. At first skeptical, Tone took the test and was offered a five-year contract. Though he didn't believe films were his future, Tone decided to try Hollywood until he tired of it, donating what was left over after his living expenses to the Group Theatre.

In Hollywood, one of his earliest successes was with Jean Harlow in *Bombshell*. In this film, he played the opposite of himself in life, an actor pretending to be the son of a millionaire. With *Bombshell*, Tone became a Hollywood star.

After the divorce from Fairbanks, Joan said she didn't plan to marry again for a long time, and *not* an actor. "Emotional involvement is tiring, draining," she said. "I knew I didn't want to be *that* emotionally involved, at least not for a *very* long time.

"With Franchot, if it wasn't love at first sight, it was *like-a-lot* at first sight. Franchot told me *he* fell in love with me at first sight."

As Fairbanks had before him, Tone encouraged Joan to expand her cultural and intellectual horizons. "Franchot was intelligent and considerate," Joan said, "and he loved the theater. He had a sophisticated background, and I appreciated a man who stimulated my mind. He introduced me to literature, music, art I didn't even know existed."

He also encouraged her to consider the stage, which Joan rejected because a live audience so terrified her. Then he suggested radio, which was at that time live, but less demanding. She was finally coaxed into performing on the air with Bing Crosby and on the *Lux Radio Theatre* in an adaptation of *Paid*. Joan found that she liked the radio medium, and continued to make guest appearances. Joan's performance in *Baby*, a 1940 Arch Oboler radio drama, is memorable. A woman is told by a doctor she is pregnant. Her reaction is apprehensive, because she doesn't know how her husband will receive the news. As she walks home from the doctor's office, she anticipates in her mind all of his possible adverse reactions. With each step, a menacing chorus of women chant, "Ba-by, ba-by, ba-by." At the end, the one possibility she hasn't considered happens. He is thrilled.

Joan loved the script. Since the program couldn't afford the $5,000 she customarily received for a radio appearance, she worked for scale.

Writer-director Oboler, sensing Joan's nervousness, allowed her to take off her shoes and perform barefoot. Joan's stage fright possibly enhanced her portrayal of a frightened, confused woman.

JOAN APPEARED AGAIN with Tone in *Dancing Lady*. This film was produced by Louis B. Mayer's son-in-law, David Selznick. He had married Mayer's younger daughter, Irene, in 1930. In addition to Clark Gable, Fred Astaire is also in the cast. It's one of Astaire's first important film appearances, just before his breakthrough role in *Flying Down to Rio*. Comedian Ted Healy appeared with "his Three Stooges," and Gable played straight man to Larry, Moe, and Curly. Joan danced with Astaire. She had only just recovered from a broken ankle.

Dancing Lady (1933)

When millionaire producer Tod Newton (Franchot Tone) offers burlesque dancer Janie (Joan Crawford) a part in his upcoming Broadway musical, it seems a dream come true for her, except there are strings attached. Janie, her virtue still intact, declines. Newton, truly in love, raises the ante. He will give her the part, with no implied commitments, except that if the show fails, she has to marry him. Confident the show will be a hit, she accepts. Newton then sets about sabotaging his own show.

The director, Patch Gallagher (Clark Gable), believes in the show, but not in Janie. He feels that she has been foisted upon him by a lecherous producer, but as they work together, she dispels all doubts. She quickly becomes the true star of the show.

Meanwhile, Newton works against the success of the show in every way he can; but with Janie's charisma, and the help of such diverse talents as Fred Astaire and the Three Stooges, Patch directs a hit.

Realizing Janie and Patch were meant for each other, Newton departs.

One week after *Dancing Lady* began filming, an exhausted Gable collapsed on the set. "It was terrifying," Joan remembered. He was rushed by ambulance to the hospital, but soon returned to work.

THERE IS A scene in *What Ever Happened to Baby Jane?* in which crippled, wheelchair-bound Blanche Hudson (Joan Crawford) is intently watching a television program starring herself, twenty-five years younger and dressed in a costume designed to show off her beautiful legs. The film being rerun is *Sadie McKee*, and Joan really is watching her younger self.

Sadie McKee (1934)

Michael (Franchot Tone) is in love with the family maid, Sadie McKee (Joan Crawford), but she loves Tommy (Gene Raymond), an unskilled worker in the factory Michael's family owns. When Tommy is fired, Sadie blames Michael. Michael spoke against Tommy because of jealousy, but Tommy deserved to be fired.

Sadie quits her job as a maid and goes to New York with Tommy, who has big plans, including marriage. He stands her up at city hall for another girl, a vaudeville performer named Dolly (Esther Ralston), who offers him more glamorous opportunities.

Through a new friend, Opal (Jean Dixon), Sadie gets a job as a social hostess in a nightclub. There, she meets alcoholic middle-aged millionaire Jack Brennan (Edward Arnold). She doesn't love Brennan, but when he proposes, she accepts. Though his drinking makes married life with him difficult, Sadie adjusts, and they become fond of each other, though she can't forget Tommy.

Tommy comes back into her life again when she sees him onstage with Dolly. Show business hasn't been what he hoped it would be, and he wants to be back with Sadie. She wants him, too, but she can't hurt Jack. Shortly afterward, Sadie learns Tommy has died.

Michael happens to meet Sadie in New York, and this time they fall in love. Understanding she is trapped in a loveless, if amicable,

> marriage, he suggests that she get a divorce, and *he* will marry her.
> She could never do that to Jack.
>
> With her help, Jack overcomes his dependency on alcohol, and
> Sadie tells him of Michael's offer. Not wishing to stand in the way
> of her happiness, he agrees to a divorce.

Franchot Tone was very excited about a play that would soon be
opening at the Group Theatre in New York. It was Sidney Kingsley's
Men in White, and Tone had invested in it. He considered Kingsley
a genius and the play a socially-conscious, responsible drama. He
yearned to be part of that kind of theater.

He wanted to go to New York to see the production—with Joan.
She resisted making a trip with him because of the press. He encouraged her, telling her that it was something they had to do, and that
they could avoid the press. She was still worried about their being seen
traveling together and about what might be written.

"We'll travel together, but we *won't* travel together," she said he
told her. "You will get on the train with all the fanfare. The press will be
told that you are going to New York, and they will see you off. Meanwhile, I'll sneak on the train, slightly disguised, and I'll hide until the
train leaves. Then, we'll be together on the train, where there won't be
any press, until we're about to pull into Grand Central. You will step
off alone, be photographed, and I'll sneak off."

Joan agreed. She had the largest reception of press and fans, including her fan club, that she had ever had, and she glowingly answered
their questions. The question most asked was, did she plan to marry
Franchot Tone? Her answer was very well received by the audience,
and by Tone, himself, who exited unnoticed from the coach section.

"She said, "Time will tell." It did.

"CLARENCE BROWN WAS a fine, fine director, and I liked him," Joan
said. "He knew what he wanted, but he liked to let us find our own
way, and then he'd make suggestions. The only problem any of us had
with him on *Chained* was how softly he spoke.

"I have always had very good hearing, but sometimes even I missed what he was saying. And Clark! Poor Clark. He couldn't hear him at all.

"We were supposed to stay on our marks, but he was back there behind the camera, and we couldn't hear what he was saying. He was a real hearing test, I have to say.

"Clark would go up to Mr. Brown and say, 'What did you say?' Or he'd turn to me and ask, 'What did he say?'

"During *Chained*, I remember Clark coming over to me, looking a little desperate. He'd had to step out of the lights in order to hear what our director had just said.

"Clark whispered, 'Did *you* hear what he said?' I said no, I didn't hear a word. That seemed to make Clark very happy. He grinned that wonderful grin of his and whispered, 'Thank God! I thought I'd gone deaf.'"

Chained (1934)

Diane Lovering (Joan Crawford) is having an affair with a wealthy older married man, Richard Field (Otto Kruger), who wants to marry her, but he cannot. His wife (Marjorie Gateson) won't give him a divorce.

To sort things out, Diane takes a cruise to South America and on the ship she meets young, virile Mike Bradley (Clark Gable). They are instantly attracted to each other, but Diane resists her feelings because of Richard, who is back in New York awaiting her return. Finally, they do admit their love for each other and enjoy a shipboard romance until Diane has to return to Richard in New York.

There, she is surprised to learn that Richard's wife has finally agreed to a divorce, and Richard and Diane can now marry. Mike, however, continues to pursue Diane, and he wins her when Richard realizes that he would be standing in the way of her happiness if he didn't release her from her commitment to him.

In 1934, during the filming of *Chained*, Joan met her birth father for the first and last time.

A man in Waco, Texas, wrote to her claiming to be her father. It wasn't the first time that this had happened. After she became famous and apparently rich, she received several letters from people claiming to be relatives, even "fathers." She wrote back to the man from Waco and asked for a photograph. It was sent, and Joan showed it to her mother, who confirmed the identity of the husband who had deserted her in her youth, leaving her to support their two children. Joan wondered if her mother would mind if she met this father who hadn't been heard from until Joan was a movie star. Her mother had no objection.

It was Joan's brother, Hal, who called Joan one day at the studio and said that their father had arrived in Los Angeles. Hal brought him onto the set of *Chained*, which was for Joan the worst and most intrusive place he could have possibly come into her life. It was just like Hal to want to show off Joan at her expense, she felt.

"I met him only out of curiosity," Joan told me. "I had no desire to show my success to him. He had never been part of my life, and I had never been extremely curious about him or given him much thought. I didn't wish to be rude.

"My brother came toward me with this older man, who looked strangely familiar. I think it was his eyes. He was dressed neatly, but in clothes that had been to the dry cleaner too often. He and they looked faded. He smiled nervously and extended his right hand. It was shaking.

"I had planned to avoid contact if he tried to kiss me, but I couldn't stop myself from taking that hand and squeezing it tightly.

"We sat down during a break in shooting and spoke awkwardly. I had been prepared to hate this tall stranger for what he had done to my mother, more than for what he had done to me. But I found myself pitying him for what I felt he had missed. It was like a scene from a film I never made, but lived.

"I think he wanted to tell me something, but he couldn't get it out. He was shy, as I had been, as I still was, inside. It was probably that he was going to say he was sorry, but that wasn't worth much at this point.

"A few days later, the day he left Los Angeles, he came back to the set, alone. I was busy with the director, but I saw him out of the corner of my eye. He waved to me. He blew me a kiss. Then he left. I think there was a tear in his eye. There was in mine.

"I never heard from him again. In my twenties, my need for a father was not the same as when I was a baby named Lucille and Daddy Cassin filled a little girl's need."

FORSAKING ALL OTHERS was adapted from a Broadway success starring Tallulah Bankhead. It was the first of many Joan Crawford pictures produced and, later, directed by Joseph L. Mankiewicz. "Joe did a lot of the writing, too," Joan said, "but sometimes he didn't take credit." I asked Mankiewicz about this and he said, "I don't remember, but usually when I didn't take credit, it was because I didn't want to take the blame."

Mankiewicz had been impressed by Joan on his first visit to her home. "She was sitting at her writing desk like a lady of the nineteenth century. She had been writing notes on thin, monogrammed blue paper. She looked like the true movie star, and I complimented her on her lovely dress.

"She said, 'It's one of my dresses for writing letters,' and she wasn't joking. She hadn't known I would be coming by to leave some material. I had expected to leave it for her with the maid, so she hadn't dressed up so beautifully for me. She had dressed like that for herself.

"She invited me for lunch. She took off her sleeve guards and said she was going to change for lunch. I said, 'It's not necessary. The dress you're wearing is beautiful.'

"She said, 'I know, but it's one of the dresses I wear for doing my correspondence. I'm going to change to one of my eating-lunch-at-home afternoon dresses.'

"When she returned, she had changed to another lovely dress, a beautiful shade of pale green. She had also changed her accessories and was wearing matching shoes with very high heels with ankle straps, and several green Bakelite bracelets. I felt I should be very flattered, but she said, 'This is what I was planning to wear, but I thought I'd be having lunch alone.'

"Joan Crawford was a real star, and she always played her part, even when she was asleep, I'm certain, even though I never had that experience with her.

"I did, however, make many films with her."

George Folsey, who shared cinematography credit with Gregg Toland, became Joan's favorite cinematographer. Folsey, she believed, was the first cinematographer to understand exactly how to light her face and give it that distinctive "Joan Crawford look." He worked on eight of her films, starting with *Chained*.

Forsaking All Others (1934)

Mary (Joan Crawford), Jeff (Clark Gable), and Dill (Robert Montgomery) have been close friends since childhood. Mary likes Jeff, but she loves Dill. While Jeff is vacationing in Europe, Mary and Dill decide to get married. Jeff is heartbroken to learn this when he returns, but he is a good sport about it.

Dill, who is undependable, stands up Mary at the altar, going off instead with his mistress, Connie (Frances Drake). Jeff steps in to console Mary, and she thinks that now she is falling in love with him. Then Dill returns, tired of Connie. He has changed his mind and wants to marry Mary, after all. Mary thinks she wants him back, and they plan another wedding.

Suddenly, Mary comes to the realization that it is Jeff she has loved all along. She tells Dill, who does not mind, and cheerfully sees them off on a European cruise.

When director Edward H. Griffith fell ill while making *No More Ladies*, George Cukor was called in to complete the film, uncredited. Joan had never worked with Cukor before.

"The director who, hands down, helped me the most was George Cukor," Joan told me. "He didn't just help me to do better in the films he directed me in, but he helped me to be *me*. His words stayed with me always, so he was actually directing me later when I did films with lesser directors, and everyone was a lesser director compared to Mr. Cukor. I heard his words in my head, even words he never said, but which I *thought* he would have said. It was as if I could hear not only his words, but his thoughts. He had a profound effect on me. If I could have selected a man to be my father, he would have been George Cukor."

I was with George Cukor while he was filming *Rich and Famous* in New York City. One day, after he shot a scene at Cartier's on Fifth Avenue, we went down to New York University, where he was guest director for a graduate class in acting.

As he directed some student actors in scenes, his most frequent criticism was that the actors were not listening to each other. He considered listening to the other actors' lines as important as speaking your own lines. I noticed that he listened intently to every word that was spoken by the actors, and he seemed to be drawing the performance he wanted out of them by the sheer will of his concentration. When he liked something, he registered unmistakable approval, and his enthusiasm inspired the students to do even better. I could understand Katharine Hepburn, Joan Crawford, and all of the other actors wanting to win this approval.

No More Ladies (1935)

When it comes to love, Marcia (Joan Crawford) believes it should be with one person, forever. Such "old-fashioned values" are not prevalent among the idle rich, so Marcia ought to be grateful when she finally finds such intensity of feeling in Jim (Franchot Tone). She isn't. She chooses Sherry (Robert Montgomery), who is a womanizer, believing that she will cure him of his need for variety in love.

She doesn't. Even marriage can't satisfy Sherry's appetite for women in the plural. Marcia resorts to drastic measures.

She gives a party to which some of Sherry's romantic victims—deceived husbands and jilted boyfriends as well as ex-girlfriends—are invited. Then she announces that she is going off to have an illicit affair with Jim, who is still willing and waiting.

True to her nature, however, she cannot consummate her proposed affair with Jim, and she goes back to Sherry, who is contrite and has, perhaps, learned his lesson, at least for the time being.

In spite of a fine cast, costumes by Adrian, cinematography by Oliver T. Marsh, George Cukor directing, and Irving Thalberg producing, *No More Ladies* wasn't successful.

Joseph Mankiewicz wrote the screenplay for *I Live My Life*, as he had for *Forsaking All Others*. "I liked writing Joan Crawford pictures," he told me. "She brought so much back-character to the screen that you hardly had to establish her. She just fit right into the story without having to explain why."

I Live My Life (1935)

Bored with a life of endless parties, polo matches, and fashionable charities, wealthy Kay (Joan Crawford) leaves the New York social scene to look for more enduring values. She chooses a Greek holiday. In Greece, she meets the man she is looking for in the person of a handsome young archaeologist. He challenges all of the values she herself is beginning to question. His name is Terry (Brian Aherne), and he is sufficiently enamored of her that he accompanies her back to America.

Terry fits into the New York social scene in a peculiar way. Although he questions all the values of the people in her world, sometimes rudely, he is accepted as an eccentric and even nicknamed "Quaint." Predictably, Kay sets out to change him, but it doesn't work. He is the one who changes *her*, but when they finally do agree to marry, she can't go through with it.

To help her save face, he agrees to appear at the church on their planned wedding day and to allow her to jilt him. At the last moment, however, Kay does appear, and they are married. It is hoped that a happy compromise between New York café society and his Thracian archeological digs will take place.

At this time, Franchot Tone was working with Bette Davis at Warner's on *Dangerous*. The Davis-Crawford rivalry may have started during that film when Bette was attracted to Tone, and then learned he was already involved with Joan. Bette lost Franchot, but won Oscar.

• • •

THE GORGEOUS HUSSY is based on episodes in the life of Margaret O'Neill (1799–1879), an early advocate of women's rights. Her name is spelled O'Neal in this film.

The Gorgeous Hussy (1936)

President Andrew Jackson (Lionel Barrymore) has come to know Peggy O'Neal (Joan Crawford) through his visits to the inn of her father, Major O'Neal (Gene Lockhart). Jackson is impressed by her intelligence, charm, and outspoken ideas on the subject of women's suffrage, and finds her a wise advisor. Soon, she is a regular guest at White House social affairs, an outrage for those who look down on her as an innkeeper's daughter. Since she is beautiful as well as intelligent and charming, she also has many male admirers.

She is not shy. When she lets John Randolph (Melvyn Douglas) know she would not be averse to being his wife, he rejects her. Later, he becomes a senator. Naval Lieutenant "Bow" Timberlake (Robert Taylor) is more receptive, and they marry. After Timberlake is killed in action, she meets John Eaton (Franchot Tone). Their marriage is a happy one. He becomes a cabinet member.

Peggy is now an influential unofficial figure in Washington, and many are jealous of her. They start to spread rumors impugning her loyalty to the Union. States' rights advocates have already begun agitating for independence from the Union.

The president is outraged at her treatment and begins an investigation, but Peggy begs him to stop. She does not wish to cause him any problems, so she takes leave of Washington. Andrew Jackson and those who knew her, however, can never forget the breath of fresh air she brought into the White House.

After *The Gorgeous Hussy*, Joan and Franchot went to New York City for a few days. He introduced Joan to his friends, among them Alfred Lunt and Lynn Fontanne. Joan was impressed by the renowned theater couple, whose marriage had lasted many years. "If Lunt and Fontanne can be successful acting together, why not Tone and Crawford?" Joan said. A marriage that was also a professional relationship appealed to her.

Tone proposed and Joan accepted.

On October 11, 1935, Joan and Franchot married secretly at the mayor's residence in Fort Lee, New Jersey. Afterward, they were met by the press and photographers at the Stork Club in Manhattan, where the couple was having a private dinner party.

A photographer asked Joan when Tone and she were getting married.

"It won't be in the near future." Joan answered. "That was true," Joan told me, "because we had been married in the near *past*.

"I had resigned myself to never having the fairy-tale Pickfair-type wedding I had dreamed of. It wasn't in the stars for me, but I no longer cared. My life was a fairy tale, and I understood that the wedding wasn't the important part. It was what came after that mattered, that wonderful 'happily-ever-after.'"

They spent their honeymoon at the Waldorf-Astoria.

Many years later, Joan jokingly told TV host Joe Franklin the reason she had hesitated in accepting the marriage proposal of Franchot Tone. "Do you realize," she said, "that it meant I would be Joan Tone?"

Love on the Run was Tone's sixth picture with Joan. In none of them does he co-star with her. In this film, Clark Gable gets Joan at the fade-out.

Love on the Run (1936)

Michael "Mike" Anthony (Clark Gable) and Barnabas "Barney" Pells (Franchot Tone), Paris correspondents for the same New York newspaper, compete with each other for stories. When Mike is assigned a routine story about a high-altitude flyer called The Baron, (Reginald Owen), he decides to steal Barney's assignment, the marriage of American millionairess Sally Parker to an exiled European prince (Ivan Lebedeff).

Barney is tricked into interviewing the Baron. Mike encounters Sally, who has tired of the fortune-hunting prince and of being a press target. "No self-respecting man could accept money for prying into people's lives," Sally tells Mike, not realizing *he* is a reporter. She wants to get away from it all.

Mike helps her flee from Paris in the Baron's high-altitude plane, which Mike doesn't really know how to fly. Mike correctly suspects that the Baron is a spy.

Surviving a crash, they take refuge in a French castle. There, in 18th century costumes, as they dance a minuet with the mad caretaker (Donald Meeker), Sally realizes she is falling in love with Mike. Barney appears at the castle wanting his story back. The Baron and Baroness (Mona Barrie) also appear, demanding the return of a secret map that Sally took from their plane. Mike and Sally escape with the map. The spies and Barney follow in hot pursuit.

After a wild chase by train, automobile, and on foot, the police get the spies, Barney and Mike get their story, and Sally gets Mike.

During one of the train sequences, Joan and Tone are seen playing backgammon. This was one of their pleasures in real life, and it remained Joan's for the rest of her life.

Tone, who didn't enjoy sitting by the windows of restaurants where everyone could see them, was increasingly upset by finding fans and press ever-present, knowing his and Joan's plans, wherever they went, or rather, everywhere Joan went. It was uncanny.

He understood how it was that crowds would be waiting for Joan at a beauty salon where she had an appointment to have her hair done. It seemed obvious that the salon wanted the glamorous promotion or perhaps someone had provided the tip to journalists for a small payoff.

He wondered, however, how they knew when the two of them were going out on a Saturday afternoon for a totally spontaneous lunch or a shopping spree. On arrival, they would find the place surrounded, and it took at least an hour for Joan to sign autographs. Joan wouldn't stop until she had signed every last one.

"I have to show consideration for my fans," she always said. She couldn't bear to leave any disappointed fans. Tone wondered if he would do better to bring along an autograph book and ask her to write in it, "To dear Franchot, bon appetit." He also considered bringing along a sandwich to satisfy hunger pangs while waiting to enter the restaurant.

Finally, he said something to her to the effect that her fans must be psychic, or else must have a private detective following them around everywhere in order to be able to get there ahead of them.

Joan explained. "It's simple. Of course someone lets them know where I'm going to be. The only person who could. Me.

"I only have to let one key fan know, and the others hear, and a few photographers, and the word gets out."

The Last of Mrs. Cheyney (1937)

Jewel thieves Fay Cheyney (Joan Crawford) and Charles (William Powell) operate successfully in English upper-class circles, she as a woman of mystery and he as a butler. Working together with a team of professional confederates, they infiltrate the weekend parties of the rich, whose jewels they steal.

At the party of Lord Arthur, Fay meets Lord Kelton (Frank Morgan), who recognizes her, but cannot say anything because he once sent her an incriminating letter. The caper seems to be going smoothly until the thieves are discovered and face arrest.

When Fay threatens to reveal the contents of Lord Kelton's letter, in which he makes damaging charges against his so-called friends, Lord Arthur is willing to come to a compromise. Fay and Charles leave without incident.

A film Joan *didn't* make was important in her career—*Parnell*. Clark Gable wanted to do the film, and he wanted Joan to be his leading lady. Gable was extremely enthusiastic about the character of Parnell.

The story bored Joan. She turned down the role of the married woman whose love affair with him ruins his career. Instead, Myrna Loy played the part. Gable told Joan that she would be sorry because the film would be "a big hit." To the contrary, the film was unsuccessful, but Joan was sorry to be right and sorrier that Gable was disappointed and, from then on, more distant toward her.

She had given as her reason that she didn't want to play a character with a foreign accent again after the criticism she had received for her

British accent in *Today We Live* and *The Last of Mrs. Cheyney*. By the time they made another film, *Strange Cargo* in 1940, their eighth film together, he was married to Carole Lombard.

THE BRIDE WORE RED was the last of seven films in which Tone appeared with Joan. She had requested him for it. Originally, Joan's part, Anni, was to have been played by Luise Rainer, who had just won the best actress Oscar in two consecutive years.

"I thought it was my moment to be strong and negotiate for good parts," Rainer told me in London in 2000. "The original play was by Molnár, but I had some suggestions, and they didn't want to listen to me. They were listening to their lion roaring.

"So, I left Hollywood, and people have said for years that I threw away my great career with both hands, and why would I do it? Perhaps it was because it all came so easily to me that I didn't value it. Joan Crawford 'won' the part, though I don't think 'won' is the right word for that film. I never saw it."

The film was directed by Dorothy Arzner, one of the few female directors in Hollywood at that time. It is based on Ferenc Molnár's play *The Girl From Trieste*.

The Bride Wore Red (1937)

Count Armalia (George Zucco), a wealthy Italian aristocrat, enjoys playing games of chance with the lives of others. For his next "wheel of life" divertimento, he chooses Anni (Joan Crawford), a struggling cabaret singer in Trieste. He offers her two weeks alone at an expensive resort in the Tyrol with an unlimited expense account. All he wants in return is to observe what effect sudden wealth can have on such an impoverished, cynical person as Anni. In the past, his games with people have not ended well for them.

Dressed as a millionairess, she arrives at the Tyrolean resort, where she is immediately welcomed into the most elite circles. Both men and women are eager to know her. Among those pursuing her is Rudi Pal (Robert Young), a wealthy and well-connected nobleman. While she likes him, she is also drawn to Giulio (Franchot Tone), the village postman. He has eschewed wealth in favor of the simpler life, which he enjoys.

As the two weeks draw to a close, Anni wonders what her new friends will think of her when her coach turns into a pumpkin. She has become accustomed to her new way of life.

The two weeks end, and all of her new "friends" abandon her when she announces the truth. All except Giulio, who loves her for herself. The count's "wheel of life" has for once brought happiness to its players.

"I was not a Method actress," Joan told me. "I never considered myself one. I took dancing lessons and later, singing lessons, but I did sometimes draw on something in my own life, a memory. I remember in *Mannequin*, I tell how it made me feel old because I was responsible for everything, working to support my mother, father, and brother. The girl in the film reminded me of me. The heroine is told by her mother, who has lived a hard and unfulfilled life, that she must dare to live her own life, not just to follow a husband in what life he has, not just to share a man's life, especially if she has chosen the wrong man and the wrong life."

Mannequin (1937)

Jessica "Jessie" Cassidy (Joan Crawford) escapes poverty and a bad marriage as a professional model. She finds security and upper-class social status in a marriage with shipping magnate John L. Hennessey (Spencer Tracy) that catapults her from Hester Street to Park Avenue. The only problem is, Jessie still thinks she loves her ex-husband, Eddie Miller (Alan Curtis).

Any feelings she has for Miller, however, quickly disappear when he comes back into her life, threatening to expose her sordid past unless she meets his blackmail demands. At the same time, Hennessey's business fails, and Jessie ignores Miller's threats as she devotes herself to her husband's needs, realizing that it is *he* she really loves, not his money and social standing.

"I was quite thrilled when I learned that Spencer Tracy had the male lead," Joan said. "I thought I'd learn something from working with him and that each of us had a following to bring to the film. When I met him, I didn't find him very attractive. I smelled alcohol on his breath, and for me that was a turn-off, even though we were not working at that moment, and he was never guilty of drinking when we were on the job.

"Spence was the person who taught me to ride a horse. It wasn't something I really had any enthusiasm for, but he seemed passionate about polo, and I didn't want him to think I was a scaredy-cat just because I was. Given a choice to be one of the girls or one of the boys, I chose to be one of the boys.

"I learn rather quickly and well, so I was pleased until I was thrown. I was black-and-blue for quite a while, and it was lucky for me I wasn't hurt much worse. I hadn't really thought of the repercussions. An injury to my face could have ended my career. An injury to my ankle or leg could have ended my dancing. I was riding a polo pony, and I have to admit it was all probably my own fault. I pulled up short, and a sophisticated polo pony wasn't expecting a novice rider. The polo pony had been a gift from Spence when it seemed I learned to ride so quickly, easily, with no sign of fear. What an actress I could be!

"I was so enthusiastic, I went overboard and bought a second horse, so they would have company, but they didn't seem to care for each other."

Joan named her gift horse Secret. It was whispered by the local whisperers that the provocative name inferred a secret, intimate relationship between Tracy and Joan at that time. Whatever the inference, neither admitted to anything clandestine, only to an open friendship, and one that did not endure, especially after Secret showed insufficient respect for Joan as a rider.

"It was Spence's horse who decided he'd rather have me on the ground than on his back. Well, I wasn't going to let him have that victory. I got right up and rode him for an hour and rode him the next day for good measure, and then, in front of him, so he could hear, I said, 'Sell him, and the other one, too.'

"It was only years later that I thought about it. I really should have offered to give him back to Spence. I wonder what Spence thought, or if he even noticed. I was really angry at the horse, and I no longer associated him with Spence."

It was with *Mannequin* that Joan received her famous "Box Office Poison" label. After several years as one of the most popular Hollywood stars, Joan was described in a trade paper article by theater chain owner Harry Brandt as one who kept audiences home. She was in good company. Also in the group were Katharine Hepburn, Greta Garbo, Mae West, and Marlene Dietrich. The phrase was quickly picked up by the mainstream press.

Joan took this quite seriously, and Tone couldn't convince her that it was the Great Depression, not any group of actors, that was keeping audiences home. King Vidor told me that the only attractions that got people into the theaters at that time were "free dishware" and, during hot summer nights, air-conditioning, which was a novelty. "People didn't care what was playing. They had to go to complete their set of dishes."

Joan had been impressed by *The Shining Hour* when she and Tone saw the Keith Winter play on Broadway. With his encouragement, she requested that M-G-M purchase the property as her next film, with Margaret Sullavan as her co-star.

The Shining Hour (1938)

The marriage of New York nightclub dancer Olivia Riley (Joan Crawford) to country gentleman Henry Linden (Melvyn Douglas) does not please his wealthy Wisconsin family, especially his brother, David (Robert Young), and his older sister, Hannah (Fay Bainter), who acts as the family matriarch. Olivia gets along only with Judy (Margaret Sullavan), who is locked in a friendly, but otherwise loveless, marriage with David. Olivia admits to Judy that she feels that her marriage to Henry is also loveless.

When Olivia is defended by David from the drunken advances of hired hand Benny (Frank Albertson), she understands that, far from disapproving of her, he is strongly attracted to her, and she to him. Judy, sensing that Olivia has become infatuated with her husband, realizes that, after all, she does love him, and she will not stand in the way of David's happiness if he decides to leave her.

Hannah, unable to cope with these developments, sets fire to the mansion in a drunken rage. Olivia, in an act of bravery, saves Judy from the flames. David, seeing his badly burned wife, realizes that he has always been in love with her.

Olivia, understanding the harm she has brought as an outsider, leaves, but not before a contrite Hannah has begged her to stay. As Olivia is driving away, Henry jumps into the open car and leaves with her.

The Ice Follies of 1939 was the second film Joan made with James Stewart. He had a small part in *The Gorgeous Hussy*. The story, that of a show business couple whose marriage is pulled apart by the wife's success and the husband's failure, was uncomfortably close to the domestic situation of the Franchot Tones.

The director, Reinhold Schünzel, wrote and directed the enormously successful German film *Viktor/Viktoria*, which later became *Victor/Victoria*, a popular Blake Edwards–Julie Andrews film. Schünzel was said to be Hitler's favorite director until the führer learned that Schünzel was one-quarter Jewish. *Ice Follies* was one of the few films he directed in Hollywood. He ended his career as a character actor, most memorably as one of the Nazi conspirators in Alfred Hitchcock's *Notorious*.

The Ice Follies of 1939 (1939)

Larry Hall (James Stewart) is an ice-skater who wants to produce his own ice shows. His bride, aspiring actress Mary McKay (Joan Crawford), encourages him in his ambitions and helps with his shows, but when they are unsuccessful, she accepts a movie studio's stock contract so they can survive.

She becomes a star overnight in her first film, while Larry struggles with his traveling ice show. Soon, they find themselves separated for long periods of time.

She tells a sympathetic studio executive, Douglas Tolliver, Jr. (Lewis Stone), that she wants to give up her successful career. She would rather be happy with the man she loves than be rich and

famous as a movie star. Tolliver solves the dilemma by hiring Larry
as a producer of motion picture ice shows starring his wife.

"One of the difficult things about our married life," Joan said, "was
Franchot missed New York and the theater. His film career did not
measure up to mine, always a strain for a man. We hoped it would
get there. His refined, almost fragile good looks didn't typecast him
for routine leads, the kind careers were built on. Sometimes I used to
enjoy just looking at him when I hoped he didn't notice.

"He wanted me to try the theater in New York. I didn't think I
could do that. I didn't even want to. I thought I would be bored playing the same role every night. Franchot told me that 'every night is
different.' I couldn't see that. I just knew I loved being on the film set.
I felt more at home there than I did at home. I was totally comfortable.
I had begun as a girl and had grown up at M-G-M. It was my first real
home. Franchot was disappointed in films, though he didn't say so. I
think that without an audience there to respond, it sort of bored him.

"While Franchot would have been happy to do a play for a year,
eight performances a week, for a film I never cared about rehearsing,
and I wouldn't have been unhappy to do only one take for even my
most important scenes. I always came to the set prepared. I put everything I had into the first take, and I never felt I got any better than that.
I always hoped directors would choose from my first takes, before I got
tired and it showed.

"Franchot admired my singing voice and encouraged me to take
voice lessons. I enjoyed singing and was told by the best voice teachers
that I had a very good voice, so that pleased me.

"Franchot persuaded me to build a small theater behind our house
on an extra lot I had purchased. I could sing there, and we could read
or rehearse. Then, he wanted to invite people in for entertainments in
which we would perform together.

"I think Franchot missed his friends. When I occasionally met some
of them from New York, I didn't feel they liked me. They enjoyed
political discussions, and I didn't know much about politics, and I
confess I wasn't very interested. I've never been able to become deeply
involved in what I didn't think I could do anything about. They also

had what seemed to me rather extreme political ideas. Mr. Mayer had always told us not to talk about our politics because we could lose some of our audience that way, those who disagreed with what we said we believed.

"Douglas's British friends, who were from the nobility and the royal family, as well as worldly sophisticates from the arts, had made the effort to bend over backwards to be nice to 'Douglas's wife.'

"Franchot's friends didn't make that same effort. It was clear they looked down on me as a movie star and thought Franchot had married beneath him. They encouraged him, in front of me, to return to the theater in New York, and they didn't mention me in that invitation, in my own house! I thought that rude. They may have assumed because I was a motion picture actress, I wouldn't have wanted to leave the movies. I didn't. They believed that only live theater was worthy, but I think of all those brilliant stage actors who gave great performances and those performances were over when the curtain came down, except in the minds of those members of the audience who had appreciated them. When all of those stage performances are lost and forgotten, my films will be there."

GEORGE CUKOR HAD been highly critical of Joan when he directed her in *No More Ladies*. As a former stage director, he was accustomed to directing actors with more theatrical experience. Far from being angry or hurt, Joan was attentive to his criticisms. She had great faith in Cukor, and she was eager to learn. He was impressed by her attitude.

He wasn't sufficiently impressed, however, to be influenced by Joan's plea to play Crystal in *The Women*. It was too important a role.

Joan spoke some of the lines for Cukor, who didn't feel she was doing it right but thought she showed great promise, and the strength of her wish to do it moved him. He felt he would be able to direct her in a fine performance, which is what happened.

Cukor considered Joan Crawford's screen self more real for her than her private self. He told me:

"The time she really came alive was when the camera was on her. As the camera came in closer, she had an expression on her face of wanting it intensely. She glowed from within. Her skin came to life. Her head fell back. Her lips parted. Her eyes were glistening. It was utterly sensual, erotic. Her close-up was ecstasy as, yielding, she gave herself completely to the camera.

"Joan Crawford and her camera. It was the greatest love affair I have ever known. She was married many times and had many lovers, and I was never in her bedroom, but I'm certain no man ever saw the look on her face that she had as the camera moved in.

"A star," Cukor said, "has a more distinctive identity than others who can be fine actresses. A star can't play as many parts, but she can play *her* part better than anyone else. That was true of Ingrid, as it was true of Bette and Kate, and as it was of Joan.

"Joan always gave me a great deal of credit for helping her, which I don't like to deny, because credit is a form of flattery, which is very nourishing for the ego, and one's ego enjoys nourishment. Really, what I did for her was to note that she did too much rather than too little, and to make her aware of that so she wouldn't do it.

"I noticed that she had distracting mannerisms. I pointed them out. Once she realized that she was doing all of those little things which distracted, she never did them again. She liked to learn, and she understood.

"The stars have an irritating quality. It's something negative, an essential fault. If they don't irritate you, you don't remember them."

After *Gone With the Wind*, *The Women* was the top-grossing film of 1939.

The Women (1939)

Mary Haines (Norma Shearer) is shocked to learn that every wife and mistress in her social set already knows: that her husband, Stephan, is being unfaithful to her with a scheming, conniving shopgirl, Crystal Allen (Joan Crawford). Mary's mother (Lucile Watson) advises her daughter to overlook the affair as she always overlooked the affairs of her husband, Mary's father, but Mary is too proud to do this. When Mary and Crystal have a chance meeting, the mistress is unimpressed by the wife's entreaties and threats. News of the affair reaches the gossip columns, and Mary feels forced to get a divorce.

She goes to Reno, where she stays on a ranch for wives waiting for their divorces to become final. Every kind of woman is represented, from women who follow divorce as a way of life (Mary Boland and Paulette Goddard) to an unhappy young wife (Joan Fontaine) who still loves the husband she is divorcing. The proprietress (Marjorie Main) of the ranch has never divorced, nor has she ever married, though she has three children.

As soon as the Haineses' divorce becomes final, Stephan marries Crystal, who instantly reverts to her true self. She is particularly unpleasant to the Haineses' daughter, little Mary (Virginia Weidler). Mary learns from her daughter how unhappy her husband is. When it is revealed that Crystal is being unfaithful to Stephan, Mary decides to fight to get her man back.

After Crystal marries Stephan, she forces his daughter, little Mary, to do things like curtsying when entering a room with an adult present, resembling Christina Crawford's description many years later of her mother's behavior. No men appear in this film. "Even the dog is a bitch," Cukor said.

"I was warned against playing Crystal by Mr. Mayer himself," Joan told me. "He said I should be aware of the danger of playing so unsympathetic a character. He said it could hurt my career because it wasn't what my fans expected from me. They wouldn't want to identify with a husband-stealing perfume salesgirl. If I did it too well, the audience could turn against me. If I didn't do it well, I would hurt the film.

"I always took Mr. Mayer very seriously. I trusted his intuition, and I knew he cared about me. I owed everything to him. But I still trusted my own intuition, and I didn't feel it was good for my future as an actress to always play it safe. Sometimes you have to pick your moment and take your chances.

"I had a lot of faith in my wonderful public. I believed they would be able to distinguish between Crystal and me. I was, after all, an actress.

"As it turned out, I was right. I was very happy I was right and Mr. Mayer was happy about it, too."

• • •

LIKE FAIRBANKS BEFORE him, Tone must have sensed that his marriage to Joan Crawford had lost its luster. Fairbanks accepted that some of the early excitement would fade, but it would then be replaced by a bond of shared experience. There would always be a certain amount of compromise necessary.

Joan was disappointed with how the marriage was going. It wasn't producing the kind of companionship that she had romantically envisioned when she accepted Tone's proposal. The union wasn't living up to her romantic high hopes.

She felt the relationship would not improve and it was more likely to deteriorate further. She still had hopes that she would find a marriage and family that fulfilled her dreams. She didn't see a good future for herself with Tone, so she invited him to leave her house and go to the Beverly Wilshire Hotel. He did. Then he moved to New York.

In April 1939, a week ahead of their divorce hearing, Joan met Tone in New York. The two of them went to Radio City Music Hall, where they attended the film premiere of *Dark Victory* starring Bette Davis. Afterward, they danced together at the Stork Club, where a little less than four years before, they had celebrated their secret wedding. They still danced well together.

The grounds for the divorce were not extreme. Joan claimed they had become incompatible, were not happy, and that her husband had been going out alone and returning late with no explanation. Joan said that above all she wanted to remain friendly with her husband.

The divorce was granted.

Joan told her friend Barbara Stanwyck that she got the divorce so that she and Franchot *could* remain friends. And they did.

AFTER SHE HAD divorced Franchot Tone, Joan drove to Las Vegas with an infant girl she had obtained from an illegal baby broker in Los Angeles. She was acting on the advice of her attorney, Gregson Bautzer, who had informed her that in Nevada she would be able, as a single woman, to adopt a child. Joan was something of a pioneer in this.

"Since I was a little girl, I'd always assumed one day I'd have a nice husband and nice babies. I never gave any thought to the idea of adoption. Life sometimes holds surprises for you, and sometimes they are good surprises, and sometimes they aren't.

"I didn't want to have babies too soon, before my career had a good start, *more* than a good start. I loved my career. Also, I needed to feel there was financial security for a baby. I believed a baby should have two parents, if at all possible. By the time I was married to Franchot, it seemed the perfect moment.

"It's a tremendous responsibility—economic and emotional, a commitment of time—giving priority to tiny human beings who are so totally dependent. And then, it's so wonderfully rewarding to see their personalities develop, each different from the other.

"Maybe if we'd had a baby who survived, it would have been a bond between us, and our marriage would have lasted. I knew that our marriage wasn't helped by my desperate desire to have a baby. Desperation doesn't help anything.

"It was understandable if Franchot saw my great desie to have children as unromantic, not very passionate, using him. He had no strong feelings about having children.

"Franchot did his part, but I had miscarriages that were painful and disappointing. No one can fully understand this sadness except a woman who has wanted a baby and experienced the joy of anticipation, only to have it end in a miscarriage.

"One of the miscarriages gave us great hope during the early weeks, and we both believed that there would be a baby. That was very sad, and I was also sick, physically as well as emotionally.

"It wasn't easy on Franchot.

"As I look back, it wasn't very good for our sex life. Always trying for a baby must have been very unsatisfying for Franchot. Worse yet, I don't think he especially wanted a child at that time, so early in our marriage, though he never said anything against it. I don't think I ever asked him. I just assumed he would want to be a father as much as I wanted to be a mother.

"I didn't have my husband anymore, but that didn't mean I couldn't have a baby. I didn't want to wait any longer.

"It didn't mean I'd given up hope. I thought I might marry again someday and still have a baby, though I had been told by doctors that my successfully having a baby was unlikely.

"I felt I had so much love to give to a child.

"A reason I had a lot of faith in adoption, perhaps the most important reason, was because the person I loved and considered my real father, the only parent I loved and who really loved me, was *not* my natural genetic father.

"It was Billy Cassin who gave me love and encouragement when I needed it. He recognized my talent and set my dancing feet on their way. His nurturing presence stayed with me even after he had gone. I wanted to keep his name because it kept him close to me. I wished he could have taken me with him when he went away. It was only much later that I understood that he couldn't take me with him because it would have been kidnapping, since he wasn't my real father. My mother told me he died. I didn't believe her because I didn't want to believe her. But my daddy never came back, so I guess it was true. If he'd been alive somewhere, I *know* he would have made his way back to see me.

"So, you see, I knew the best bond wasn't blood, but love.

"I was going to call her Joan Crawford, Jr. When I took my baby home, as a single parent, I couldn't legally adopt her in the state of California. So, months later, before her first birthday, I left California with her, so I could adopt her legally. It was important to me that when we had her first birthday party, I knew my little golden-haired angel was mine, and no one could ever take her away from me or separate us. I felt about her that she was *my* firstborn. I hoped that I would be not only her mother, but that as she grew up we would be best friends.

"Even though I thought of her during that first year as Joan Crawford, Jr., I decided there might be confusion with our having the same name. What if she wanted to be an actress? There would be the same complication that Douglas Jr. and Douglas Sr. had. I had always liked the name Christina, so it was with 'Christina' that I celebrated my own little girl's first birthday."

• • •

STRANGE CARGO, JOAN'S eighth and last film with Clark Gable, was based on a novel, *Not Too Narrow, Not Too Deep*, by Richard Sale. The part opposite Joan had been first offered to Spencer Tracy. Though she thought he was a very good actor, Joan didn't feel the chemistry was right for her with Tracy.

"My own preference in all the world was Clark Gable, and when I heard the part was open, I let Mr. Mayer know how I felt about Clark. He already knew. 'Good chemistry,' he said.

"'Too good,' I think he thought."

Strange Cargo (1940)

Prisoners plotting an escape from a French penal colony off the Guianas are joined by Verne (Clark Gable), his girlfriend, Julie (Joan Crawford), and Cambreau (Ian Hunter), a charismatic religious figure. Verne is a hardened criminal, while Julie is a café singer who was imprisoned for fraternizing with him when he was in town on a work patrol.

One by one, the escaping convicts die in the jungle or on the boat, each one being blessed by Cambreau after they repent their sins. Finally, there are only he, Verne, and Julie. They plan an escape to Cuba, but Julie, not feeling worthy of Verne, drops out.

On the boat, Verne resists Cambreau's efforts to convert him. Angrily, he fatally injures the holy man, who blesses him as he dies. Realizing the error of his ways, Verne returns to the penal colony to serve out his sentence, and Julie promises to wait for him.

"Clark was terribly disappointed," Joan said, "when with *Gone With the Wind* receiving so many Oscar nominations and so many Oscars, he was the only person not to take one home. He didn't say anything to anyone else because of his male pride, but for him to mention it at all, even to me, I knew he was deeply hurt. He loved being an actor, and the recognition of his talent, not just his looks and voice, meant a great deal to him. He mentioned it only once, and never referred back to it, but I'll never forget when he said to me, 'What would *Gone With the Wind* have been without me?'

"It was a question I couldn't answer. I could only ask it myself. What would *Gone With the Wind* have been without Rhett Butler?

"I didn't think Clark would make a good husband—a great lover, a fine friend, but I imagined him as an unfaithful husband.

"I didn't think he would be satisfied with only one woman, even me, and he would face endless temptation. He never had to ask. I don't know if he even knew how to. There was always an endless supply of attractive young things, who knew quite well how to ask, throwing themselves at him.

"I was also certain that he would prefer not having as a wife an actress with a career on a par with his, that he would prefer someone who could be happy simply devoting herself entirely to him.

"I was wrong in the way I judged him. I thought he liked to live in the moment, to be free of responsibilities.

"Then, along came Carole Lombard.

"He wasn't interested in adventures, and he became a devoted husband."

WHEN NORMA SHEARER, who was forty at that time, learned that she would be playing the mother of a fourteen-year-old daughter in *Susan and God*, she declined, saying it would be damaging to her career. George Cukor, who was to direct the film, suggested Joan as Susan.

Louis B. Mayer called to inform Joan that the part was hers if she wanted it, and she accepted immediately. She did it before reading the script. "I was never coy," she told me.

"Norma Shearer's foolish vanity was my good luck. I always prided myself on recognizing luck and, what is it they say? 'Seizing the moment.'"

Susan and God (1940)

Susan Trexel (Joan Crawford), a wealthy New York matron, returns from a European trip with a radical new religious belief that promises universal happiness. Her well-intentioned attempts to convert her family and everyone in her social set to her new faith results only in unhappiness for all, especially her husband, Barrie (Fredric March), who leaves her after being driven to drink. For the sake of their confused and insecure adolescent daughter, Blossom (Rita Quigley), Barrie returns, and Susan realizes that something more than just her new belief is necessary for lasting happiness.

Susan and God was based on a play by Rachel Crothers. Gertrude Lawrence created the role of Susan on Broadway. The film closely followed the style of the play.

In 1940, when Joan learned that *A Woman's Face* was going to be remade as a Hollywood film, she wanted the part. "I loved the Swedish film, but I assumed they would want Ingrid Bergman to repeat her performance in English." David Selznick, however, had other plans for Ingrid, his overnight sensation.

"I went directly to Mr. Mayer and asked him to buy the property for me. It was a wonderful part, and I knew I could be great in it. I wouldn't be Ingrid Bergman, but I would be Joan Crawford.

"When George [Cukor] told me that I would be playing opposite Melvyn Douglas, I was happy and I was sad. I was glad to be working with a real actor, but I felt the audience would be disappointed by the way he looked.

"I think Melvyn Douglas is a terrific actor. If anyone asked me, I would say the most underrated actor in films, as far as I'm concerned, is Melvyn Douglas. The test is, what would a great picture be like if you tried substituting someone else? Everyone knows it was the great Garbo who made *Ninotchka* the wonderful film it is, but what would *Ninotchka* have been without Melvyn Douglas? Not the same. No one could have equaled his performance.

"What has been his problem? As a younger leading man, it was the way he looked. He just wasn't handsome enough for audiences. He was so wonderful that it made him look better, and his portrayal of the character distracted you from the way he looked, but if only he'd been handsomer, he could have done anything. Anything. As an older man, he's proven that.

"Working constructively and worrying constructively is important. George [Cukor] taught me about working constructively. I taught myself about worrying constructively. I determined I should only worry about what I could do something about. If I couldn't do anything about it, there wasn't any point in turning good time into worrying time. Later I think my Christian Science leanings helped me to gain and enjoy perspective.

"Before I met George, I was very hardworking, but much of it was wasted, thrashing about. I had *so* much energy, but I didn't know what to do with it. I was a whirling dervish. You know, I used that expression for years before I found out what they were. I saw a picture of one, and I didn't want to be a whirling dervish anymore."

Joan had hoped for an Oscar nomination for her part in *A Woman's Face*. She was extremely proud of her performance. She felt that Cukor had helped her tremendously and that he was very pleased by her achievement. "With George, you could tell if he wasn't pleased by what you were doing. Nothing subtle. He let you know, but he let you know how you could do it better."

A Woman's Face (1941)

After Anna Holm (Joan Crawford) has her badly scarred face made beautiful by Dr. Gustaf Segert (Melvyn Douglas), a plastic surgeon, her attitude toward life changes. She stops feeling justified in a life of crime, and strives to reform. She hopes she can achieve change with an aristocrat, Torsten Barring (Conrad Veidt), who found her attractive even before her operation.

Barring, however, only wants her to help him assure his inheritance by participating in one more crime, a murder. Blinded by love, she follows his plan and becomes the governess of Barring's young nephew, Lars-Erik (Richard Nichols), the obstacle to Torsten inheriting the Barring fortune when old Magnus Barring (Albert Bassermann) dies.

Dr. Segert, fearing that he has made Anna an even more evil creature, is relieved when she thwarts Torsten's attempt to kill the child after being unable to do it herself. Instead, she kills Torsten, and in court she is acquitted of murder. Anna has experienced a moral as well as a physical transformation, and she and Gustaf realize they are in love.

Although *A Woman's Face* was a film Joan had very much wanted to do, it wasn't successful. Neither was her next, which she *hadn't* wanted to do.

When Ladies Meet is a remake of a 1933 Myrna Loy–Robert Montgomery film of the same title. Like *Susan and God*, it was based on a Rachel Crothers play.

When Ladies Meet (1941)

Novelist Mary Howard (Joan Crawford) is seriously involved in a relationship with her publisher, Rogers Woodruff (Herbert Marshall), who is married. Pursuing Mary is Jimmy Lee (Robert Taylor), who is in love with her, but cannot compete with Rogers for her respect and affections. He disapproves of Mary's intention to break up Rogers's marriage so that she can marry him.

Jimmy arranges for Mary to meet Rogers's wife, Claire (Greer Garson), at a friend's house without her realizing who she is. They become friends and confide in each other their problems with men. Mary confesses she loves a married man. Claire says her husband is an habitual womanizer, but she loves him and will always take him back. When Mary realizes they are talking about the same man, her feelings about Rogers change, and she no longer wants to take him from his wife. She returns to Jimmy.

"When Clark first told me about Carole [Lombard]," Joan explained, "he said she reminded him of me in some ways. He said, 'She's a man's woman.'

"I had certainly made a wrong evaluation of Clark, judging him to be poor husband material. I didn't think he was a one-woman man. I didn't see him as a man who could love one woman for a long time, a lifetime, his or hers.

"I didn't blame him for it. He had endless opportunity. I loved Clark, but I thought if I married him, he would break my heart, because what we had was too good to last.

"When he married Carole Lombard, it wasn't possible to find a more faithful husband. He was not only faithful in his actions, but in his thoughts. I don't think he ever even had an unfaithful thought, and you can't say that for many men.

"He was in love with her, and he loved her. Those aren't the same things, you know, and it's heaven if you can get the two things, passion and lasting love.

"I liked Carole, and I told myself I was happy for Clark, and for her, too. I never considered myself an envious person, because I wasn't one. But if I tell the truth, I did have a few times when Clark told me about how wonderful she was. I didn't exactly enjoy hearing those words, so many of them, pouring out of Clark, who never had had that many words to spare during the years I knew him. Carole must have been divinely happy.

"But then, the tragedy happened. The plane crash. And she'd been working for our country on a bond drive. It was terrible. She was supposed to take a train, but she took a plane to get back faster to Clark."

On January 16, 1942, Carole Lombard and her mother were killed in a plane crash while taking off from the Las Vegas airport. She had been traveling by train on a national savings bond tour and was returning to Hollywood from Nevada in a commercial aircraft.

"There were some vicious people who spread gossip that she was rushing back in order not to leave her handsome husband alone too long. That was ridiculous. A terrible thing to say, anyway, and especially in light of the brave sacrifice she had made. I know why she wanted to rush back. Not because she didn't trust her husband, but because she loved him so much.

"Clark was inconsolable for a long time. He had such terrible regrets about letting her go at all. They were both very patriotic. He hadn't been able to go with her because of a film, but still he blamed himself for not stopping her. He never really stopped blaming himself. But she was a very spirited girl, and that was what he loved. He wouldn't have wanted to change her. I don't think he could have, although she wanted very much to please him. She learned how to do everything he enjoyed, fishing, hunting, which he'd always done with his men friends. With her, they could do those things alone, or he could bring her along.

"Clark could never get over her loss. A part of him died when she died. The vibrant, exciting life force that was Clark had gone. He was still a lot of man, but the spark, the electricity went with her."

After Carole's death, Clark went to Joan's Brentwood home for dinner at the end of shooting for *Somewhere I'll Find You*. "I offered him a shoulder to cry on, and he accepted it. It was also important that he got a good warm meal provided with comfortable company."

In tribute to her friend, Joan offered producer Edward Kaufman her services in his upcoming film, *They All Kissed the Bride*, which was to star Carole. Joan arranged for her salary, $125,000, to be donated to the Red Cross in Carole Lombard's name. Mayer agreed, and Joan was loaned out to Columbia for this picture.

Then Gable enlisted in the Army Air Corps.

He and Joan remained good friends until his death in 1960.

They All Kissed the Bride (1942)

Everyone is terrified by domineering trucking heiress Margaret J. Drew (Joan Crawford) until crusading journalist Michael Holmes (Melvyn Douglas) tames the shrew with a series of articles exposing her harsh management practices. Repeating the *Ninotchka* formula, Michael wins the formidable Margaret with his dedicated persistence. It seems likely that they will soon be living happily-*never*-after.

For the first time in more than a decade, Joan had the opportunity to show what a fine dancer she was, jitterbugging with Allen Jenkins. It was her most vigorous dancing since *The Hollywood Revue of 1929*.

When Joan returned to M-G-M, she made *Reunion in France*, which was produced by Joseph Mankiewicz, directed by Jules Dassin, and co-starred her with John Wayne. It was her first war picture since *Today We Live* in 1933.

Reunion in France (1942)

Wealthy Parisian socialite Michele de la Becque (Joan Crawford) leads her frivolous life as she always has, oblivious to World War II. She only becomes involved during the German occupation of Paris when she suspects that her lover, industrialist Robert Cortot (Philip Dorn), may have become a collaborator. She fears that his factory is manufacturing weapons for the Germans.

Her patriotism awakened, she becomes romantically involved with an Allied pilot, Pat Talbot (John Wayne), who has been shot down and is now hiding from the Gestapo with her help. In spite of her attraction to Talbot, she cannot forget Cortot.

She is reunited with Cortot when she finds out that he is not a collaborator, but a member of the Resistance. The weapons his factory is making for the Wehrmacht are deliberately manufactured with defects.

PHILLIP TERRY WAS born in San Francisco in 1909. His real name was Frederick Kormann, and his father was an oil rig operator. Working with his father in the oilfields of Oklahoma, Terry developed a muscular physique. At Stanford, he made the varsity football team, then coached by Glenn "Pop" Warner. Terry's real interest, however, was theater, and after Stanford, he went to London to study acting at the Royal Academy of Dramatic Arts.

Returning to the United States, he tried Broadway and then Hollywood, where he was signed as an M-G-M contract player. His ruggedly handsome features, trim six-foot-one frame, and excellent background would seem to have endowed him with leading man potential; yet he only starred in a few low-budget films, mostly loan-outs, or appeared as a supporting player in more important productions. He had a small part in Joan's *Mannequin* in 1937, but he is best remembered as the long-suffering brother of Ray Milland in Billy Wilder's *The Lost Weekend*.

Wilder told me, "When Phil Terry came on the set to do *Weekend*, I said, 'Where are your glasses?' He had the kind of face that didn't look right without glasses. But he didn't like to wear them, even though he could have used them, because he wanted to be a leading man."

When Phillip Terry expressed interest in meeting Joan Crawford to her friend, publicist Harry Mines, an afternoon tea was arranged at her home. Joan was impressed, and when Terry called to ask her out the next day, she accepted.

After her divorce from Franchot Tone, Joan had said, quite emphatically, as she had after her divorce from Douglas Fairbanks, Jr., "I won't be marrying an actor again."

Joan and Phillip Terry were married on Tuesday, July 21, 1942, at a friend's home in the San Fernando Valley, just as she was starting *Reunion in France*. She and Terry had known each other for six weeks.

Joan had always thought that she would enjoy some time at home, without the responsibility of having to work, time with her child, her garden, her home, her husband.

She didn't have so much time with her husband because when he didn't have a part, or even the immediate hope of a part, he took a job in a war plant. Joan was too patriotic to object and she understood about masculine pride.

"The money he contributed," Joan said, "was just a drop in the bucket, but I was careful not to make it seem that way. We used it to buy groceries, which made it appear more important and immediate.

"He didn't want to stay home with me, and he couldn't just wait by the phone or keep calling his agent. I called *my* agent much too often."

She felt it was selfish to have household help during World War II, when there was a labor shortage. Since they didn't have any money coming in, Joan decided she could keep her own house as well as anyone.

Joan prepared lunches for Terry to take to work. He liked to have a few drinks when he came home in the evening. Joan began to drink more than she ever had before, and she moved from champagne or wine to vodka.

She learned something about herself. Although she had always considered herself rather domestic, she found out she wasn't as domestic as she had imagined.

She was bored.

"AFTER CHRISTINA WAS a few years old," Joan told me, "I was so pleased with my little girl that I knew I wanted to have another child. I didn't want her growing up alone. This time, I wanted a boy, since I already had a girl. That's one advantage of adoption.

"I was offered a baby boy with blond hair, and I was told that he was Irish and French, which just happened to be what I was. I also have some Swedish." Joan named the new baby Christopher.

She was thrilled and happily shared her good news with the press, with whom she had a good relationship. She saw no reason why this happy news should be kept secret. There was, however, a reason to keep it secret.

When the story was printed, the mother who had given up her baby for adoption read it. Joan had included so many details about the baby that the mother had no difficulty recognizing her son, realizing that he had been adopted by a famous and rich woman.

Joan was approached by the woman, who claimed she hadn't wanted to give up the child. She demanded that Joan return her baby. She also asked for money to compensate her for the emotional pain she had endured during the experience. She threatened to go to the press and create a scandal.

After trying to avoid doing so, Joan gave up the baby. She paid the woman money to settle the matter.

Later, Joan was told that the woman "sold" the baby to someone else.

The brief experience of holding "Baby Christopher," far from discouraging Joan's feelings about adopting another baby, encouraged her. Undaunted, she adopted another blond baby boy, naming him Phillip after her husband. When Joan and Terry later separated prior to a divorce, she renamed the baby Christopher.

"Joan was trying to create a family," Myrna Loy told me, "so she decided on the name Christopher, which she liked as a good name for

Christina's new younger brother. It made it seem almost as if they were twins."

She changed the baby's name because she didn't want Terry to have a claim that could jeopardize her sole custody. Terry, however, would never have considered causing a problem. The idea to adopt had been entirely hers, and he had cooperated only so she would be happy.

"As a child," Joan said, "'Tina' had a lively imagination, but always for the negative. For years, she had to have a light on when she slept. When she was very little, I thought it seemed natural, and I didn't question her about her fears. I assumed they would just go away as she grew a little older. But they didn't. If anything, her fears grew greater.

"For a long time, she wouldn't say what it was. Then we learned she was afraid of rats that would come and eat her. That was a strange fear, because we had the cleanest house in the world. I thought the rats must stand for something else.

"It wasn't very convenient leaving lights on at night so Christina would never be in the dark. I tried one of those Lone Ranger masks without eye slits, but it bothered me, and I couldn't sleep. I never adjusted to the lights. I think Christina's younger brother was bothered by the lights, but he worshipped Christina and would never say anything."

Above Suspicion was Conrad Veidt's last film. He died shortly afterward of a heart attack while playing golf. He had been one of the leading actors in Germany when the arrival of the Nazis motivated him to leave his country of birth permanently and become an English citizen. His wife was Jewish and he was extremely anti-Nazi.

While he never again achieved the exalted position he had held in the German cinema, he had an estimable career in England and Hollywood. His specialty was playing aristocratic villains and merciless

Nazis, exactly the opposite of his true beliefs. During World War II, he donated a considerable part of his earnings and savings to British war relief. He is best remembered for his portrayal of the arch-Nazi Colonel Strasser in *Casablanca*.

Above Suspicion (1943)

Newlyweds Frances (Joan Crawford) and Richard Myles (Fred MacMurray), respectively an American student and a professor at Oxford, plan a continental honeymoon. Since this is shortly before World War II, the British Foreign Office recruits them to help locate a missing scientist who is also being sought by the Germans. He has developed a formula that will neutralize a top-secret German weapon that is to be used in their upcoming invasion of Poland.

In Paris, clues are uncovered that lead them to Salzburg and the assassination of a high Nazi official during a concert. At the concert is one of Richard's acquaintances from Oxford, Sig von Aschenhausen (Basil Rathbone), now a German officer. Richard finds out that the dead Nazi official was a former commandant of a concentration camp. The assassin (Bruce Lester) was also working for the British Foreign Office. His sister had been a victim of Nazi brutality.

Frances and Richard finally locate the scientist, Dr. Mespelbrunn (Reginald Owen), who is being held by Aschenhausen's Gestapo agents. They manage to escape with Mespelbrunn, who entrusts his formula to them. Through a mysterious man they met in Salzburg, Hassert Seidel (Conrad Veidt), they obtain forged passports that will enable them to escape Austria by way of Italy.

Before they can leave, however, Frances is captured by the Gestapo and tortured. She is saved by Richard, who arrives with British agents, who kill Aschenhausen. They escape over the Italian border disguised as a German SS unit.

Joan said, "Richard Thorpe, the director, did a perfectly adequate job, but just think what Alfred Hitchcock could have done with it! I think it was a Hitchcockian kind of story, and I would have worked free to be directed by him. Well, almost free. It would have changed my life. I probably wouldn't have left M-G-M. I would have just faded away. I wouldn't have been at Warner's to do *Mildred Pierce*, and I wouldn't have taken home my Oscar.

"Alfred Hitchcock wasn't an M-G-M director, and our professional paths never crossed, though I did ask him to keep me in mind, and I'm sure he did. We would have had a lot of giggles together because we had the same sense of humor. He was not only a wonderful director, but a wonderful friend."

After *Reunion in France*, Joan had been offered roles in two films, *Cry Havoc* and *The Heavenly Body*, both of which she declined. The role she really wanted, the title role in *Madame Curie*, went to Greer Garson. Joan felt that her position at M-G-M was being usurped.

Long dissatisfied with the parts she was being offered and with the ones she *wasn't* being offered, Joan asked Louis B. Mayer to release her from her M-G-M contract. He did not wish to do it, but when it became clear that Joan had made up her mind, Mayer agreed. She had to pay a penalty of $50,000.

Douglas Fairbanks, Jr., remembered Joan later telling him that she was "ruffled and saddened" over the $50,000 she had to pay to get out of her contract.

"It had shocked her that Mayer had gone along with that and not interceded in her behalf, as she originally had assumed he would. I didn't say it, but I thought it was probably Mayer's idea. Personally, I think she was less effusive about how wonderful 'Mister' Mayer was after that."

Afterward, Joan had mixed feelings about her decision to leave the studio that had been her home for so many years.

"I did not understand fully, no, I didn't understand at all what it would be like to leave Metro and make films anywhere else. Metro had been my home, and it was my very good home. I had been there something like eighteen years. I'd never had any other home for that long.

"Losing Louis B. Mayer was, as it turned out, a little like losing Daddy Cassin, only I didn't know it was going to feel the way it did. After all, I was the one who made the choice. After I did it, that made it even more difficult knowing it had been my own decision. If I'd done the wrong thing, I would have no one to blame but myself.

"I thought it was something I had to do for my career. Mr. Mayer couldn't have been nicer about it. I was certain I was doing the right thing. I *had* to be certain to be able to do it at all.

"Afterwards, though I wouldn't admit to anyone that I had even the shadow of a doubt, there were times when I had *more* than a shadow of a doubt. I was almost overwhelmed by self-doubt about what I had done. I couldn't lie to myself. That is the most terrible thing anyone can do. Anyway, I wouldn't know how to do it.

"At the time, it had seemed absolutely right, but I didn't have a crystal ball. Afterwards, there were times when it seemed absolutely wrong. It was probably neither. Probably more of a mixed bag. You can really only look back in hindsight, and even hindsight isn't twenty-twenty. To know, you would need one of me who stayed with Metro and one of me who ventured out on her own, and then we would have needed someone to decide who among the two of me had the best career."

Joan's new agent, Lew Wasserman, who also represented Bette Davis, negotiated a new contract for her at Warner Brothers. She was to receive $500,000 for three pictures. This was less than she was earning at M-G-M, but she would have almost complete artistic control over what she did. This meant she could choose her scripts, her directors, and her leading men.

"WHEN CHRISTINA WAS little," Joan's friend and longtime secretary Betty Barker told me, "Joan liked mother-and-daughter dresses. She had her dresses copied for Christina. Christina was a pretty little girl."

Christina lived in a world of lavish birthday parties. "Part of it," Joan told me, "was parents who *could*, wanting to give their children

the best, and some of it, I suppose, was parents' wanting to show off."
"The gifts were very expensive, and the birthdays were elaborate social occasions. I wanted Christina to have birthday parties which would fill her mind with beautiful memories.

"I remember one wonderful birthday party I had for her when she was about five.

"We invited many children, and they were all beautifully dressed, with lovely little outfits and their hair shining and clean little hands. The children all brought the most wonderful, handsomely wrapped gifts.

"I coached her so that she would know exactly how to behave, like a little lady. I explained to her that she should follow the same ritual that was the procedure at the parties of the other children of her age. The birthday boy or girl would open a gift and then would take the gift around the room to show it to each of the guests as a token of respect for the gift and its giver.

"About halfway through, I noticed my little girl becoming cranky and tired, and not taking the gifts around. She didn't look happy. She looked like she was going to cry. I think she was getting tired of opening the packages and showing what she had received.

"I rose to help her, and as I bent down to pick up one of the gifts to show, she whispered in my ear, 'Mommie, I'm tired of the party. Do I have to open the rest of the gifts?' I said, 'Of course we do, or we'll hurt the other children's feelings, and you wouldn't want to do that, would you?' She didn't answer.

"I had asked her to be careful about the way she unwrapped her gifts. Some of the people had paid extra for the special packaging, and the gifts came from the most elegant shops. Since so much effort had been put into making works of art of the wrapping, she should open the presents as carefully as possible, so as not to insult those who had given the gifts and were there watching, folding the gift paper as soon as she had opened the gift, following as closely as she could the creases in the paper. This lasted only briefly, and after the first dozen gifts, I had to fold the paper.

"I thought about my birthdays when I was a little girl. It didn't take any time at all, because my birthday was never celebrated. I don't think my birthday was a cause for celebration for my mother, my father having left, and I was just another mouth to feed.

"My own birthday is March 23, and when I was a little girl, that day would come and go just like any other. There was no thought of a party, no extra money for it, and my mother had no time or energy because she was always tired from working to support us. I think she was too tired to remember I had a birthday.

"My brother, Hal, was too stingy with a good word to say 'Happy Birthday,' even if he remembered, which he probably didn't.

"I didn't have friends when I was a child to invite to a party. I was looked down on by the other girls and their families, so even if I had invited anyone, their mothers probably would not have wanted their daughters associating with me or my mother.

"People told me later that I should be glad that I didn't have to know a lot of false friends who didn't have the right values. I don't feel that way. I wish I could have been a little bit popular. I would have liked some girlfriends. These didn't have to be lifetime relationships, carefully examined, but I think they would have been fun in their moment.

"The only person who celebrated my birthday when I was a child was my Daddy Cassin. He always remembered. First thing in the morning, he would say 'Happy Birthday' to me. If he had a show rehearsing or playing, he took me with him to his theater. That meant everything then. Those were the great days of my life up to that time. They were magical. I saw the world of make-believe, which was much better than what I saw of reality.

"My daddy always made time for our sodas on my birthday. He offered me a second one, which was really too much for me, but he encouraged me to get it by telling me I could have as much as I wanted of the second one, and then he would finish the rest, so it wasn't wasted. That became our 'shared soda.'"

DURING WORLD WAR II, Joan went to the Hollywood Canteen at least one night a week, generally more, sometimes as often as three nights a week. Usually, she worked at the snack bar, and during the night she wrote dozens of postcards home for every serviceman who wanted one or more, and everyone did. It was her idea. She would address the card and say that the soldier or sailor was there with her, that he was looking well, and having a good time at the canteen. Then she would sign the card, Joan Crawford. She never left while there was even one person in military service who wanted one of those cards sent home for him.

More than thirty years later, I was with her and John Springer when a man approached us. "Miss Crawford," he said, "my wife has your postcard, the one you wrote for me at the canteen.

"You wrote that I was fine, and she treasured the card and had it all the while I was missing in action.

"Then, she kept it all during the time after she learned I was a prisoner of war. When I came back, she handed it to me.

"Now we're saving it for our grandchildren. Thank you, Miss Crawford."

Hollywood Canteen was written and directed by Delmer Daves. He also wrote the earlier *Stage Door Canteen*, which was directed by Frank Borzage. Like the first film, the story centers around servicemen who visit the canteen, but in Hollywood instead of New York. Most of them are back from the war in the Pacific or are going there. The entire Warner Brothers stock company appear as themselves in cameos. Joan appeared before Bette Davis in the credits, since the actors were listed alphabetically. Joan's brief appearance is her Warner Brothers debut.

Hollywood Canteen (1944)

Two soldiers (Robert Hutton and Dane Clark), finishing sick leave and about to be shipped out to active duty in the Pacific during World War II, unexpectedly find themselves honored guests of the Hollywood Canteen because one of them (Hutton) is the millionth GI guest. His prize is Joan Leslie as a date. Clark's prize is dancing with Joan Crawford.

"At the canteen," Joan told me, "it was my goal to dance with every serviceman who wanted to, and it seemed they *all* wanted to. It was easier for the better dancers, but I encouraged everyone to dance with me. I thought a big part of it was that they wanted to be able to say they danced with Joan Crawford. I wanted to make it true for every one of them, and I wanted them to feel they danced well, even some who began by saying they had never danced before at all. It was a challenge, I have to admit, but I had the technique, I think. I wanted every one of them to believe he was a wonderful dancer, at least that once, and to look good in front of his friends. My mission was to make each one feel like Fred Astaire. I said to each one, 'I enjoyed our dance,' and it was *so* true. I think it meant as much to me as to them. It was wonderful to be able to make them so happy.

"Once in a while I got tired, exhausted, and then I felt ashamed. The thought that never left my mind was that some of those wonderful brave young men, so very young, would not be coming back. I couldn't bear it. And in that room, there were some who were going to be terribly injured.

"They didn't seem to be thinking that way. I wished I could be carefree the way they were. Maybe they weren't as carefree as they seemed. Maybe they weren't really, and they were just better actors than I.

"When I wasn't dancing, I was serving at the snack bar. I would make little sandwiches and pass them out, and of course, I would write the postcards they could mail home. I can honestly say I never left a serviceman un-danced-with, hungry, or without a postcard or postcards if he wanted them to mail to parents, sisters, girlfriends, wives. I'd write Joe or Tom or Bill is looking well and having a good time, or whatever they wanted me to write.

"When I went home, I cried until my pillow was all wet. I cried myself to sleep when I thought about the ones who wouldn't come back or wouldn't come back whole.

"One of the people who was devoted to the canteen was Bette Davis. She came all the time. She was one of us who were willing to do anything. She would have been willing to work in the kitchen, wash dishes or clean. It was the way Marlene Dietrich and I felt, too. But it wasn't what the young soldiers wanted, because they enjoyed seeing the movie stars.

"Bette played a part in creating the canteen. It was John Garfield's idea, and maybe Bette's, too. Anyway, Bette was the one who facilitated it. She went straight to Jack Warner, who really got behind it.

"The USO [United Service Organizations] does a wonderful job during peacetime, which isn't so well known except by the military people who go there. They aren't facing war, but they are still young and lonely. They need a place to go, somewhere they don't have to spend money and where they feel welcome. They can meet other servicemen and make friends at the USO, and they can meet local people and feel more comfortable in a strange city."

Joan said she wished she had more money to give to the USO, but she planned for them to be a prime beneficiary in her will. Throughout her life, Joan was not very politically active, "except to vote," she said, but she was intensely patriotic.

6

The Early Warner Years

(1945–1948)

"D O YOU KNOW what words meant the most to me in my life?" Joan asked me. "I don't think you would guess.

"It was hearing the words 'Mommie, dearest' said to me by my little girl, Christina. It made me so happy. It was like applause.

"She was very little, and we were standing together in my bedroom looking at ourselves in the full-length mirror. We were wearing mother-daughter dresses. I liked our mother-daughter dresses, because for me they showed our bond.

"I told Christina and Christopher that I liked to have them call me 'Mommie, dearest.' Christina understood that she could use it to get what she wanted from me. I didn't understand that, though, and it always worked. When she and Christopher said it to me as little children, I loved it, but looking back, I understood that when they said it in a chorus and looked at each other, they were mocking me.

"When she was grown up and not very friendly to me, she would come by once in a while to get some money, and she would begin in a wheedling tone, 'Mommie, dearest,' preceding her request.

"When she was a little girl, she really had my number. She was precocious in Mommie psychology. She read correctly how anxious I was to have my children love me and respect me. If you had asked me which mattered most to me, I would have said respect. But it wasn't really true. It was their love that meant the most to me."

• • •

JOAN REJECTED NUMEROUS scripts because they were not the kind of material she had been hoping to find, in search of which she had left M-G-M. She could not accept what she considered poor material, but she believed it was unfair to continue to be on salary while she waited for the right script. She told Warner's they didn't have to keep her on salary, and they were happy with that arrangement. Then came *Mildred Pierce*.

There were those at Warner's who expected Joan to make her appearance on the set of *Mildred Pierce* as a prima donna; haughty, aloof, demanding, spoiled. A person who was most certain that Miss Crawford would be a horror to work with was Michael Curtiz, the number one director at that time at Warner's. He had long been considered one of the best directors in Hollywood, but his reputation had soared with *Casablanca*.

Joan realized immediately that Mildred Pierce was the part of a lifetime. Curtiz, however, opposed her selection.

When Joan learned of this, she anticipated that there would be conflict on the set that could only be disruptive. More important, he might keep her from getting the part if he protested strongly enough against her.

Her answer was a surprise, a shock, to everyone. She offered to take a screen test and to let Mr. Curtiz decide on the basis of the test whether he wanted to have her play Mildred Pierce or not.

Jack Warner was amazed. It was unheard of for a star with her reputation to try out with a screen test. It was not necessary for her to do this, Warner explained. Producer Jerry Wald and others conveyed the same sentiment, that she need not try out. Joan insisted.

After seeing the screen test, no one had any further doubts about her qualifications for playing the role nor could there remain any doubts about how *right* she was for it. Even Curtiz was convinced, though he was still wary, saying, as Joan mimicked the director's Hungarian accent, "Not only are her shoulders too beeg, but her head iss too beeg, too."

This comment was reported to Joan by her friend Wald. He thought that she should be prepared for a struggle, and some antipathy. He was afraid Joan would be hurt, but her concerns were professional, not personal. She was determined to do everything for this film, in which she had such belief. She felt it represented her best chance to restore her career, and she had already come to the conclusion, as she told me, "that my work is my life."

She volunteered to work with several of the featured players and contract players on their screen tests. It wasn't only an act of incredible generosity, but Joan admitted it was also beneficial for her because she was at a new studio. She wanted to get to know the crew as she had at M-G-M, to establish rapport with them as individuals, to observe their style, and to know how they worked.

More than thirty girls were tested for the part of Veda, Mildred's spoiled daughter. Ann Blyth was one of the last. Joan liked the sixteen-year-old immediately. She encouraged Blyth and invited her into her dressing room, where she coached her and fed her lines. She had found the perfect actress for the part.

There was a special reason Warner's didn't want to select Ann Blyth. She was under contract to Universal and they didn't want to create a star for another studio. They saw the part as a great opportunity for one of their own contract players, but Joan insisted.

Ann Blyth said she owed Joan so much, possibly her career, and Joan had been the kindest person, "like a wonderful older sister or mother."

Before filming began, everyone around the set was surprised when Joan came on the set wearing a dress she had selected and wanted to show to the director for his approval.

Curtiz looked at her dress and screamed, "None of those Adrian dresses, and no shoulder pads!"

It was very quiet. No one spoke. No one moved. No one even breathed.

"I bought this dress at Sears," Joan said. "And it doesn't have any shoulder pads."

By the end of the film, Joan had established rapport with Curtiz. He paid tribute to her talent, cooperativeness, and "sweetness."

She gave him a gift of a pair of oversized shoulder pads.

. . .

"THE THING I most appreciate about Bette Davis," Joan told me, "is that she turned down *Mildred Pierce*."

"Do you know that I turned down *Mildred Pierce*?" Bette Davis asked me. "I don't think they told that to Miss Crawford. She might not have appreciated being offered my leavings."

"Bette wouldn't have been good in it anyway," Joan said. "I suppose she understood that. The part wasn't right for her. I honestly believe that she regretted turning it down when I got my Oscar, but she got plenty of Oscars, and if she had taken the part, she *wouldn't* have gotten an Oscar for it.

"I didn't resent her getting first choice at Warner's. It was the way it should be. Bette Davis was the queen of Warner's then, and deservedly so. She'd spent the great years of her professional life with them, the way I did with M-G-M. She had first choice for every script worth anything. I would've expected to always have first choice over her at M-G-M if she had moved there, even if the part she was playing was Bette Davis, in which case I would have let her have it because she could play Bette Davis better than I could, and she would have been welcome to it."

There was one thing that irritated Joan about being compared to Bette Davis:

"So many people have written that I was a star, not an actress. They wrote that Bette Davis was an actress *and* a star, a *real* actress.

"I knew I was as much an actress as she was. But I wasn't as hurt as you might think because I loved being called a star, and even more *being* a star. But it was nice with *Mildred Pierce* to finally be certified as an actress."

Mildred Pierce (1945)

At police headquarters, restaurateur Mildred Pierce relates the events leading up to the murder of her present husband, Monte Beragon (Zachary Scott).

In flashback, housewife Mildred Pierce supports her family with home baking, while her husband, small-home builder Bert Pierce (Bruce Bennett), looks for work. They have two daughters, Veda (Ann Blyth), 16, and Kay (Jo Ann Marlowe), 11. Kay is a tomboy, while Veda is a pretentious, vain young lady with expensive tastes that Mildred tries to satisfy.

Suspecting Bert is involved with another woman, Mildred insists on a separation, though it's not what either one really wants.

Veda is humiliated when she finds out her mother has become a waitress, but Mildred tells her it is part of a plan to become wealthy. Mildred is going to open a restaurant called Mildred's. She has already found an appropriate site on the ocean.

Wally Fay (Jack Carson), a real estate agent who likes Mildred, arranges for her to meet the property's owner, Monte, a charming playboy with extravagant tastes. Mildred persuades him to let her use the property for a restaurant, paying him as she is successful.

Mildred's is so successful, she opens a chain of restaurants. Meanwhile, she becomes romantically involved with Monte.

Veda is even more precious to Mildred when Kay dies of pneumonia after a vacation with her father and sister. Mildred feels guilt as well as grief, because she was with Monte while, unknown to her, her youngest child was dying.

The Mildred's chain of restaurants makes her a wealthy woman, but her affection for Monte diminishes as she realizes he is more interested in her money and Veda than in her. She pays him to leave, his "tip."

Veda secretly marries a young millionaire, and then forces his family to pay $10,000 for an annulment, claiming she is pregnant.

Mildred tears up the check when she realizes her daughter is not pregnant, and Veda slaps her, saying she is ashamed that her grandmother had to take in laundry. Mildred orders Veda to leave.

Mildred learns from Bert that their daughter has become a honky-tonk dancer. Veda is willing to come back, but on her own terms: a large amount of money and social status.

To provide the social status, Mildred marries Monte, who agrees to this only after he receives a third of the Mildred's restaurant chain. Veda returns.

Needing more money, Monte sells his share of Mildred's, and Wally joins him rather than risk his investment, forcing Mildred toward bankruptcy. Then she realizes that Veda and Monte are having an affair.

Holding a gun, Mildred confronts the couple in his beach house. Monte easily disarms her.

After Mildred leaves, Monte tells Veda he couldn't love a little tramp like her, and she shoots him with Mildred's gun.

Veda persuades her mother not to call the police, pleading for another chance, blaming Mildred for the way she is. The flashback ends.

To protect her daughter, Mildred confesses to the crime, just as Bert had already done. Veda, picked up by the police as she is leaving town, unwittingly admits that she is the real killer. Still haughty, she is led off to a cell.

As Mildred leaves the building, Bert is waiting outside for her in the light of dawn. Silhouetted in the foreground are workers scrubbing the floors.

Joan won her first and only Oscar for this film. "You can't imagine what receiving my Oscar meant to me," she said. "I had always wanted to win one, and I treasure mine. I gave a good performance in a fine picture, but the truth of it is, as I see it, I won more of a lifetime Oscar which they gave for the sum of the best of my films, *A Woman's Face* and *Grand Hotel*, and a few others, with extra points for sticking around so long."

In 1946, the Oscar ceremony took place at Grauman's Chinese Theatre in Los Angeles. The nominees for best actress were Greer Garson for *The Valley of Decision*, Jennifer Jones for *Love Letters*, Gene Tierney for *Leave Her to Heaven*, Ingrid Bergman for *The Bells of St. Mary's*, and Joan for *Mildred Pierce*.

Bette Davis's film that year was *The Corn Is Green*. Bette was very proud of her performance, playing a schoolteacher much older than she actually was. Bette always said that she loved to play old until she *was* old. "Then, I wished I could play young," she told me, "but that's impossible, to play much younger than you are. What a shame."

Bette was not nominated that year, and as she herself noted, *"Mildred Pierce* far out-grossed *The Corn Is Green."*

. . .

JOAN DIDN'T GO to the Oscars. She believed that Ingrid Bergman would win for her role in *The Bells of St. Mary's*. Joan thought Ingrid, as a fine actress, truly beautiful, and playing a nun, was a sure thing.

Everyone assumed that Joan would go from her home in Brentwood to the Oscars ceremony. She knew that producer Jerry Wald wanted her to be there, but the very thought of it sent Joan into an agony of uncertainty.

"Jerry found *Mildred Pierce* for me," Joan said, "putting me forever in his debt. He was a person who did everything well. He was a fine producer, with good taste. He had a writer's heart. I'd said I would do anything for him, and this was all that he wanted. How could I say no to him?

"But how could I say yes? I was terrified, and with every day that passed, I was more terrified. I was afraid of two things.

"I was afraid of losing. The tension is so terrible when you're sitting there waiting. Waiting for best actress means sitting there almost the entire evening. You have to look composed and applaud at all the right moments when you're so confused you can hardly concentrate on who's getting which award. I'd be so nervous I couldn't bear it.

"Then, when you lose, and I was certain I would, you have to sit there through the last awards wearing your best face. You can't wear a loser's face and depress others and humiliate yourself. You can't wear a winner's face because you *aren't* one. And I wouldn't know what part to play after I heard the words that someone else had won, probably Ingrid Bergman.

"Even though you know you're going to lose, you can't be one hundred percent certain of losing, and you can't go without a speech.

"The only thing worse than losing was winning. I would have to go up to the stage and make a speech as myself. I didn't like to face a live audience, and these were all people who were in the business, as they say. I would be judged by them. If I did badly, and I'd *think* I did badly, no matter what happened, I would have to move from my house in Brentwood and go somewhere and hide. What if I stood there, and the applause stopped, and I opened my mouth, and nothing came out?

"I fretted so much that I couldn't sleep at night. I could scarcely eat, and I developed a temperature. My doctor said I had to go to bed and rest. Well, that was the worst thing for me, to go to bed with my dilemma.

"So, I had nothing to do but get sicker. Then, I *really* couldn't go. The decision was made for me.

"There were people who thought I just lied. I could never have done that. The most I could do was to make myself genuinely sick."

When she did win and her Oscar was delivered to her home, Joan looked so well that her reported illness was said to be feigned because she didn't want to be there unless she knew she would win.

"I did my best to look my best," Joan told me, "but I really *was* ill.

"I've never prided myself on being a good loser. I've always wanted to be a good winner, whether it was a dance contest or the Academy Awards. One could never have too many prizes. But the Oscar was the most special."

The announcement that she had won was made by Charles Boyer.

Michael Curtiz and Jerry Wald presented the Oscar statuette to Joan in her Brentwood home. The press had been notified, and there was a tremendous crowd.

That night, Joan slept with Oscar.

WARREN COWAN REPRESENTED Joan during her time at Warner Brothers. He was considered the dean of Hollywood publicists. I met him with Groucho Marx, for whom he also worked, when I was writing my first book, *Hello, I Must Be Going*, which was about Groucho and the Marx Brothers.

"For Joan Crawford," Cowan told me, "I started 'the Oscar campaign,' as it's known today. What we did for her was the first one directed to members of the Academy.

"When we started handling her, she'd just been named 'Box Office Poison' by the theater owners of America. She had left M-G-M and signed with Warner Brothers.

"About two or three weeks into the shooting of *Mildred Pierce*, I sat at my typewriter and wrote an item. That's what publicists did in those days. The item said, 'The front office at Warner Brothers is jumping with glee over the early rushes of Joan Crawford in *Mildred Pierce*. They say she's sure to be nominated for an Oscar this year.'

"Well, much to my surprise, Hedda Hopper ran that item exactly. She never checked on 'the front office,' whoever that is, and when I saw it in print, I remember thinking, 'We should repeat this story over and over again to attract the attention of the Academy members and hopefully get her nominated.'

"We did all kinds of stories tied in with 'they say' and groups that were picking her for awards, and we took the first ads in the trade papers directed to the Academy, about Joan Crawford. By the time the picture came out, that whole label of her being 'Box Office Poison' was forgotten, and she did, indeed, win the Oscar.

"The first time I met Joan was when I drove to her home one morning. I knocked and rang the front bell, and there was no answer. So, I walked around the back of the house, and there was a kitchen door, which was half door and half window. I looked in, and there was the maid scrubbing the kitchen floor, wearing a bandanna on her head. I rapped on the door, and she saw me and came to the door. I said, 'Excuse me, is Miss Crawford at home?'

"She said, 'You must be Warren. It's *me*, Joan.' She really cared about cleanliness.

"She was incredible. She answered all her fan mail. There was a ton of it, but she thought she owed it to her fans.

"She was the most disciplined person. She once told me that when she drove, her back never touched the seat. She said, 'I sit erect to keep my posture.'

"I remember sitting in her den one day, and she asked me if I had the number for the Hollywood Roosevelt Hotel. I said no.

"She dialed information, and instead of saying, 'What is the number for the Hollywood Roosevelt?' she said to the operator, 'Hello, dear. This is Joan Crawford. What is the number for the Hollywood Roosevelt?'

"I found her fascinating. Very kind. I loved her."

• • •

"DAVID NIVEN WAS a great friend of mine," Douglas Fairbanks, Jr., told me. "He and his beautiful young wife were terribly happy after the birth of their baby, and they weren't going out, but there was a neighborhood party at Ty Power's.

"They played hide-and-seek. Primula had just had a baby son, with her handsome husband, and she was full of fun when she pulled open a door, thinking it was a closet she could hide in. It wasn't a closet, and she fell down a flight of stairs. She was rushed to the hospital with her desperate husband by her side.

"Joan wasn't at the party, but when she heard what had happened, immediately she called and offered to take the baby until his mother was well. It was so like Joan not just to say, could she help, but to step in and take responsibility and do what was needed.

"Primula died. She was only twenty-seven. It was tragic."

GREG BAUTZER WAS a tall, handsome, sun-tanned lawyer who was as well known in Hollywood for his romantic escapades as for his legal practice. He possessed many of the qualities Joan admired, among them being a wonderful dancer. Although she considered it frivolous to judge a man by the way he danced, "I couldn't help it," she admitted.

He had worked his way through the University of Southern California law school to become a prominent Hollywood lawyer, working with many of the major stars. Athletic, an outstanding tennis player, he was socially graceful and frequently escorted actresses to parties. He had great energy, working at his practice all day and playing just as hard at night. Though they were mutually attracted, their affair wouldn't begin until 1947, after Joan had divorced Phillip Terry and had won her Oscar for *Mildred Pierce*.

HUMORESQUE WAS BASED on a Fannie Hurst novel that had been made into a silent film. The ironic title is most often used to characterize a short whimsical piece of music. Joan immediately let producer Jerry Wald know that she was interested in playing the part of Helen Wright.

"I had kind of a sexy scene in *Humoresque* with John Garfield," Joan told me. "I rode a horse, and I was supposed to ride into a tree branch and be knocked to the ground. John was to rush to my side and be on top of me. I must have been crazy because I said I wanted to do my own stunt. They must have been crazier, because they let me do it.

"I must say that lying there on the ground with Johnny on top of me, I was very happy. I liked Johnny, but the reason I really was so happy was because I was still in one piece.

"My happiness was short-lived. The powers-that-be had decided that it was too racy to have Johnny Garfield there on top of me. We had to reshoot that scene so that I ended up on top of him. That passed. I couldn't really understand what was the difference, him on top of me or me on top of him.

"Well, the difference was I had to fall off the horse again. I did, and I lived to tell the tale."

Humoresque (1946)

Wealthy Helen Wright (Joan Crawford) has many flirtations and affairs with younger men, which are overlooked by her aging husband, Victor (Paul Cavanagh). Her current affair is with a talented violinist, Paul Boray (John Garfield), who intrigues her more than the others because of his total dedication to his art. His independent spirit especially attracts her. She falls in love with him, and he with her.

Through her social connections and wealth, she is able to guide his career. Personally, they have problems. Paul's mother (Joan Chandler) strongly disapproves of the relationship, and Paul himself cannot understand Helen's complex, often contradictory nature. For her part, Helen worries that her destructive possessiveness threatens not only their love, but Paul's future as an artist.

After a quarrel, she sees him with a young woman and becomes irrationally jealous. They quarrel, and Helen realizes their relationship is not only in trouble, but doomed, like all of her others.

At her seaside house, Helen grows depressed while listening to Paul playing on the radio, and she commits suicide, walking into the ocean.

I met violinist Isaac Stern at New York's Photosphere shop on Sixth Avenue, and we talked about *Humoresque* as we waited for our pictures. We continued talking as we walked toward Carnegie Hall. This was a few years before Stern would save the historic building from demolition.

He was music advisor on *Humoresque*, and he provided the sound of John Garfield's violin. He very much liked Joan Crawford, and they became good friends. He said she was respectful toward him to the point of being "reverential, worshipful, even awe-struck.

"Of course, I can't say I didn't enjoy it, but it also made me self-conscious and nervous. Not when I was in the recording studio dubbing the music, but in front of other people, socially, it embarrassed me a bit.

"But then I thought, 'How would it be if she suddenly stopped her wonderfully absurd behavior because she found out that I was just an ordinary man who knows how to play a very expensive fiddle?' I stopped being embarrassed.

"It isn't well known, but Joan had a real appreciation of music. It is well known how she could dance, but she sang, too. She sang for me, and I was surprised by her trained voice. It was a light voice, but very pleasant and distinctive. When I played Isolde's Love-Death for the sound track, I thought of her and her very lovely soprano voice. Imagine. A beautiful Isolde who weighs only a hundred pounds!"

Stern enjoyed his film work, and he said he was proud to have made a contribution to *Humoresque*. "I was twenty-five and I'd recently made my Carnegie Hall debut. I felt a little like John Garfield myself. If only I could have *looked* like him, too!"

ALTHOUGH JOAN HADN'T planned it that way, she found herself a single parent with two difficult children.

"Though they were in no way related," Joan said, "and Christina was older than Christopher, the first two children I adopted very much resembled each other in looks, and strongly in personality. I don't think any two siblings could have been more alike. They enjoyed tormenting me. They were allies and each, because of having a confederate, was stronger.

"I told my daughter when she was very young, 'Tina, I promise you will not have the kind of childhood I had. I want you to have everything I never had, everything I can give you.'

"She was so young I wasn't certain she was grasping what I said, maybe hearing the words, but not fully understanding the meaning. She grasped what I said, her way.

"For her, I think my promise meant instant gratification."

"The daughter was the troublemaker," producer-director-writer Joseph Mankiewicz told me.

"The little boy admired his sister so much, and I think she knew how to play him. Maybe the older girl resented getting a new baby brother and only pretended to be pleased about it. Joan said Christina really loved him, but who knows?

"Joan loved her and saw what she wanted to see. She was clearly the apple of Joan's eye."

THE BACK-TO-BACK SUCCESSES of *Mildred Pierce* and *Humoresque* prompted Lew Wasserman to request Joan's contract with Warner Brothers be renegotiated, something Jack Warner was willing to do. His Bette Davis films were not doing well, and she was acting as if she wanted to be let out of her contract. Joan Crawford was viewed as a replacement.

Under the terms of the new five-year contract, Joan would do two pictures a year for $250,000 a picture, with complete script, director, and co-star approval. She was also free to work on a loan-out to other studios, should she desire.

Betty Barker, Joan's longtime personal secretary, told me that the second *Possessed* was one of Joan's favorite films. "She liked that movie very, very much. She would show that often in her little theater behind her house."

Possessed (1947)

Like a sleepwalker, Louise Howell Graham (Joan Crawford) aimlessly roams the deserted streets of downtown Los Angeles at night. She has just killed the man she loves.

In a flashback, before she married multimillionaire Dean Graham (Raymond Massey), Louise was his invalid wife's nurse. Although the wife believes that her nurse is having an affair with her husband, Louise is obsessively in love with a young engineer, David Sutton (Van Heflin), who, after showing interest, rejects her. After Mrs. Graham dies, Louise stays on to take care of the Grahams' young son, Wynn (Gerald Perreau). Unable to win David, Louise accepts Dean's offer of marriage, although she does so with the disapproval of his adolescent daughter, Carol (Geraldine Brooks), who believes her late mother's accusations.

David, now working for Dean's company, becomes involved with Carol, who doesn't know of Louise's obsession with David. Louise, learning that David and Carol are going to marry, goes mad and kills him. Found walking the streets in a catatonic state, Louise is diagnosed as not being responsible for her actions. Dean, who loves her in spite of everything, offers her his support while she recovers from her illness.

This was the film on which Joan said she "had to work the hardest" in her life.

"It's not easy to play a crazy person. You have to be able to convey that you *are* crazy, but you can't be continuously crazy at the same pitch. And you can't be so crazy you'd be locked up, or the audience gets bored or irritated, and wants to run out of the theater, and often does. The balance of unbalance is necessary. I did my homework. For six weeks, I went to some hospitals and mental institutions and rest homes to observe the mentally ill. I talked with psychiatrists, and I got advice, which I followed. In the film, I mean!

"In the hospital wards I visited to learn about the character I was playing, I saw people who seemed perfectly sane, but then they might switch suddenly. For no reason at all, a woman would begin crying hysterically.

"It seemed like each one was in a shell. Sometimes they were walking as in a dream, and they really believed what they were seeing and hearing. It was only in each person's mind, but it was so totally real to that person, more real than reality. Poor souls. I couldn't bear it. I felt so sorry for these tormented people who had lost themselves.

"At first, I could barely watch. I felt like a spy or an intruder, that observing their illnesses was too deep an intrusion. But they never seemed to mind. Usually, they didn't seem to pay attention to me at all, and they were scarcely aware I was there, I think. But *I* was very aware. It was a terribly hard experience for me because my heart was breaking for them.

"One thing I noticed was when they talked, even when you didn't notice anything wrong with them, they didn't look into anyone's eyes when they spoke with them. When these poor, sick people spoke, they turned their heads to the side. They never looked their doctors in the eye.

"I loved doing that film, and I felt so lucky to be nominated for an Oscar, me and that part."

Joan was nominated as best actress. She lost to Loretta Young, who won for *The Farmer's Daughter*.

JOAN AND GREG Bautzer had been seeing each other, often. She told friends that he was perfect for her at that moment, since neither one of them wanted marriage.

She liked Bautzer's refined manners—quick to get the car door, or to light her cigarette—and she loved his not being an actor. It was very important to her that he was *not* an actor. He automatically stepped aside when pictures were being taken of her unless she beckoned him into the photograph. She said it was wonderful to be with a man who had his own different successful career.

She was pleased that he took an interest in her son and that Christopher looked forward to his coming over and playing ball with him. She had failed to establish any good rapport with Christopher.

• • •

HENRY FONDA TOLD me that *Daisy Kenyon* wasn't "his cup of tea," but he was very happy with Otto Preminger as a director and, Fonda added, "I have known some of the best."

"I enjoyed talking about art with Mr. Preminger, who was a sophisticated art collector. He wasn't an artist with a brush or a pencil, but his art was making films."

Joan admitted that she found Henry Fonda extremely attractive. "He was just the kind of man I liked. He was not only so handsome, but he was a wonderful artist. I admired his drawings and paintings. He was as talented as an artist as he was as an actor.

"There was never anything between us, except a film, I'm sorry to report. I was surprised to learn much later that Bette Davis had liked him, too. Well, who wouldn't?"

Daisy Kenyon (1947)

Daisy Kenyon (Joan Crawford), a New York commercial artist, is dissatisfied with her backstreet relationship with lawyer Dan O'Mara (Dana Andrews). He is married with children, and although he is unhappy with his wife, he refuses to get a divorce to marry Daisy.

Daisy accepts this until another man appears in her life. He is Peter (Henry Fonda), who is quite the opposite of the selfish and overbearing Dan. She falls in love with Peter, and they marry.

Daisy's marriage to Peter doesn't stop Dan from pursuing her. He even divorces his wife. Being confident of himself, he believes Daisy will divorce Peter and marry him, as soon as he is available.

Peter leaves the decision to Daisy, who chooses Peter, not Dan.

"Daisy Kenyon wasn't a great movie, but I think it was a good one," Joan said. "I had wanted to do it primarily because of the opportunity to work with Otto Preminger. He'd done *Laura* just a few years earlier, and I wanted to work with all of the good and great directors I possibly could. I always wanted to continue to learn.

"I'd first met Mr. Preminger at a party for him when he came to Hollywood. When I heard that I would be working with Henry Fonda, too, that was chocolate frosting on a chocolate cake. He was an extraordinary actor and a lovely man. And Dana Andrews, an under-estimated actor who wasn't fully appreciated because his style was to underplay, which is so difficult.

"People didn't seem to like dear, sweet Otto. They would say to me, 'He's a Nazi, you know.' And I would say, 'But he's Jewish. He had to flee Austria for his life.' He was the kindest, sweetest man.

"How can people who don't know the person, or anything about the accusations they're repeating, believe such untrue rumors, and then spread them?"

"I enjoyed working with Miss Crawford," Otto Preminger told me. "We were alike because we were both people who tried hard. There are some people who scorn those who seem to be trying too hard. Miss Crawford and I were people who believed there was no such thing as trying too hard.

"We did not have the greatest film to make because that depends on the writers and, in this case, the choice of a book, and then the script. Audiences notice the stars. Sometimes they pay attention to who directed a film. They do not notice who writes it.

"It was clear that we couldn't make a masterpiece out of what we had, but to her credit, Joan worked as hard as if we had a masterpiece going. She came early, she knew her lines and probably everyone else's, too, and she was always there, trying as hard as if we were making some great film. Well, you have to feel you are doing something worthwhile or you can't go on, and she helped me to feel that way.

"She did her best every day, and I did, too, because that was the way we were made."

Otto Preminger's Manhattan town house, which was close to Joan's apartment, had a small but precious garden. Such gardens are rare on Manhattan's Upper East Side. After lunch, we went into the garden, where a large Henry Moore sculpture of a woman dominated with her serenely graceful presence.

Neighbors had expressed admiration for the figure, but complained that they could only see her back.

Preminger then had the figure mounted on a revolving pedestal so that everyone else, on occasion, had a chance to observe the figure from all sides. When I said something about how much I liked "his" Henry Moore figure, he corrected me. "She's not mine.

"When I die, she's not mine anymore. When Henry Moore dies, she's always *his*. That's the test."

Glancing at the figure, Preminger said, "Did you notice how feminine she is? That's something I want to tell you about Joan. The most surprising thing I learned about her, as we worked together, was that she was a very feminine woman. No matter how severe the suits, how large those shoulder pads, there was a tiny feminine woman who cared greatly about everything.

"They weren't shaped the same. Joan was a tiny girl, and Henry Moore's is a big lady, but they were both *all* woman, and you know, if you happened to bump into tiny Joan, you were shocked to find she had a body as hard as the statue."

IN EARLY 1947, Joan adopted twin infant daughters. She named them Cynthia and Catherine, following her preference for names that began with C. They were always called Cindy and Cathy.

Her affair with Bautzer continued, though not without friction. The disparity in their incomes was always a problem with the men in her life. He was extremely successful, but she was more successful.

Joan had always enjoyed giving gifts to people she cared about and for Bautzer she would select Cartier cuff links. He was appreciative and wore her gifts. He also gave her gifts, shopping at Cartier for earrings that cost more than he could afford. He told her that he would prefer not exchanging expensive gifts because he couldn't afford it. "Actually, I couldn't either," Joan admitted, "but I really enjoyed buying the things for him. I told him he didn't have to reciprocate at all. He could just give me a token. But he didn't like that. Male pride should never be underestimated.

"It reminded me of when I saw the house I wanted and *had* to have it, and it was more than Douglas could afford. I just *had* to have it, and I could do it, so I did, but I don't think Douglas was ever truly at home there because he hadn't paid half of the price of the house and couldn't afford half of the expenses. It didn't seem he should mind, but he did, I think, as I look back."

Joan enjoyed being envied by other women, who found Bautzer attractive. She found she didn't enjoy it when Bautzer would escort one of the Hollywood actresses who "pursued" him to a premiere or Hollywood party or his being in the newspaper columns having lunch with one of them, even if she was his client. He was accustomed to being pursued by women. "I suppose I preferred a man who pursued *me*," Joan said.

For her next film, Joan was reunited with some of the key people from *Mildred Pierce*. Zachary Scott was her leading man, Michael Curtiz her director, and Jerry Wald her producer.

Flamingo Road (1949)

Sheriff Titus Semple (Sydney Greenstreet) runs Bolton City. A carnival has not paid him off, so he sends his deputy, Fielding "Field" Carlisle (Zachary Scott) to disperse it. Field finds only sideshow dancer Lane Bellamy (Joan Crawford) still there. Feeling sorry for her, he helps her get a job as a waitress.

He falls in love with Lane, but Sheriff Semple expects his deputy to become a state senator and forces the weak Lane to marry wealthy and socially appropriate Annabelle Weldon (Virginia Huston). Semple arranges everything through Dan Reynolds (David Brian), a builder who runs the state political machine.

Semple has Lane fired from her job. When she confronts the sheriff, she is arrested on false prostitution charges.

Vowing revenge, she becomes a hostess in a roadhouse One of its clients is Reynolds, who is staying there on election night. Reynolds falls in love with her, and they soon marry.

Field, now a senator and still in love with Lane, resists Semple's plans to make him governor. When Reynolds refuses to back Field, Semple threatens a labor dispute that will disrupt an important local building project. Semple decides to run for governor himself.

Field commits suicide after becoming an alcoholic. Semple starts the rumor that Field killed himself because of his affair with Lane. Reynolds believes the lie and leaves Lane.

Lane confronts Semple with a gun. In a struggle, he is killed. As
Lane awaits trial, Reynolds returns and vows to stand by her.

"Both Christina and Christopher were attention hogs," Joan told
me. "It seemed they couldn't get enough. They were voracious con-
sumers of attention. But I must say, they never competed with each
other for attention, only with the rest of the world.

"Christopher knew just how to do it. He seemed to enjoy only bad
attention and didn't try for any other. That seemed to be the only kind
of attention he knew how to apply himself to. His goal seemed to be
to punish me by being a bad boy. He was very good at achieving that
goal, if no other.

"They were very unified from the first moment Christopher was
old enough to begin worshipping his sister.

"Christina had been a dear, beautiful little blond baby, affectionate, sweet. She didn't cry and was no trouble, until later. It began
with her fear of the dark. Then, the whispering began with her little
brother.

"At first, I thought that was cute, their two little blond heads
together. I wondered what my babies were gossiping about.

"Later, I understood it was about *me*. I was the one they were
talking about, and what they were saying wasn't nice, but it was only
much, much later that I understood that. If I had known at the time, I
don't know what I could have done. I couldn't return them.

"I don't know if I should have been stricter, or less strict. Nothing
seemed to work. They were difficult children, and it only got worse as
they grew up. Their difficulties grew up with them, even faster than
they did.

"I remember how sorry I felt for Bette Davis when I heard that the
baby girl she had adopted turned out to be mentally retarded, brain-
damaged. I admired the way she and her husband, Gary Merrill, handled the situation, totally responsible. I never mentioned it to Bette
because I didn't think she cared about having my admiration, and
I knew she would only resent my sympathy. She certainly wouldn't
want my pity and probably would show disdain for my expression of
sympathy.

"One thing I did envy her. I envied her that she had a child of her own, a little girl.

"Mine was a different problem. As a small baby, Christopher was a beautiful child, but he had a strangely cold personality. He didn't smile or laugh, even when you tickled him. He only looked like you were bothering him. He didn't like it when I held him and especially if I tried to cuddle him or touch his face and beautiful gold hair. He seemed uncomfortable. He would use the strength in his little body to pull away.

"He seemed complete unto himself. It was as if my tender attention made him feel uncomfortable. I tried to attribute it to a boy baby being different from a girl baby. As his little body grew, and he had enough strength to do so, he would squirm, as if he wanted to get away from me.

"Christopher was the most energetic child. Someone told me that it was because boys are different from girls. Christina was such an easy baby and when she was a little girl, she never got her dress dirty. She sat where I put her, with her hair bow in her golden hair.

"Christopher was always on the move, from the time he was a baby. He seemed never still. I thought he would outgrow all of that over-abundant energy, but the opposite. He grew more energetic and very strong.

"As soon as he could walk, or something like walk, toddle, he moved forward, head-down, face-forward, always looking for danger, steps to tumble down. I didn't know what to do about my fearless child.

"As soon as he could walk on his little legs, he began to try to run away. He was running away from something or someone. He often succeeded. He ran away a lot of times. He didn't have anywhere to run to, so it became clear he was running away—from me.

"I tried as soon as I thought he could understand my words, but I couldn't persuade him about danger because he was too young really to understand. Later I thought when he understood what danger meant, he went more strongly toward it.

"I couldn't lock him in his room like a prisoner in a jail cell. If I did, my precious baby would be trapped, and it would take longer to rescue him if we had a fire.

"I considered putting a dresser in front of the door. That made me like his jailer. Even worse, I didn't want *him* to feel that way, that I was holding him against his will by force. I was at my wit's end.

"I tried having him sleep in Christina's room. That lasted quite a while, but it was a problem because Christina had to sleep with a light on.

"When we had people in, Christopher would come out with his sister, she wearing a pretty frock, and he would be handsomely dressed in little short pants. He would bow to each guest, the way I had taught him to, and Christina would curtsy. Sometimes, it was funny when he would bow so low, he almost fell on his face. I thought it was because he loved me and wanted to please me. I explained to him that he needn't bow *that* low. He gave me this cold look. Then, the next time I introduced someone, he bowed even lower.

"I wasn't teaching Christopher, he was teaching me. He was training me, so I would know what my place was, so I would learn my lesson. The lesson I was learning was that whatever I said to Christopher, he was likely to do the opposite.

"My voice was like a red flag to a bull. My voice seemed to irritate him terribly.

"Sometimes when I went out to dinner with a man, I would see how interested my little Christopher was in a big person who was male if the man spoke with him. Or it could be a gardener, a repairman, a delivery man, and it meant more than when I said anything.

"The only thing he seemed to be good at was running away, and he was too good at that. They say practice makes perfect.

"I remember the first time. We searched everywhere. I thought we would find him under one of the beds, playing a private game of hide-and-seek. But after we had searched under all of the beds, everywhere, and I could not think where to look anymore, I felt true panic.

"If Christina didn't know where he was, I became afraid that he had been kidnapped.

"It was a fear the successful, well-to-do parent knows. It had hovered in the back of my mind.

"I prayed if they had him that they would send a note. I would do whatever they said. If only they would return him unharmed, I would pay the ransom. Fortunately, he was too young to identify the kidnappers, so they could let him go. I hoped they would leave him in a safe place.

"Then I noticed that one of the windows was open slightly. It seemed too little a space for even young Christopher.

"I rushed outside, and there he was, sitting on the grass.

"We had to sleep with the windows closed, which was a shame, because the air was so fresh and good where we lived. I like cool rooms.

"That continued until Christopher was strong enough to open the window himself. After that, there was no point to not having fresh air in the house.

"One of the times, my little boy ran away and we couldn't find him for many hours. He was about eight or nine. The police brought him back.

"I didn't know how to greet him. I wanted to throw my arms around him and hug him, but I thought he'd probably pull away. And I didn't think I should give him the satisfaction of knowing how desperately frightened I'd been. He seemed to like the two policemen and want to stay with them. He certainly didn't look happy to be returned like lost property to me. He sat stiffly on a chair, not showing any emotion.

"I asked him, 'Why did you run away, Christopher?'

"No answer.

"I didn't bother asking him again. I knew I'd received the only answer I was going to get, no matter how many times I asked the question.

"I no longer got any respect from him. I was a little embarrassed in front of the detectives, especially when one of them asked if he could have my autograph.

"I wasn't much in the mood because the personal Joan Crawford was suffering, but my professional self couldn't let down a fan. The second detective asked if he could have an autograph for his nephew, 'Pat.' I said, 'Of course.'

"Then I asked them if they had questioned Christopher about why he had run away.

"They said they had, and he told them that it was because his mother wouldn't let him have chocolate sauce on his ice cream.

"He'd caused me a lot of pain, but he didn't get his victory. The next time we had vanilla ice cream for dessert, he didn't get hot chocolate sauce on his ice cream.

"Christina ate all of hers with great zest, but Christopher, who had vanilla ice cream without sauce, left his ice cream untouched and stared at me with a look of palpable hatred, which I could feel.

"The battle of wills had begun. I suppose it had begun well before the chocolate sauce, but I had wanted to overlook it.

"From then on, no matter how much I wanted to, Christopher never let me overlook it.

"When I was in school at Rockingham I ran away because I was working like a drudge to earn my board. I hated it.

"When they noticed I was gone, which I suppose they did when there wasn't anyone to make their beds, they didn't bother to look for me. I guess they thought I'd be back, and I was. I didn't have anywhere to go.

"I thought about it when Christopher ran away. I thought I should understand what Christopher was feeling and doing.

"I tried having him sleep in my bedroom. We brought in a bed for him, but he didn't like that. He didn't need much sleep, and he went to bed earlier than I did. I considered having him stay up later so he could sleep through the night.

"Someone told me about a restraining harness which might keep him in bed. It had been created for children like Christopher who left their beds and then their houses and wandered around the neighborhood during the night.

"It seemed a wonderful idea. I knew Christopher wouldn't like it. No, I knew he'd *hate* it. But I was at a loss. I couldn't face the situation.

"He was quite precocious in his attempts at roaming and running away. I simply didn't know what to do. I thought of him going out into the street and being hit by a car. That was my great fear.

"Or that he might go onto someone else's property and fall into a swimming pool and drown. I had read stories about that happening to young children.

"I had this unbearable image in my mind of my beloved child floating face-down in a neighbor's pool. I taught him to float and then swim before he was two. I wondered if that protected him or created a greater danger because he liked the water. Would he look for a swimming pool? Would he panic and forget what he had learned? It could happen to a little boy, wandering around at night, he could—and I can't even say the word—drown.

"The restrainer didn't work. Clever Christopher quickly figured out, Houdini-like, how to wiggle out. He also figured out how to get back in, so I didn't know.

"As soon as he was old enough, he accused me of 'kidnapping' him. I learned much later that he had been telling that, over the years, to any man in our neighborhood who would listen to him."

Betty Barker, who had worked for Joan from before the time she adopted the children to after they were grown, said about Christina and Christopher: "They were willful children.

"People said Joan was controlling. I never saw that in thirty years. And, also, I never saw her out of control. In thirty years, I never saw her do anything wrong with her children. I would swear to that. She deserved a lot better than she got back from the two older children she adopted."

"I never thought about *not* telling my children they were adopted," Joan said. "I saw it as meaning that they were wanted and they would know that. I thought that if I told them late, after they believed I was their natural mother, they would be terribly shocked, and it would be difficult for them to adjust to such news.

"Along the way, who could I say was his or her father? It was certainly a question I would be asked.

"I never wanted to lie to them. I never did. Never.

"I couldn't imagine seeing it any other way. But I guess two of my children *didn't* see it that way."

JOAN PLAYS ONLY a cameo part in *It's a Great Feeling*, a satire on Hollywood moviemaking starring Jack Carson, Dennis Morgan, and Doris Day, in her first starring role. Other cameos are contributed by

Gary Cooper, Edward G. Robinson, Danny Kaye, Ronald Reagan, Jane Wyman, Eleanor Parker, Patricia Neal, and Errol Flynn. Some famous directors appear, too—King Vidor, Michael Curtiz, and Raoul Walsh. Almost everyone plays himself.

It's a Great Feeling (1949)

Jack Carson and Dennis Morgan, playing themselves, want to make a movie with their new discovery, waitress Judy Adams (Doris Day), but their producer, Arthur Trent (Bill Goodwin), can't find a director willing to direct the "difficult" Carson. Carson solves this problem by volunteering to direct himself. In the end, he directs himself out of winning the girl. Errol Flynn wins her instead, which may be a happy ending for Doris, or not.

Joan appears as herself at a fashion house, where she sits knitting. She overhears Carson and Morgan talking about Doris Day as if they are both having an affair with her, and as if she is merely a property, not realizing they are talking about a movie they are making. She confronts them with a parody of her speech from *Mildred Pierce*, in which she tells Veda to leave, and then, in defense of Doris Day's honor, she slaps them both. "I do that in all my pictures," she says, rushing off. This was one of Joan's few opportunities since silent days to play comedy, and she loved doing it.

Some of the strain in Joan's relationship with Greg Bautzer began to show in public, which she hated. She had never liked any kind of quarreling. "Personally it disturbed my sense of balance. Professionally I could not allow personal stress to intrude into my performances, for which I needed all of my concentration. I found it embarrassing to allow private feelings to hang out like wash on a clothesline. Though I must say that Greg tried hard to make it work, ours was a passionate relationship which became *too* tempestuous.

"Several times we quarreled and stopped speaking, but each time he persisted, and he was quite a romantic fellow. I found that as I resented his attentions to other women, we quarreled about other things—never about the true source of my irritation.

"I couldn't say to him, 'I'm jealous and I don't want you seeing other women, even though we don't have an exclusive arrangement.' I couldn't lose my pride to that extent. It would have been mortifying, humiliating. And it wouldn't have done me any good because I think any attempt to cage him would have made him feel trapped, and he would have flown away. He was all grown up and set in his ways.

"So, instead, I began to speak sharply to him over something petty that didn't matter and did not make for a good romantic relationship. Sharp words and nagging are very bad for sex. I'd caused him to move further away in our relationship. I don't wonder. I'm surprised he didn't run for cover sooner. I'm surprised I didn't, but I knew that Greg Bautzers didn't grow on trees.

"The affair ran its course. When we quarreled, I would suggest we stop seeing each other. I would tell him not to call again. I don't know why I said it, because each time, I was afraid he *wouldn't* call again. Then, when he did, I wouldn't answer. After the phone had rung many times, and I assumed some of the calls were from Greg, finally I would answer. We would always get together again—until we didn't.

"The last time we had words about something, I don't remember about what, we were out in my car. I was driving. He offered to drive. He got out of the car to switch with me, and I drove away, late at night, far from where he lived. He was wearing new shoes and he had to walk home, a long distance. I drove away from our relationship."

JOAN'S NEXT PICTURE was one with an original story that had not been written yet, and it was to be directed by Vincent Sherman.

7

The Later Warner Years

(1949–1951)

VINCENT SHERMAN TOLD me that he had "a black silk panty affair," with Joan Crawford. "It began," he said, "when she gave me a glimpse of her black silk panties. It went on when she whipped them off, which she did numerous times. And finally, it ended when she showed me the back of her black silk panties."

At the time I first spoke with Sherman, he was well into his eighties. I was with director Curtis Harrington, whose work Sherman admired, at the Directors Guild Theater in Los Angeles. Sherman enjoyed talking about films, especially his own, in which he took great pride. He had enjoyed his career tremendously.

We continued talking on other occasions. He told me about his professional as well as his personal relationship with Joan Crawford during the time he was making three films with her. Their first film together, originally called *The Victim*, became *The Damned Don't Cry* (1950).

"*The Victim*," Sherman explained in a slightly lingering southern accent, "was based on the life of Virginia Hill, a young woman from a poor family down south. While she was still in her teens, she ran away to the Chicago World's Fair of the thirties, where she got a job as a cooch dancer in a sideshow. There, she met an accountant who fell in love with her, and he introduced her to some members of the mob for whom he worked. Eventually, she became the mistress of a New York gangster named Joe Adonis, who was said to be related to Frank Costello, and high in mob circles.

"She lived a life of luxury for several years in New York. Then, she was allegedly sent to Las Vegas, where she was supposed to spy on Bugsy Siegel. He was, you know, the man largely responsible for establishing that town when it was only a small desert oasis. The mob suspected him of cheating them, and they wanted evidence that he was skimming their profits. Her mission was to make a play for Siegel and, if he was guilty, to expose him. The mob would take over from there and finish the job.

"She took to her job too well and, unplanned for, she fell in love with Siegel. She was living with him as his mistress at the time of his murder by the mob. It was reminiscent of so many of Crawford's early M-G-M vehicles, the rags-to-riches struggle of a woman, and the consequent wages of her sins.

"Naturally, I hoped we could bring something a little fresh to this formula. I was very anxious to do something that wasn't pat, that wasn't trite, as it was an important step in my career, I hoped. I loved directing films, and even if I never made it to be a real 'name' director, I wanted to keep working in Hollywood and have a chance to make some good films.

"Jerry Wald, the producer, had asked a writer named Harold Medford, who was under contract to the studio, to write a treatment. But then he informed me that he was bringing out Jerry [Jerome] Weid–man, a well-known novelist, from New York to do the screenplay. It was already beginning to look complicated. More writers doesn't necessarily mean a better script. Usually, it means just the opposite. It's not easy to put people together and make a successful collaboration. A meeting was arranged with Crawford, Wald, Medford, Weidman, and me. We discussed the story and how it should be developed.

"This meeting took place in Crawford's dressing room on the Warner lot. This was my first glimpse of her in person. I was very impressed. I found her to be an attractive and impressive woman. I have always admired strong women and avoided clinging-vine types, but her reputation was such that I made up my mind I was not going to get personally involved with her even if an opportunity occurred and if it turned out she liked me. I had made the same resolution when I first met Bette Davis, for what it was worth. I felt I had learned my lesson. These women were both very powerful stars and wielded a lot of influence at the studio. They were both small, but each had a large presence.

"Weidman retired to his hotel room and went to work on the screenplay. As he finished his drafts, he sent them to us, and Medford and I would review the pages as they came in and we'd confer. What I did not know at the time but found out later was that Wald had told Weidman to write the screenplay as he saw fit and not to consult with us. So the meeting was only window dressing, an attempt to make us feel part of it.

"At this time in my career, I wanted to work closely with the writer, preparing a step-by-step outline with him in which every scene would be thoroughly gone over. I believed in a lot of preparation. Only in this way did I think we could deliver the story in the most exciting form possible. After I learned what Wald had done behind my back, I didn't like it, but I decided to just wait to see what Weidman came up with before lodging any protest. I didn't really have any choice. At that stage, I didn't want to be thought of as a troublemaker or time-waster.

"In the first two weeks, he completed seventy-five pages of script, an unheard of amount of writing in such a short time. Obviously, he really could write a lot, fast. His dialogue, I thought, was excellent and the scenes were good. Nonetheless, I became pretty alarmed. The story had hardly begun and there was already over half a script. At this rate we were going to wind up with more than three hundred pages, which was almost enough for three films. Extensive cutting would be more difficult and take longer than writing to approximately the right length. I could see trouble ahead.

"I confided to Wald my worries about the length, which coincided with Medford's worries. I asked if I could talk with Weidman to see if we couldn't get the script down to more workable proportions. We ought to be able to tell the full story in something like 130 pages. We had to. But Wald insisted we should let Weidman continue writing to see what he might come up with. Only if he was free to write it as he saw it would we have the full benefit of his talent. Wald was very sold on him. My earliest sense of trouble ahead grew much greater.

"In those days, you wanted a film that was between one hour and forty minutes and two hours. To dare to go beyond that, you would need an unusual story, one of epic proportions or one with great production values. I have come to appreciate what Harry Cohn, who was head of Columbia Pictures, once said: 'After an hour and forty-five minutes of sitting, my behind begins to get tired,' or something to that effect, though he put it a little cruder.

"In my opinion, there is no reason the average story cannot be told in two hours. I believe it was Hitchcock who said the same thing, only he added the need to go to the bathroom every so often. Beyond a certain amount of time, you are asking for an intensity of physical and mental concentration that tends to diminish as you continue. In spite of Miss Crawford's recognized star power, I did not think she could produce that kind of concentration, unless we gave her fantastic material, and I didn't think our story was going that way. It wasn't even fair to expect her to carry that much of the film with the story we had, which was clearly not *Gone With the Wind*.

"After not having spoken with me since our first meeting. Miss Crawford phoned to ask me if I had read the pages that had been written so far. She was worried because Jerry had told her that he thought they were great. He had told her or implied that I thought it was going well, just as it was. She knew nothing of my concerns about the length of the script, it seemed to me, and she was having second thoughts about my judgment. She probably had decided I was incompetent or crazy, or both.

"She found out that Jerry had lied to her. I probably was too frank and said more than I should have. She became angry and insisted that we all meet so that she could personally express our misgivings to him. Weidman. Medford and I agreed.

"Weidman had promised that he would compress whenever possible from then on, but he asked to be allowed to finish the script before making any changes on what he had already written. I guess he was protective of his artistry. Maybe he also understood that it was a damned hard job, without having the fixes make it seem choppy. Although we agreed, I informed him that in the meantime Medford and I were going ahead with condensing the first batch of pages. He didn't say anything. There was a loud silence, and I knew he wouldn't like it. He was proud of what he had done, and he wasn't going to appreciate our putting our hands on it. There was no way we could do well from his standpoint. We were on our way to a lot of personal tensions.

"During that meeting, I had a chance to observe Joan carefully. I realized that even though she was still very attractive—very—she could never be made up to look like an adolescent girl who chooses to run away from a dreary home life. This was the whole basis of our story the way it was being written.

"I noticed lines in her face, crow's-feet around her eyes, and her neck was starting to show wrinkles. I studied her not from my standpoint as a man, but as a director. I took a very hard professional look.

"This preyed on my mind, and I told Medford. We decided to have a talk with Wald, who finally agreed that we had better take Joan's appearance into consideration and write a different opening for our film. He thought she was very attractive, too, but she couldn't play a girl. It was all very delicate.

"Meanwhile, I was out looking for locations and preparing the production, glad to be busy and away from all the problems.

"Weidman finished the script and it was, as I had feared, more than three hundred pages long. Even though there were many good scenes, we would have to cut them down. Even more important than good scenes, the scenes had to work together to develop the story and the characters, and one scene had to lead to another. With what we had to add, unless we cut a lot, the script could run four hundred pages. There wouldn't be anyone left in the theater, even to watch Joan Crawford.

"Feeling that he had completed his work, Weidman wanted to go back to New York. He was not attracted to the tedious business of cutting and compacting, and besides, his contract time was up. Crawford now demanded that Wald turn the script over to me and Medford for the final draft. She indicated wonderful confidence in us. I was very pleased by that. It was very flattering. In the meantime, Weidman went back east.

"Our first task was to write a new opening that would establish Crawford's character believably while stating our theme. I recalled a conversation I once had with Sinclair Lewis in which he told me how he came to to write *Dodsworth*.

"His first wife was not only socially ambitious, but, as she approached fifty, she worried about still being attractive to men. She was convinced that once a woman passes fifty her sexuality ends. Not that she was contemplating unfaithfulness, but she enjoyed the attention of men besides her husband, and she wanted to cram in as much flirtatious excitement as possible before it was too late, which she feared was imminent. This was all the inspiration Lewis needed.

"Medford and I agreed that was an appropriate, good starting point for our story. We would write a new opening in which Crawford was living a drab life as a bored housewife married to an oil field worker. Her seven-year-old son wants a bicycle, so she buys it for him. Her husband says they can't afford it, and he demands that she take it back.

"Not wanting to disappoint the boy, she pleads with her husband to let their son keep the bike, but the husband is adamant. Joan's character realizes that it will be humiliating for their son to be without the bicycle after he has already shown it to his friends, but she can't persuade her husband.

"The son, who is just up the street with his friends, is ordered by the father to come back home at once. As he starts back, he is run over by a truck. With his death, Crawford, who was staying with her husband only for the sake of her son, has nothing left to keep her in this dismal situation.

"She leaves her dull, domineering husband and her mother and father, with whom they have been living, and she goes to New York, where she is determined to find a better life while she is still young enough and has her looks.

"The big thing was, what would Miss Crawford think? Would she like it? It was a big change. How would she feel about our having made her older? Would she be insulted? We certainly would need her support.

"We sent this opening to Crawford. She liked it. From then on, she phoned me almost every day to discuss some story point, or she would come to the studio to talk about her wardrobe. I found her excellent to work with. She was intelligent, perceptive, and presented her thoughts in a way which was never high-handed. She could have been imperious, but she never was. She always asked rather than told.

And she listened. She appreciated being part of the process of working on the script, even though she had such power. It's hard for me to communicate how much power she had. She could whisper in Wald's ear, anytime.

"As we talked about the script, Joan revealed to me more and more of herself. Our conversation that was professional remained professional. But we also began to have some personal conversation.

"She tried to get me to tell her about Bette Davis. She was very curious about how I found it, working with Bette, but I avoided the subject. She was seriously curious about Bette. I know that I was surprised to learn that despite their different backgrounds and supposed hatred for each other, which I don't personally think was true, Joan and Bette Davis were very much alike, or so it seemed to me.

"Joan told me about her childhood, with a father who deserted the family, which had a devastating emotional effect on young Joan, maybe even greater than on the wife, her mother, who was just able to get someone else. As she told it, her mother was pretty able in that department and not too finicky.

"I was fascinated by the parallels with Bette, who had lived through the same situation, which left her subconsciously seeking a father. And I personally think Bette was seeking a father she could emasculate. I felt that despite their vastly different backgrounds, they were really sisters-under-the-skin.

"While Joan constantly professed a great love for Hollywood, I detected an underlying cynicism on her part. Also, beneath that facade of toughness, I could sense the heart of an incurable romantic. I felt she was more of a romantic than Bette. She was still looking for Prince Charming! And she was still expecting him to arrive, in a white convertible, if not on a white charger. It was an appealing quality, a kind of naïveté that I hoped we could capture in our film.

"We had some time one morning after some wardrobe tests, and she suggested that we run *Humoresque*, which I had not yet seen, because she wanted to discuss the various hairstyles she might use. We had something to eat first and, with the help of a few martinis, she volunteered a little more about herself, showing a softer side, confiding how much she was looking forward to our working together.

"In retrospect, I recognized this as Joan's dance of the seven veils. Later, we went over to the projection room, which was located at the lower end of the Warner lot, and we began running *Humoresque*.

"I thought the film was very well done in all respects, and Joan looked positively ravishing. Then, the last veil dropped. I happened to compliment her on a very sexy scene, and she took my hand and pressed it against her breast. There was no missing that hint.

"You can imagine how surprised I was. No words. I was stunned but I was also aroused. Then, before I could say or do anything, she stood up and, lifting her skirt, she pulled off the pair of black silk panties she was wearing. It was dark, but from the light reflected from the screen, I could see more of her than I had ever expected to see. Never had I encountered such female boldness. Bette Davis had been forward enough, no shrinking violet she, and she liked sex, but nothing like this.

"Despite my excitement, my first thought was to lock the door to the projection room. I hoped the projectionist was loading another reel or something. As I rose to lock the door, she pulled me down on top of her, holding me close. I informed her as to my concerns about the unlocked door, but nothing seemed to distract her from the matter at hand. I couldn't get the projectionist and the door out of my mind. I imagined the door opening, and Jack Warner would be standing there with Louella Parsons and a photographer, maybe even my wife.

"We kissed. I stole a look up at the projection booth. Fortunately, the projectionist seemed otherwise occupied, possibly reading a fan magazine about what it would be like to make love to Joan Crawford.

"I got up and went to lock the door. I saw there was no way I could lock it from the inside.

"I persuaded her to exercise some restraint and wait until the end of the picture we were seeing, so we could go to her dressing room. I tried to make it clear that it was because I didn't want to interrupt her performance, that I was anxious to see it as a whole to the end without breaking it. The truth was, I needed more privacy.

"She relented reluctantly, but needless to say, my concentration on the rest of *Humoresque* was greatly impaired. I was thinking about what had happened, what was going to happen, what the repercussions might be for my career. These were not the best thoughts a good lover, or even an adequate one, should be having.

"Later I came to believe that she had been aroused by her own eroticized image on the screen. I came to think that she had been more excited by herself than by me. It seemed we had switched roles, as I believed from whatever previous sexual experience I had had. I was confronted here with a female who went after what she wanted with a masculine approach to sex.

"I pondered her motives. What was she thinking? She had no reason to think I was available. She didn't even know if I was happily married and therefore wouldn't be interested in her. Maybe she liked the idea that I was married and thus only available for a fling, and of course it was possible that someone had told her about my affair with Bette Davis, despite my efforts to keep that quiet. Or maybe she was just concerned that I had not made a pass at her or indicated in any way that I desired her. Was she testing me? Or was she testing herself?

"The truth was that an affair with Joan was far from my thoughts. I didn't like the idea at all of being compared to all of those other men who who had been in her life.

"Most of all, I was determined to spend more time with my wife and children. Hedda and I had been experiencing marital difficulties, which weakened any reluctance I might have had in becoming even slightly involved with Crawford.

"Joan, too, was at a vulnerable point in her personal life, having just broken up with Greg Bautzer, a handsome and successful attorney, with whom she had been involved in a long-standing affair. Despite my resolve to avoid any entanglements which might threaten my own marriage, I took the path of least resistance. I suppose I was curious about her, and to know what would happen and how it would be. Whatever happened was for the immediate pleasure without becoming involved, of that I was sure.

"We were both silent as we took the long walk from the projection room to her dressing room. I don't know what she was thinking, but by the time we got there, the sudden rush of passion that had come over her in the projection room had passed, and our attempt at love-making was anticlimactic. I was grateful that I was adequate, which was about all I could hope for in my nervous state. I didn't want to think my career was riding on *that*.

"Before we started shooting, Joan and I had dinner at Don the Beachcomber. She was a regular there and had her own table reserved in a secluded corner. I also ate with her at her home in Brentwood on Bristol Avenue.

"It was exactly what you'd expect, a movie star's palace. You entered via a circular driveway, where she had two Cadillacs parked if they weren't in the garage.

"The front door opened on to a small entry hall. To the right as you entered, there was this very large living room done luxuriously in white by Billy Haines, a former M-G-M star and a successful decorator who was her friend. To the left, there was a den with a bar, a breakfast room, and a large formal dining room. The kitchen was huge, and there was a pantry and a laundry room, as well as maid's quarters, all of this on the ground floor.

"In the back was a large patio around a huge swimming pool, and beautifully landscaped grounds, with trees and flowers situated along carefully groomed pathways. There was a wonderful smell in the air from the flowers and the greenery. She had a projection room in a small building to the right as one came out of the house.

"I met her four adopted children. Christina, the eldest, was thirteen years old, Christopher was ten, and Cindy and Cathy, the twins, three. They were charming and polite, though I should mention that I did notice that they seemed a trifle stiff and ill at ease when they bowed and curtsied. This was long past the time when children were taught to do such things. Mine certainly weren't. It represented something from long ago, very out of style, but Joan didn't seem aware of that. Joan introduced me as Uncle Vincent. I wondered how many 'uncles' they thought they had and what meaning the word 'uncle' would have for them, the older two, that is. The twins were still babies, very sweet.

"The children were sent upstairs to bed, and we had dinner. It was just for the two of us, but still quite formal. Being an old southern boy, I knew what a woman who thinks she's Blanche DuBois expected. She waited for me to pull back her chair before she sat down, and then she thanked me for unfolding her serviette and handing it to her. Actually, I considered spreading it out on her lap, but I didn't want to overdo it and gild the lily.

"The table was laid out with what I judged as very expensive silverware and chinaware, highlighted by an elegant candelabra. The fine dishes were very thin china and made me a little uncomfortable, because I didn't want to be responsible for dropping one. This made my hand shake a little, which I tried to hide, because I didn't want her to think I was unmanly. I was afraid she might assume the shaking was over her, not the china.

"Everything was beautifully arranged. In my past experience, nothing in the wealthy homes I had visited, and I have visited a few, surpassed it. An excellent dinner was served by a woman dressed, I suspect, just for that evening in a black outfit.

"Everything was of the highest quality, the best that money could buy. I sensed that Joan had made a thorough study of etiquette and proper social behavior because, coming from a poor and humble background, such refinement hadn't come to her as her birthright. This was worthy of the legendary Pickfair, which she knew well through her marriage to Douglas Fairbanks, Jr. I suspect that someone more secure would have been less concerned with being so correct in such informal circumstances as ours, but obviously, she had innate good taste.

"After dinner, I was taken on a grand tour of the house. Joan showed me her upstairs living room, which had several large walk-in closets. One of these was for shoes, and there were at least a hundred pairs in it, probably many more, all arranged neatly. Another closet was cedar-lined, and it was for her fur coats, and there was yet another, for her suits and dresses. Adjoining this room was her bedroom. At each end, there was a king-sized bed, both of them covered with silk sheets and pillow covers and beautiful down comforters. We were followed everywhere we went by Cliquot, her white French poodle, who regarded me with polite suspicion. Like all of her children, her dog's name began with C.

"The tour ended, and I was about to go home, when she asked me if I would like to join her in a shower before she went to bed. I had rehearsed several scenarios in my mind as I drove there, and all of them had ended with dinner and some polite conversation. None of them included talking in the shower. I hesitated, but after the excellent dinner, the good wine, and the luxurious surroundings, as well as Joan herself, any resolve I might have possessed to resist any invitation that could lead to sex melted.

"We got undressed in one of the bathrooms. I wasn't surprised that her body was so lithe and well shaped and her breasts so firm yet soft, but I hadn't expected her to be so small. Totally naked, she seemed much shorter than I had thought her to be. It must have been the way she carried herself that made her appear taller, that and her high-heel shoes. She noticed me staring and waited for me to say something. I complimented her on the way she looked, and I meant it. She smiled demurely and said, 'I still have to lose a few pounds here and there,' running her hands over her trim body. I couldn't imagine where she meant, but I found it rather enticing the way she ran her hands over her body.

"We got into the shower stall. It was big enough for more than two. I won't tell you what thoughts passed through my mind. After she turned on the water, the seventh veil dropped, as the warm shower streamed down onto our bodies like a tropical waterfall.

"I remarked that it was a shame that censorship prevented us from showing on the screen the full range of her talents. Perhaps she guessed what I was thinking.

"'The ideal wife is a lady in the living room and a whore in bed.' I had heard that line before, but never so memorably. Through the years afterward, whenever I heard it, I thought of Joan. I stayed until midnight, then drove home.

"I couldn't fool my wife, Hedda. She sensed what was going on. She asked me outright, 'Have you been sleeping with her?'

"I never lied to Hedda. I certainly wasn't a perfect husband, but I would never lie to my wife. I had told her about Bette Davis's advances and admitted right away that the same thing had happened with Crawford. I said, 'We took a shower together.' I didn't feel it was untruthful not to fill in the details.

"She hesitated, then said, 'Are you in love with her?'

"I said, 'No,' and she knew I meant it. She understood. I never lied to her. In that way, she could trust me, and she would have recognized a lie when she heard it from me. She knew me very well. She was my best friend, and as such, deserved the truth from me.

"Hedda was a remarkable woman. She just sighed and said, 'Well, I guess it's too much to ask of any man that he turn down the opportunity to sleep with Joan Crawford.'

"I realized once again what an extraordinary woman I had for a wife. How many women would have accepted a situation like that? I marveled at her lack of jealousy, though to this day I am still not sure whether she was hurt and resented it. If so, she didn't reveal it to me. I hoped she felt so secure in the knowledge that I genuinely loved her and would never leave her that she had no reason to be jealous of a passing male fling. I couldn't imagine life without Hedda. That's what I once told her in the midst of the crisis with Davis.

"Whatever happened between Hedda and me, I could never forget our early years, what we had meant to each other, the love and respect we felt for each other. I told Joan how I felt about Hedda and she seemed to accept my loyalty to her, just as Hedda seemed to accept my relationship with Joan. Still, Joan was curious and wanted to meet this woman who had such a hold on her husband. Maybe she thought she could learn something.

"After two weeks of shooting, Joan gave a lavish, old-fashioned Hollywood party at her home, and Hedda and I were invited. In the backyard, a large tent had been put up. Contrary to what you've heard, it often gets chilly in southern California. It was pretty chilly that evening, so charcoal burners were placed all around the tent to provide heat for the guests.

"It was crowded with Hollywood celebrities. Louis B. Mayer, Joan's old boss at M-G-M, was there, and so was her new boss, Jack Warner. It was quite a dinner party. Hedda and I didn't know many of the guests, but Joan introduced us to everybody. In advance, I *had* been a little worried. I knew Hedda was curious about Joan. But whatever concerns I had anticipated, it was a lovely evening and we had a wonderful time.

"When we arrived home, Hedda said, 'She's still a stunning woman, and you know, there's something about her I like and admire.'

"I asked her to explain.

"'Well,' Hedda continued, 'I found her gracious and considerate. And if you look beneath all the Hollywood crap, you can detect a woman who's refused to become a loser, who's pulled herself up from nothing and made something out of her life.'

"I don't think anyone's ever described Joan better.

"I enjoyed every moment working with Joan. On the set, she understood right away whatever it was I wanted, never disputing my direction, and even anticipating me. If she had an idea, she always presented it in a way that never undermined my authority, which she could have done if she'd wanted to, with her star power. It was always that way of asking, never telling. That attitude gave me even greater authority with the others on the set.

"Her suggestions were usually helpful. I had never worked with an actor who knew so much about filmmaking and was so cooperative. She was also intelligent, an attribute I value highly in a woman. She never did anything that made me look less, only more.

"Professionally, we got along perfectly. Personally, it wasn't so smooth. The first sign of personal problems with her came when we went on location to Palm Springs. Using her clout as a big star, she managed to arrange through the studio to get us booked into the Racquet Club with my room next to hers with a connecting door, *chambre séparée*, as they say. I only learned about this on my arrival. It bothered the hell out of me that she had gone ahead and done this without telling me, but I said nothing. I don't know that I minded the whole thing, except not being told about it. It seemed that I, as the man, should be in control, or at least consulted. Of course, I was in no position to get us rooms at the Racquet Club.

"During the shoot in Palm Springs, Hedda unexpectedly drove down for a visit. She was with Freda Lerch, an old friend. Freda, who had been Willy Wyler's secretary and script supervisor, was curious about Crawford. We were shooting an exterior when they arrived, and I took them over to Joan, who was sitting in the shade to protect her skin from freckles, so that they could say hello. Although Joan was polite, she wasn't her usual gracious self.

"I invited them to have lunch with us, but first they wanted to use my room to freshen up. Naturally, I was concerned that Hedda would find out that it was next to Crawford's room. Although she knew about our affair, I did not want to embarrass her by making it public. I certainly didn't want to embarrass her in front of her friend, and I didn't want any stories to spread. The connecting door was fortunately locked, and I heard nothing about it from Hedda. Joan was the one who got riled up about it. Joan was full of surprises.

"As soon as Hedda left, Joan confronted me angrily, saying I should not have allowed her to come. It was our first argument. I tried to convince her that I did not know that she was coming, and even so, how could I stop her? She was, after all, my wife.

"Suddenly I thought I understood why she had seduced me so soon after we met. She was trying to take control of me and the film.

"That evening, she didn't have dinner with me as we customarily did. She ate alone in her room with the door between us locked. It seemed she resented my wife. Just as well. I was annoyed, too, and I was determined not to let her take control of me or of the film.

"After dinner, she avoided me, taking a walk instead with Steve Cochran, a tall, handsome, young actor who was playing Bugsy Siegel in the film. This was, no doubt I felt, an attempt to make me jealous and, moreover, to punish me. I didn't feel punished at all. I decided I wanted to be out of it all with the inevitable complications.

"The next day, I made no mention of it. She was aloof all day until the shooting ended, and then she asked if we could have dinner together that evening. I knew I had done the right thing. As long as I could hold the reins tightly, all would go well. But if I let loose for just one second, I was certain there would be hell to pay.

"That night she asked me how I felt about getting a divorce and marrying her. She wondered if I'd been thinking about it. She said she loved me and that she believed I felt the same way about her. She had evidently forgotten that I had told her from the start that whatever problems Hedda and I had, I still loved her and could never leave her or my children.

"She said she could not understand Hedda's lack of jealousy or how she could permit our relationship. I had told her that Hedda knew, probably a mistake to have told her that. She believed it could only mean that Hedda did not really care for me, but was merely holding on to me for other reasons.

"What really puzzled her was that Hedda still occasionally came into my bed. That was totally unacceptable behavior for Joan. She threatened that if she ever found out that I was unfaithful to her with anyone besides Hedda, that it would be the end of our relationship! Obviously, she didn't understand that I was still physically intimate with my wife. I believe the way she saw it was that I was being unfaithful to *her*, Joan Crawford. I assured her that I had absolutely no interest in anyone else, not counting my wife, and that was true. More than true. I certainly hadn't been looking for adventures on the side. Then she calmed down and we finished shooting in Palm Springs without any further problems.

"It was not possible for me to refrain from being amused at such an outlandish situation. On one hand, we have a wife who can accept sharing her husband with another woman, but on the other hand, this woman resents having to share the husband with his wife. I believe it was the difference between true love and possession.

"Back at the studio, Joan made arrangements to spend Monday through Friday nights in her dressing room, which was the size of a small apartment. Since I lived only a few minutes away from the studio, it was more convenient this way for me to see her at the end of the day. On Friday night, she would go home for the weekend to be with her children.

"People often ask me how the devil did we ever keep our affair out of the gossip columns? To my knowledge, never a word leaked out. If it did, I didn't see it, and nobody ever told me about it. The truth of the matter is that we weren't the only ones who were getting away with this kind of thing, privately, that is.

"At about the same time, several important, and married, stars were rumored to be having torrid affairs that the press, probably pressured by the studios, was being protective about: Errol Flynn and Patrice Wymore, Gary Cooper and Patricia Neal, and others. Maybe they were. Maybe they weren't. Surely some of them were. Nowadays, people do not realize how all-powerful the old-time Hollywood studios were and that their influence extended far beyond the studio gates.

"Hedda had met Joan, and liked her. Quite perceptively, she understood that our affair was a temporary affinity created by the nature of the work, and it would come to an end with the end of the picture. The picture would wrap and so would the affair. It would be wrong, she felt, for a husband and a wife who really loved each other to allow a temporary sexual dalliance to break up a very good marriage.

"Though most people would have thought Crawford embodied the new liberated woman, it was really Hedda. Joan Crawford, her reputation to the contrary, in truth remained a slave to convention, even when she broke the rules.

"The emotional demand of our work, that of creating believable people and situations on the screen, requires an unimaginable intensity of feeling with an inevitable breaking down of protective psychological barriers. It can cause a director and his star to reveal things to each other that they might never reveal to their spouses, things very deep down in their psyches.

"The good director tries to get to know everything he can about his star in order to help her summon up the feelings called for in the script. There is a kind of close rapport between a male director and his female star over the length of the film, sometimes many months, that can and often does lead to a closeness on the set that can lead to something more off the set. I imagine that a similar relationship can develop between patient and psychiatrist, causing some women to fall in love with their analysts."

THE DAMNED DON'T CRY, the new title of *The Victim*, resembles *Mildred Pierce* in many respects. Both films open with a murder that is explained in flashback. The heroines are mature housewives who suddenly have to face the world alone, and do so with style and success. Each loses a child early in the film. The films share Jerry Wald, a successful producer of this kind of film. He also produced *Humoresque* and Joan's 1947 *Possessed*.

The Damned Don't Cry (1950)

A man's body is found on the Nevada desert. Police identify him as Nick Prenta (Steve Cochran), a notorious member of the crime syndicate. They suspect a gangland killing. Home-movie footage links Prenta with Lorna Hansen Forbes (Joan Crawford), an enigmatic Texas oil heiress, who has disappeared. In spite of her wealth, Lorna's background is unknown.

She is really Ethel Whitehead, ex-wife of construction worker Roy Whitehead (Richard Egan). Fearing both the underworld and the police, she has returned in panic to the house of her former husband's family in a midwestern factory town. In flashback, the events that brought her full cycle from poverty to riches and back are shown.

Ethel is an unhappy housewife whose husband is more concerned with saving for the future than spending money on what he considers luxuries. One of these luxuries is a bicycle for their small son, Tommy. On her own, she buys him one on credit. The son is killed riding it. Ethel, distraught and no longer able to endure her drab, oppressive life, leaves the small factory town for the big city.

In the city, she finds work at a cigar counter, as well as jobs as a part-time model. At the cigar counter, she meets a clever accountant, Martin Blackford (Kent Smith), whom she introduces to a nightclub operator who has bookkeeping problems. When Blackford solves them ingeniously, she invites him to meet ruthless crime syndicate boss, George Castleman (David Brian), whom she has come to know through modeling. Blackford accepts a job as Castleman's accountant only because he has fallen in love with Ethel and will do anything to please her.

Castleman is so impressed with Ethel that he gives her a new identity at a high salary. As Lorna Hansen Forbes, she can now move in high social circles as an oil heiress while furthering his criminal operations.

Ethel, now Lorna and believing herself in love with Castleman, obeys his order to go west and lure his archenemy, Nick Prenta, into a situation where he can be killed. Instead of following

Castleman's orders, Lorna falls in love with the young, attractive Prenta. Blackford, learning that Castleman is aware of Lorna's betrayal and intends to kill her along with Prenta, travels cross-country to warn her.

Castleman comes west to kill both Prenta and Lorna, but is persuaded to spare her by Blackford, who convinces him that she may be of use later. Prenta is killed, but Lorna escapes, and she returns to her roots as Ethel. Castleman follows with Blackford.

In a shoot-out in front of her old house, she is wounded, but will recover, and Blackford kills Castleman.

"With the completion of the picture," Sherman continued, "I asked [Jack] Warner if I could take a few days off to rest, and he agreed. I had planned on taking Hedda and the children away on a short vacation trip. I felt that the wrap marked the end of the affair with Joan. Then Joan called, saying it was important we talk.

"She asked me to read a script Columbia Pictures had submitted to her. They wanted to start the picture in a few weeks. If I liked the script, she'd talk to Harry Cohn, head of Columbia, and Bill Dozier, the producer, about our doing it together on a loan-out from Warner's. When I told her I would be glad to read the script while I was away with my family, she asked me to postpone my trip a few days.

"'I have a better idea,' she said. 'We'll drive up to Carmel. You can relax there while you read the script, and then we can discuss it. They want a yes or no by Monday morning.' It was Thursday, so I said I'd call her back. As usual, Hedda understood that it was not a pleasure trip but business, and she accepted my promise that the moment I returned we'd go to Yosemite for a week.

"The next day, while Joan drove us up to Carmel, I read the screenplay, which was called *Lady of the House*. I soon realized that it was a rewrite of *Craig's Wife*, a play by George Kelly which had been made into a film with Rosalind Russell years ago. When I finished reading, I advised her against doing it. I felt it was too dated for today's audiences even if an attempt was made to update it.

"She'd asked for my advice, but that wasn't really what she wanted. What she wanted was for me to say yes. Then, I was to convince her that she was right, that it *was* a good script and she *would* be wonderful in it. But I had too much respect for her and for myself to do this project, and too much to lie to her about it. Still, Joan wanted to do it. Couldn't I figure out *something* to make it work?

"I told her I wouldn't touch it even if she felt she *had* to do it. She was disappointed because Warner's didn't have anything for her at the moment and she needed the money. At that time, she was getting $200,000 a picture.

"We stayed in a suite with a fireplace she had reserved at the Carmel Inn. At sundown, she had it lit and we ordered a delicious dinner with a bottle of vintage French wine. All of this was, of course, conducive to making love afterwards. The next morning I reread the screenplay but it hadn't gotten any better. Before I left Joan, I told her that I had a different title in mind for the picture we had just made.

"A few days later, Rudi Fehr, the editor of *The Victim*, showed me his first cut. After we made a few changes, we ran it for Warner and Wald. Everybody seemed happy, and I suggested the new title, *The Damned Don't Cry*. This was taken from an old novel that Warner's had bought years before but never used. Everyone agreed it was a better title than *The Victim*. Joan was pleased when I called to tell her the reaction.

"Meanwhile, she followed my advice and turned down *Lady of the House*, and I took my postponed vacation with Hedda and the children. Two weeks later, I got a call from Steve Trilling [an assistant producer], and I was asked, 'Are you ready to come back to work?' I said yes.

"'That's good, because we've just arranged for you to direct Margaret Sullavan at Columbia.'

"I had never been loaned out, and I was looking forward to it with enthusiasm. Sullavan was a fine actress with a distinctive manner and voice. I asked what the picture was.

"'I haven't read the script, but it's called *Lady of the House*.'

"'Oh, shit!' I almost said aloud. Instead, I told him about my talk with Crawford. 'What happens if I turn it down?' I asked.

"'You can't,' he said. 'We've already made the deal. Twelve weeks, and you start Monday. And if you refuse, you'll be breaking your contract. You don't want to do that, do you?'

"Well, he was certainly right about that. I was getting $3,000 per week, and my next raise was to $3,500, and then $4,000. I later learned that Columbia paid Warner's $60,000 for my twelve weeks. That's a profit of $20,000.

"I reported to Columbia and [producer] Bill Dozier's office on Monday morning. I found him easy to talk to. He was intelligent, and knowledgeable about films, which is more unusual among Hollywood producers than you might imagine. I told him about Joan and how I felt about *Lady of the House*.

"After listening to me politely, he explained to me that Cohn had always wanted to remake *Craig's Wife* and had personally asked him to produce it. He suggested I reread the script. Since I was committed to doing it, he thought I should make some notes about what changes I might have in mind. I was assigned an office, and I went to work.

"Later that same day, Harry Cohn, whom I had never met, sent for me. I had heard many stories about him, so I was more than a little curious to meet him. He was one of those people everyone talked about.

"He was seated at the far end of a huge office, at an enormous oak desk with a multitude of buttons and phones. He was a grim man with a slightly terrifying face and sharp, angry eyes. At least in appearance, he lived up to his reputation. I felt as if I were entering the ring with a tough heavyweight fighter, and here I was an inexperienced lightweight.

"Before I could even introduce myself, he snarled, 'I hear you don't like this project.' I sensed this was a man who would only respect strength.

"'Right,' I came back as strong as I dared. 'Why are you spending your money to borrow me for something I have no enthusiasm for? I believe I'd be far better suited for something else you have.'

"'What do you have in mind?'

"'*Born Yesterday*.' He was silent for a moment. Then he asked me why I thought I was right for it.

"I explained that since I understood the characters and it was such a damned good play, I knew I could make a hit film out of it.

"He pondered this for a moment, then said, 'I'll let you read the script. Then you can tell me what you think.' I was elated.

"The script made from Garson Kanin's stage play was written by Julie and Phil Epstein. They were the best screenwriters in the business and my two favorites. But as I read their adaptation, I started to have reservations.

"The play is confined to a single set, a hotel room. The Epsteins, in their understandable effort to open up the play for the screen, had lost some of the dramatic tension.

"The next day, I went up to see Cohn and give him my reaction. He wasn't pleased. 'I paid the Epsteins a hundred thousand dollars to write that script,' he said. 'Are you telling me now I should scrap it?'

"'No, of course not,' I explained. 'The Epsteins are two of the best writers in Hollywood. I'm only suggesting that you don't sacrifice the tension of the play by leaving the hotel room when you don't have to. You should only leave it when there is a need and a definite advantage.'

"He listened without comment and then said he'd think about it. Meanwhile, he requested that I concentrate on *Lady of the House*. I promised him that I would give it my best shot.

"Although I can't explain it, there was something about Harry Cohn that I liked and respected. It seemed that under his formidable exterior there was a vulnerable human being. Later I learned that I was correct. While I didn't get to direct *Born Yesterday*, George Cukor did. I was gratified to see that he did pretty much what I would have done. I believe Harry Cohn had listened to me and then given Cukor greater artistic freedom than he would have otherwise had. Like me, George had a strong stage background, and so did Cohn, who, someone told me, came out of vaudeville.

"The day after I talked with Cohn, I received an urgent call from Joan, very upset. 'You're a fine friend,' she said, loud enough for me not to need a phone. 'You told me to turn down *Lady of the House*, and now you're *directing* it.'

"I tried to explain to her what had happened, but without success. She was, understandably, very angry. I should have been the one to have called her up and explained it, at least *tried* to explain it. I was a coward.

"She made some calls, letting it be known that she would now do the film because I would be directing it, and in short order, Cohn arranged for a Joan loan-out from Warner's. Margaret Sullavan was assigned elsewhere. I strongly suspected that Cohn knew what he was doing all the time and was behind everything that happened.

"As I reread George Kelly's play, *Craig's Wife*, I realized that my original objections to it as a Joan Crawford vehicle were wrong. Having had the opportunity to observe Crawford in her home, I recognized that in many ways she was the embodiment of the play's central character, Harriet Craig. She had the same obsessive attitude toward her home. She distrusted men, whom she tried to manipulate. She was very old-fashioned in how she believed a man should treat a lady. She expected doors to be opened for her, chairs to be pulled back for her, cigarettes to be lit for her. In return, she would be the lady of the manor and a meticulous housekeeper, even doing the actual work herself, sometimes, and always directing it.

"I hoped to capture these characteristics in the film—which was now called *Harriet Craig*—but I was afraid Joan would object. I was afraid she might recognize herself. She didn't, although she certainly could have taken it personally.

"I even considered that maybe she didn't notice what we were doing, but Joan was far too intelligent not to be aware of this. In retrospect, I think she could step back and view herself just as she would a character in a film. Then, just like a fictional character, she wouldn't be able to do anything about it because her character in life had already been written.

"*Harriet Craig* turned out to be an enjoyable and rewarding experience. I was fortunate to be working with one of the best cameramen in the business, Joe Walker. He had been Frank Capra's cameraman on all those great films Capra made at Columbia. We worked together beautifully."

Harriet Craig (1950)

The only passion in the life of Harriet Craig (Joan Crawford) is total control of her environment and the people in it. This is seen in her perfectly maintained household, of which her successful husband, Walter (Wendell Corey), is a part of the furnishings. Though not happy with her obsessive behavior, he is so easygoing that he doesn't realize that Harriet hates all men, himself included. This is the result of her irresponsible father abandoning his family when she was a child.

When her husband is offered a new assignment that will force her to move and thus upset her established routine, she persuades his boss (Raymond Greenleaf) that Walter will be more valuable to him where he is. She does this so subtly that Walter's value to the company is not undermined, but he does lose the opportunity that will uproot Harriet.

She interferes in the lives of others, as well. When her visiting young cousin, Clare (K. T. Stevens), falls in love with a young man (William Bishop) of whom she disapproves, Harriet manages to spoil their romance.

One of the few pleasures left to Walter is the companionship of his old friend Billy Birkmire (Allyn Joslyn). Harriet makes Billy so unwelcome that he stops visiting Walter.

Finally, Walter has had enough of Harriet's insidious manipulations. In a rage, he smashes her favorite antique vase, and then leaves her to a life in her sterile domestic Utopia, alone.

"As Joan had done at Warner's," Sherman continued, "she made arrangements with Columbia to spend nights in her dressing room while she was shooting *Harriet Craig*. She had a kitchenette and a small bath, and sometimes she'd have dinner sent in and I'd join her. For the sake of the film, we put aside our personal problems. That wasn't easy, but it paid off. Everything went smoothly on the production, and the producers were very satisfied with the results. She was so good in the film that sometimes I wonder if even I didn't get confused about Joan and the character she played. I wonder if I didn't get Joan and Harriet Craig mixed up in my mind.

"The reviews were good, and the picture did well at the box office, much better than I had ever expected. I was happily surprised. I was glad to have been so wrong. Joan's performance was wonderful, and I received many compliments on how I had worked with her from critics and from the studio. I had thought I knew everything, and I didn't. After the rocky way the project had begun, this was all very gratifying to me.

"Joan told me that she had 'fallen in love,' and I was worried she was going to say with me, but she had fallen in love with *Goodbye, My Fancy.*"

"IF TRUTH BE told," Joan said, "I didn't feel I was the best possible choice, but I thought, I *knew* I could do it. Madeleine Carroll had starred on the stage, and Katharine Hepburn and Roz Russell were naturals for the part. But *I* got it."

Goodbye, My Fancy (1951)

Congresswoman Agatha Reed (Joan Crawford) returns to the college that once expelled her to receive an honorary degree. More important to her, she is returning to renew her relationship with the man who was responsible for her expulsion.

Twenty years earlier, it was discovered that she had spent the night off-campus with a man. Although Agatha was subsequently expelled, she never revealed the man's name. He was Dr. James Merrill (Robert Young), then a young professor, now the president of the college.

Following Agatha wherever she goes is Matt Cole (Frank Lovejoy), a magazine photojournalist. He is interested in her, but she doesn't take him seriously.

Agatha and Merrill's relationship appears to be rekindled until small differences become larger irritations, and Agatha realizes that their separate worlds are incompatible. Hers is not the comfortable, secure world of the college campus, but the uncertain, exciting world of politics, and her liberal views clash with the conservatism she finds in the school.

> She is not ready to give up everything she has struggled to achieve, and she recognizes that Cole fits better into her world than would Merrill.

Fay Kanin spoke with me about her play, *Goodbye, My Fancy*, and the making of the film version with Joan Crawford.

"I did not think that Joan Crawford was the perfect casting for it," Kanin told me. "It was done with Madeleine Carroll on the stage. I couldn't think of two people quite so different as Madeleine Carroll and Joan Crawford. My play first came to life for me with Madeleine Carroll, who was perfect, just the way I imagined the character. So I was already set in one conception of the character. But Joan felt she had fallen in love with the play, and she wanted to make a film of it. She talked Warner Brothers into doing it with her in it. It was all her desire to do it that got it made. But I think it needed a little gentler casting. Anyway, we got it done, and I was really very grateful.

"I'm sure she liked what she did. She was very good.

"I got to know Joan when she did *Goodbye, My Fancy*. I didn't get to know her a lot, but I liked her. She didn't play the big star. She came, and she did her work.

"I remember, we, my husband [Michael Kanin] and I, had lunch with her. She had a dressing room that was really like a little cabin, and she kept inviting us to lunch, Michael and me. Then, she would serve the lunch. I never got over that. She loved to put on an apron and pass the food to us. It was wonderful. That was something that pleased her. We got on very well.

"We didn't do the screenplay. It's something else if someone else writes the screenplay. Of course, you aren't involved in the same way. When it was done originally, it was a play, and I loved it. I liked it better than this film. Madeleine Carroll was so lovely, and it worked so well. It wasn't possible to do it better.

"I liked the director, Vincent Sherman. I knew him as a director, but I also knew him as a friend. I knew his wife, Hedda. I also know that he and Joan got on, shall we say, *very* well.

"Hedda was an interesting person. And very tolerant. She ran his business. She did all the managing. I liked her a lot. And I liked Vincent, who did a good job."

"As soon as I had finished *Harriet Craig*," Sherman told me, "I was informed that Warner's had bought the play *Goodbye, My Fancy* for Crawford and that I was to be the director. That was very exciting. It had been a hit on Broadway with Madeleine Carroll and Sam Wanamaker, and was written by my talented friend Fay Kanin. The screenplay was being done by Ivan Goff and Ben Roberts, who were also two old friends of mine. They, too, were very talented. I hadn't seen the play, but I enjoyed reading it, and I looked forward to directing it with Joan.

"Meanwhile, there was my own relationship with Joan. She continued to tell me she loved me and how she appreciated all my help on *Harriet Craig*. The professional and the personal were always linked with her. Joan gave me some gifts: a gold Cartier watch, Cartier cuff links, initialed linen handkerchiefs, silk pajamas, and an expensive camera I've kept all these years. I pleaded with her to stop. The things were wonderful, but it was embarrassing. But she said, 'If it gives me pleasure, why should you mind?'

"I was exhausted at the end of *Harriet Craig*. It had gone smoothly, but directing a movie is hard, hard work.

"When I reported back to Warner Brothers, I was given the *Goodbye, My Fancy* screenplay. After reading it, I asked for a few changes and began casting.

"The president of the college, who had been Joan's secret love, was Robert Young. Ideal. The newspaper reporter, who is currently pursuing her, was Frank Lovejoy. Not ideal. I balked.

"Frank was a fine actor and a good friend, but I did not see him as the right one for Joan to go off with at the fade-out. For me, their chemistry did not ignite. I complained to Henry Blanke, who was the producer, and he agreed, but our protest was ignored by Jack Warner. Frank was under contract, and Warner was adamant, so we had to use him. It wasn't very good for my friendship with Frank. After that, there wasn't much *love* or much *joy* when he saw me.

"Eve Arden was cast as Joan's secretary, and she would provide the laughs. She and Joan were friends from *Mildred Pierce*.

"My problem was not the cast, but with Jack Warner himself. Early in the shooting, it was relayed to me that Warner wanted me to stay away from any close-ups of Joan, "because she is getting too old" I was told, and to do only full figures or knee shots of her.

"I asked if that meant no more close-ups of anyone in the picture from now on?

"I was told, 'No, just Crawford.'

"This was ridiculous because how could I make close-ups of everyone except Crawford? She would be the first to notice this, and how could I tell her what Warner had said? Even if I tried to fool her by using a wider lens, she would know right away. And besides, the shot wouldn't look right in the completed picture. She was very intelligent and educated about the camera. Most of all, how on earth could the picture be cut smoothly without any Joan Crawford close-ups?

"Joan was the star, the story was about her. Her fans came to see her, not just her name in the credits. They weren't coming to see Robert Young or Frank Lovejoy, or me, or Jack Warner.

"This was the first time Jack had ever interfered with my authority in such a manner. I handled the situation as best I could. I compromised and only made close-ups that I deemed absolutely necessary. I should also mention that the character Joan was playing was about the same age as Crawford herself, and with Young and Lovejoy, she was not exactly robbing the cradle.

"Why someone like Joan Crawford, who had surmounted every obstacle that could possibly be put in the path of a woman in Hollywood, would ever feel insecure, is beyond me. But she did, and come to think of it, so did Bette Davis, another great film actress whom I came to know too well, personally speaking. I was worried that the thing about the close-ups would hurt Joan's feelings.

"The film was too political and too cerebral for Joan Crawford fans, I think. Neither Joan nor Bette Davis had that light touch which is necessary for this sort of comedy.

"When the picture was over, I was told that Jack Warner was displeased with it and with me. I had ignored his order not to shoot close-ups of Crawford. He reminded me that his name, not mine, was on the studio gates, and that unless I could follow orders it would be best for me to leave.

"It was sad to leave Warner's. I had put in over fifteen years there, and I took away with me many memories. Joan left after making *This Woman Is Dangerous* a year later. Our three pictures there together were respectable productions that I am proud of, and I think Joan felt the same way."

8

The Pepsi Generation
(1952–1960)

WHENEVER ASKED WHICH of her films she liked the best, Joan would have to think for a moment before answering. "Oh, I love them all, but since I got my Oscar for *Mildred Pierce*, that *has* to be a favorite. And I also liked *Grand Hotel* and *The Women* a lot, too."

Asked which was her *least* favorite film, she would answer without hesitation, *"This Woman Is Dangerous."* She didn't wish to discuss *why* she didn't like it. She said, "That would take all day. I've always said that I thought there was something of value in every picture I ever made, but I can't for the life of me think of what it was for this one. In that way it's a perfect picture."

This Woman Is Dangerous (1952)

Beth Austin (Joan Crawford) is the mistress of a brutish gangster, Matt Jackson (David Brian), whose holdup gang terrifies New Orleans. Actually, *she* is the leader of the gang. Complaining of headaches and blurred vision, Beth is told that she must undergo an operation immediately or face blindness. After one more successful holdup, she leaves for a clinic in Indianapolis, assuring her jealous and suspicious lover that she will return soon.

At the clinic, her doctor, Ben Halleck (Dennis Morgan), is intelligent and understanding. Being with him changes her, and she falls in love. Meanwhile, the FBI has traced her to the clinic and is waiting for Matt to rejoin her.

Matt tires of waiting for her in New Orleans and travels to Indianapolis to visit her. When he realizes what has happened between her and Ben, he sets out to kill Dr. Halleck in an operating room auditorium. He is stopped at the last moment by Beth with help from the FBI.

Beth, now recognized as reformed, is sent to jail for a short term, while Ben awaits her return.

The critical response to *This Woman Is Dangerous* was uniformly negative, and Joan agreed with them. She loved success, and this, she said, "was painful." It was her last Warner Brothers picture. Lew Wasserman negotiated her release from the studio and arranged for her to make one film at RKO. This was the first time in more than twenty-five years Joan had been without a studio.

She had seen a script called *Sudden Fear* and liked it. When RKO couldn't meet her salary, she waived it and agreed to accept a participation in profits instead. She wanted Clark Gable as her lead, but he had just remarried and was unavailable. Jack Palance, who got the part, had recently become known for his performance in Elia Kazan's *Panic in the Streets*.

Sudden Fear (1952)

On a cross-country train trip, Myra Hudson (Joan Crawford), an independently wealthy Broadway playwright, meets Lester Blaine (Jack Palance), an actor she has just fired from her most recent play. There is no bitterness, however, and a romance blossoms between them. When they reach her home in San Francisco, they marry.

It seems a happy marriage until Lester discovers that Myra plans to leave the bulk of her fortune to charity. In the meantime, she learns that Lester is having an affair with another woman, Irene (Gloria Grahame). Lester and Irene are plotting to kill her before she can change her will in favor of the charities.

Myra, always imagining stories that she might use as plays,

concocts a counterplot. She plans to steal Irene's pistol and shoot Lester with it so that it appears the jealous mistress killed her lover. Lester, however, finds out what Myra is doing and confronts her.

When she flees the house, Lester follows her in a car, planning to run her down so that it seems an accident. He does run down a woman, but it isn't Myra. She is Irene, dressed like Myra. In the accident, both Lester and Irene are killed.

Myra is shocked, but she has thwarted the plot on her own life.

Sudden Fear was successful and very profitable for Joan. She was nominated for an Oscar, along with Bette Davis for *The Star*. Shirley Booth won the best actress award that year for *Come Back, Little Sheba*.

For *Torch Song*, Joan returned to M-G-M. As she remembered the moment, she was euphoric, "I was at Metro again. It had been a long time . . . As soon as I was on the set, I knew I hadn't been forgotten there. I can't begin to tell you how wonderful being there made me feel. I *can* tell you I was deeply worried that maybe I wouldn't be remembered. But then, there were all those wonderful technicians. Not only did they remember me, but I remembered them, every single one. I wondered, how did I ever bring myself to leave Metro? And I had a chance to dance again. What more could a girl, who was no longer a girl, ask for?"

Joan's singing voice was dubbed by India Adams. Joan would like to have sung all of her songs, but she accepted what she was told, that the shooting schedule was too short to allow her proper rehearsal time. "I had to assume my singing voice was rusty," she said. *Torch Song* was shot in MetroColor, one of her few film appearances in color.

Torch Song (1953)

Independent, domineering Broadway musical comedy star Jenny Stewart (Joan Crawford), though hated by her co-workers, yearns for companionship and love. She finds it with her severest critic, Tye Graham (Michael Wilding), a rehearsal pianist who was a newspaper reviewer before he was blinded in the war. It was he who gave her the rave review in her first show that started her climb to stardom. At the same time, he fell in love with her. With changed circumstances, she falls in love with Tye, and they find happiness together.

"Some people believed Mr. Mayer had let me go like an old horse," Joan told me. "Well, it wasn't true, but sometimes it seems people are more likely to believe lies than the truth. I've never understood it. But there's nothing to do about it.

"I knew the truth, and I know Mr. Mayer didn't initiate my leaving. He didn't want me to go. He tried to persuade me to stay. He tried very hard. I almost was persuaded to stay, not because I thought I wasn't doing the right thing, but because it was so hard for me to do something against Mr. Mayer. Finally, Mr. Mayer made it possible.

"All the while I was struggling to divorce myself from M-G-M, I knew what I wanted. I could never have pursued that course if I had any doubts.

"The first doubts I had, however, were as I drove away that last time, from M-G-M. There weren't many who knew that I would not be back, never in the same way. But I knew."

BETTE DAVIS ASKED me, "Did you ever see those pictures they used in the promotion for Miss Crawford in that film *Johnny Guitar*? I never saw the film. It looked like a real stinker, not her fault, we all had to do some of those. Anyway, she always was a skirts lady, and it was funny to see her in the ads wearing pants.

"She looked like the pants were wearing her."

Johnny Guitar (1954)

In a remote Arizona town, feelings are divided for and against the coming railroad. Farmers, miners, and merchants are for it, cattle ranchers are against it. Saloon-keeper Vienna (Joan Crawford) wants the railroad because it will be good for her business. She is opposed by cattleman John McIvers (Ward Bond) and by Emma Small (Mercedes McCambridge).

As an ally, Vienna has brought in one of the deadliest gunmen in the West, Johnny Logan (Sterling Hayden), known as Johnny Guitar. He gave up killing five years earlier when Vienna left him. Now, he carries no gun, only a guitar.

Another ally of Vienna's is the Dancin' Kid (Scott Brady), a former miner who leads a gang of other ex-miners.

Emma and McIvers storm Vienna's place with a mob, demanding she turn over the Kid to them. Emma claims the Kid has killed her brother in a robbery attempt. Even if Vienna knew the Kid's hideout, she wouldn't tell them.

When the Kid and his gang arrive at Vienna's, they deny the killing, but they and Vienna are told to leave town or be lynched. Vienna is not intimidated, but the Kid decides to leave after robbing the town's bank, which is owned by Emma.

Vienna happens to be at the bank during the robbery, withdrawing money to pay her employees. Because the Kid doesn't take her money and Vienna kisses him goodbye, Emma assumes that she is a part of the robbery.

Emma and McIvers form a posse after a captured member of the Kid's gang reveals their hideout. Vienna arrives first to warn the Kid. Johnny, now armed, follows.

In a shootout, Vienna, wearing a cowboy outfit, is wounded by Emma, who then kills the Kid. Vienna kills Emma, and the mob disperses.

Vienna and Johnny embrace under a nearby waterfall.

Johnny Guitar was Joan's first western since *The Law of the Range* in 1928. The film was ridiculed by critics and shunned by moviegoers. Joan enjoyed making the film, but she wasn't happy when she saw it. *Johnny Guitar* has since become a cult classic.

The Star, a 1952 Bette Davis film, was thought by many to be based on the life of Joan Crawford. When I spoke with Bette about the film she immediately made the point that *The Star* was *not* based on Joan Crawford. "There certainly were elements of Miss Crawford which caused that rumor to circulate," Bette said.

"I played a character who was not *just* Joan Crawford. If for one minute I'd thought the character *was* Miss Crawford, I would *never* have accepted the role, because I couldn't have done *in*justice to her character. She played the part of Joan Crawford better than anyone else ever could have. Absolutely."

WHILE WORKING ON *Female on the Beach*, Joan stayed late in her Universal dressing room after everyone had left to celebrate New Year's Eve and the coming in of 1955. She was too tired to drive home.

As she was sitting there, she received a call from a friend in Las Vegas who was having a party. He wished her a Happy New Year, and then he put on the phone several of his guests to do the same. One of them was a man she had met at a New York party in 1951.

His name was Alfred Steele, and he was currently the president of Pepsi-Cola. He expressed surprise that she was not out celebrating, and told her he would like to see her when he came to Los Angeles. Since Joan had met him with his wife, she assumed that he meant she would be seeing the two of them. That was not the case, however. When he contacted her shortly afterward, she learned that he was divorcing his second wife. Steele seemed to be just what Joan wanted in a man.

"One of the most attractive things about him," Joan told me, "was he wasn't an actor, as my first three husbands were.

"I would tell the press, especially after the failure of my first marriage, to Doug Jr., that I didn't feel it was a good thing for an actor and an actress to marry, especially if each one loved his or her career, and especially if the woman loved being an actress as much as I did.

"I didn't really want to have to choose between being an actress and being a wife and mother. But looking back, it became clear to me that when I had to choose, I chose being an actress. But I hoped I wouldn't have to choose, except temporarily. I did want one day to be a mother, and I was certain I would be a good one.

"I wasn't as concerned about being a wife, except of course if one were going to have children. It seemed to me that a man and a woman, as long as there were no children, could handle it another way.

"But I had grown lonely, something I never expected I would face in my adult life, the life I could make for myself, the one I could shape. I was a lonely little girl, even before I knew what the word 'lonely' meant.

"I promised myself that someday I would be surrounded by a wonderful warm family of my own and that we would all love each other very much. As a bonus, Al seemed to love children, and they loved him."

Alfred Steele was born in Nashville, Tennessee, in 1901. Like Fairbanks, he had traveled with his parents throughout Europe, and like Tone, he had lived a privileged existence. Like Terry, he had been a varsity football player. He played for Northwestern University, where he graduated in 1923.

His first job was selling advertising for the *Chicago Tribune*. Then he became the advertising manager for Standard Oil of Indiana and a vice president at the D'Arcy Advertising Company.

Steele worked for Coca-Cola before moving to Pepsi-Cola, which had never been able to challenge Coca-Cola. A year after moving to Pepsi, Steele became chairman of the board. Since Steele had joined the company, profits had increased greatly.

Joan felt that having a man in the house might do wonders for Christopher. She told me, "His favorite activity had become running away. He knew that would upset me, and he was right about that." The boy had reached his early teens. People told her that the teens were sometimes a troubled time for parents, but Joan had been having constant problems with him for almost his entire life. She could not understand it, and she said, "I did not know how to deal with it. And as he was growing up, I found him rather threatening. It's hard to imagine becoming afraid of your own child, but I had to admit it to myself, if to no one else. I was growing afraid of him. Worse yet, I felt if he saw my fear, he would become even worse, because he seemed to enjoy what he saw as a shift in the power.

"I think he looked forward to getting out of my house and being old enough for me not to be able to bring him back. Actually, I had little desire to bring him back, once I fulfilled my obligation. I have to admit, though, that when Al came into our lives, Christopher paid much more attention to what Al said than he did to me. He didn't talk back to Al. He stopped being a bully with me.

"Cathy and Cindy, my dear young twins, were very fond of Al, and they enjoyed having him come into their lives."

Cathy Crawford remembered the happy morning when she and Cindy were having breakfast with their mother and Steele. Joan informed them that she would be marrying "Uncle Al."

"We were so happy. My sister Cindy said, 'Oh, good. Now we can have some babies.'"

"When they married, we called him Daddy, and he took us under his wing."

Female on the Beach (1955)

Lynn Markham (Joan Crawford) arrives in Balboa to live in an ocean-front house that had belonged to her late husband. The previous tenant, a wealthy widow, had thrown herself into the sea from an upper-story balcony after a violent scene.

Lynn finds the house frequented by strangers who act as if they live there. One is Drummond "Drummy" Hall (Jeff Chandler), who does odd jobs. Lynn soon understands that the dead widow, Eloise Crandall (Judith Evelyn), supported him. Lynn is attracted to the handsome beach bum.

Another is Osbert Sorenson (Cecil Kellaway). He and his wife, Queenie (Natalie Schafer), provide card games for the locals. Lynn is shown the property by Amy Rawlinson (Jan Sterling), real estate agent for the Markham estate.

Police Lieutenant Galley (Charles Drake) tells Lynn that they suspect Eloise Crandall was pushed off the balcony. He warns her to be careful.

Lynn finds Eloise's diary, in which she describes how Drummy is being paid by the Sorensons to lure wealthy widows to their card games so they can be cheated and blackmailed. Eloise is furious and heartbroken.

Drummy denies he had anything to do with the woman's death. He says he loves Lynn, who reminds him of a decency he once knew.

> The Sorensons supply the police with evidence incriminating Drummy. In spite of this, Lynn marries him. They plan a honeymoon on Drummy's boat. At the last moment, they argue.
>
> When Lynn returns to the boat to apologize, she finds a crazed Amy, admitting that *she* killed Eloise. She is sabotaging the boat so that it will sink at sea, and only Drummy, a strong swimmer, will survive.
>
> Amy is subdued, and Lynn and Drummy are now free to try to live happily together.

Joan had never wanted to be a single parent. It wasn't her choice, but it happened because she wanted so much to be a mother. She wished to have a husband and for her children to have a father.

Her marriage to Al Steele gave promise that she would have that personal life for which she had been yearning and searching. Her twin girls loved their "Uncle Al" and were happy to switch immediately to calling him "Daddy" as soon as Joan became Mrs. Alfred N. Steele. Teens Christina and Christopher also seemed happy with Steele.

Joan overcame her fear of flying to travel to Las Vegas with Steele in a Pepsi-Cola private plane on May 9. They were married there the next day.

At about this time, Joan signed a contract to make *Queen Bee* and *Autumn Leaves* for Columbia. Jerry Wald would be the producer for the first film and Willian Goetz for the second. *Queen Bee*, based on a novel by Edna Lee, was written and directed by Ranald MacDougall.

Queen Bee (1955)

Imperious, domineering, vain Eva Phillips (Joan Crawford) rules over a dysfunctional family in a Georgia mansion. Her wealthy husband of ten years, Avery (Barry Sullivan), is an alcoholic and their two small children, Ted (Tim Hovey) and Trissa (Linda Bennett), are more familiar with their nanny than with their mother.

Among the eccentric members of the household is Avery's sister, Carol Lee Phillips (Betsy Palmer). She is engaged to Judson "Judd" Prentiss (John Ireland), the manager of Avery's cotton mill.

A young cousin of Eva's, Jennifer "Jenny" Stewart (Lucy Marlow), arrives from Chicago on a visit. She and Avery are immediately attracted to each other.

Jenny learns about a recurring nightmare from which Eva's son, little Ted, suffers. He wakes up screaming from a dream in which he is in a car that is about to crash into a mountain.

Hoping to spoil Carol's planned marriage to Judd, Eva tries to seduce him. When the high-strung Carol learns that Judd was once a lover of Eva's and that they may resume their affair, she commits suicide.

Eva learns from the new governess that her husband was seen in the bedroom of her young cousin. Nothing had happened, but Eva is jealous and enraged. She warns Avery about the stories she will tell in court about Jenny and him, if he attempts to divorce her.

Avery once more becomes affectionate toward Eva, saying that he wishes to begin their life together again, a second honeymoon. Eva believes him.

One night when Avery is unable to drive Eva, she asks Judd for a ride. Eva realizes that Judd is driving too fast and recklessly. He accuses her of being responsible for the death of Carol. Then he tells her that her husband had intended to kill her in an automobile accident after first establishing what a happy couple they are.

Instead, Judd is going to do it. They crash and both are killed.

Avery and Jenny are now free to marry.

"*Queen Bee* owed so much to Tennessee Williams," Joan said. "I felt like a Carte Blanche DuBois."

Joan said she liked participating in public appearances with Steele for Pepsi-Cola. Since she wasn't being offered parts, at least nothing she considered acceptable, she found the Pepsi work a rewarding way to spend her time. When she attended a conference or a speaking engagement with him, there were always fans of hers who were happy to see her, and she was happy to see them. Steele gave her expensive gifts, including diamonds that she took great pleasure in wearing.

Betty Barker remembered that Joan and Al Steele's Fifth Avenue apartment had eighteen rooms, which they had extensively remodeled, and heated floors were installed. "The renovation lasted a year, and the neighbors didn't like that very much."

Through the years, Barker had continued to do part-time work for Joan when Joan was in California and, to a lesser extent, when Joan was in New York and had work to be done in California. They continued to speak regularly on the phone during the years that Barker worked as a secretary to Howard Hughes.

Joan returned frequently to California, and Barker occasionally traveled to New York to see Joan.

"*Autumn Leaves* is a wonderful picture about an older woman with a younger man," Joan said. "That is nearly always a doomed relationship. I certainly knew it was not for me. The woman is in such a vulnerable position. She has to lose. It's just a question of time. Time ticks for all of us, but the clock ticks louder and faster for the older woman with the younger man. She has to be able to grab what she can as fast as she can. There are women who can do that, I suppose. I'm not one.

"I only know how to do what I do with all my heart, and I need to protect that heart from getting broken or even chipped. It's the only one I have.

"Cliff Robertson was the young man. I *could* have fallen in love with him. He was so handsome, such a wonderful actor in a demanding part. I did whatever I could do to help him with everything I had learned about acting.

"There is an actress in this picture, also gifted, who truly deserved a wonderful career and great parts. Vera Miles had the looks and she's a *real* actress. She's had a good career, but she deserved even more."

Autumn Leaves (1956)

Middle-aged Millicent Wetherby (Joan Crawford), still attractive but unmarried because of the years she lost caring for her ailing

232

father, meets Burt Hanson (Cliff Robertson), a younger man who is also lonely. After a short courtship, he suggests marriage, but Milly, apprehensive about the difference in their ages, rejects him. Burt is persistent, however, and she finally accepts his proposal.

After Milly and Burt marry, his ex-wife, Virginia (Vera Miles), appears, demanding a property settlement. Milly learns that the reason for their divorce was Burt's mental instability after he discovered Virginia was having an affair with his father (Lorne Greene).

Burt becomes severely depressed, and Milly is forced to have him hospitalized, paying for everything herself. She stands by him despite the fear that when he is cured, he won't need her anymore. She is wrong. When Burt is released, he rushes back to her, professing now an even stronger love for her.

Since this was the first time Joan played a secretary, she used her own secretary, Betty Barker, as her model. She studied Barker, noting how she went about her daily routine, how she handled papers and arranged them, how she answered the phone. Betty Barker looked pleased as she recalled how she was Joan's inspiration for Milly.

"I was glad to help out," she said. "Joan genuinely liked this film. She enjoyed making it, and when she saw it afterwards, she enjoyed viewing it."

Autumn Leaves was significant for another reason. It was the first time Joan had worked with Robert Aldrich, who would later direct her and Bette Davis in *What Ever Happened to Baby Jane?*

Joan's having to have a relationship with a noticeably younger man was something she had managed to avoid thus far on-screen. She felt that being romantically involved with a younger man made her seem older than she actually was. She never wanted to appear desperate on-screen or in life.

"When I was a girl," Joan said, "I could not have imagined myself not being young. It seemed getting older would take forever. I didn't even give it a thought.

"Later, time went by faster.

"I'm grateful to have started so young in my career, when I was in my teens, seventeen, on my way to Hollywood. People have asked me if I feel I missed something by starting to work so early. No. I wouldn't trade a minute of my working, dancing, acting. I find it hard to call it work."

MARILYN MONROE TOLD Laurence Olivier that Joan Crawford was one of the women she admired most in the world. "It was because of what Joan did adopting those children and being a wonderful mother to them," Olivier told me.

"Marilyn had been to Joan's house and she said," 'What a home she gave her adopted children!' Marilyn knew what it meant to be a foster-home child.

"She said it's terrible when you're little and you know nobody really wants you. Marilyn believed Joan really wanted those children. She didn't just give them a foster home. She adopted them. She didn't just take them in as foster children to try them out. Marilyn said she'd had tryouts, and it was painful.

"She couldn't say enough about what Joan had done, and Marilyn was impressed that she didn't just depend on a man to support her economically or emotionally. Marilyn admired that kind of courage, though she didn't feel she had it herself.

"She said she would have loved anyone who loved her like that when she didn't have a mother and father to love her, but she saw some children who were twisted by the experience, and they were afraid of loving anyone because they might have been given back.

"Marilyn stayed with people who threatened her all the time. If they didn't like something she did, they said they were going to give her back. She was never adopted and only stayed in foster homes, so they could have given her back anytime they wanted.

"She thought she was a saint. Saint Joan. Saint Joan Crawford!

"Marilyn told me whenever she was at a big party, and everyone was having a wonderful time, talking and smiling, and laughing, she could look around the room and see if someone there was an orphan or grew up in a foster home.

"'You know how I can tell?' she asked me. 'It's in their eyes. It's a lonely look, being alone, a lost child.' Childhood, she felt, was the most vulnerable time, and children like her had had their childhoods stolen.

"She said, 'I know that lost look well because it's the one I see in my own eyes when I look into my mirror.'"

The Story of Esther Costello (1957)

In a childhood accident with a hand grenade, Esther Costello (Heather Sears) is stricken deaf, dumb, and blind. In the remote Irish village in which she lives, she is left to survive in any way she can.

Margaret Landi (Joan Crawford), a wealthy American woman, estranged from her husband and trying to restore a sense of purpose in her life, visits the village of her birth. After making some charitable contributions there, she is introduced to the unwanted, destitute little girl by the village priest (Denis O'Dea). He convinces Margaret, who has always wanted children, that she should become her patron, even though the child's condition seems hopeless.

Margaret takes Esther to London for examinations, where the unresponsive child is unexpectedly diagnosed as healthy, but suffering from psychosomatic trauma. Back in America, Margaret lavishes all of the care she can manage on Esther, and finally Esther responds, but without regaining her sight and hearing. She becomes famous and a cause celèbre for such cases.

Esther's newfound fame lures back Margaret's husband, Carlo (Rossano Brazzi), and she accepts a reconciliation with him. His motives, however, are mercenary, and his interest in the maturing and very attractive Esther is far from paternal.

When Carlo rapes Esther, she is shocked back to normalcy and is able to see, speak, and hear again. When Margaret learns of the rape and Esther's recovery, she leaves her with a young reporter (Lee Patterson), who has fallen in love with the young woman. Then Margaret goes on a final drive with Carlo. With her driving, they enter a tunnel and crash.

When the filming of *Esther Costello* finished, Joan went flying with her husband on promotional tours for Pepsi-Cola. Joan had been terrified by the idea of flying, but she had to conquer that fear if she wished to travel on business with Steele. She did want to be with him; she also became aware immediately that she was a special asset to him. Everywhere, her fans welcomed her.

Joan accompanied her husband to the opening of bottling plants all over the United States, Canada, and South America, as well as Great Britain and Europe. It was not unusual that an executive of Steele's stature would be accompanied by his wife. What *was* unusual was that the people were waiting for Steele's wife, not just Mrs. Steele, but Joan Crawford.

For Joan, this was like a red-carpet premiere, and it was another precious opportunity to talk with fans, hers and those of Pepsi-Cola. She was the most glamorous Hollywood actress who had ever become an ambassadress for a major corporation.

She did it as she did everything, enthusiastically. Joan also attracted the press, which gave Pepsi-Cola an extra dividend.

"My husband, far from ever minding all the attention I attracted, was thrilled by it. He was so proud of me, and as a good businessman, he was well aware of my contribution to Pepsi-Cola."

She was popular with the other executives, and unexpectedly, she was particularly popular with the wives. They were enthralled by her wardrobe, some of it by Adrian, all of it perfectly accessorized, matching high heels, an Hermès crocodile bag and silk scarf, kid gloves with pearl buttons, often a high-style hat. She always had a lot of luggage and she would change as many as four times a day for whatever events were on the agenda.

A great deal of this time was, as always, spent signing autographs.

JOAN'S MOTHER DIED in Los Angeles in 1958. She was seventy-four years old. Anna had lived in Los Angeles since 1929, when Joan invited her to come from Kansas City and join Hal, who had arrived earlier, uninvited. They lived in the first house Joan had purchased for herself, and Joan moved out. Joan supported her mother as her mother had taken care of her, also providing for Hal. She was glad to be able to repay her mother's sacrifices, fully understanding how hard Anna had worked for her and Hal. Anna never had to work again, and enjoyed her life in the Hollywood Mother's Club.

In California, Anna played a minor role in Joan's life, but Joan's daughter Cathy remembered the delicious pies her grandmother would bake and bring to their house. Anna enjoyed belonging to a club for mothers of the stars. She was buried in the place of her choosing, Forest Lawn Cemetery.

Joan's brother, Hal, died of a ruptured appendix at the age of fifty-nine only five years later. He was employed at that time as a night clerk in a Los Angeles motel. His early ambition to have a Hollywood acting career remained unfulfilled, despite what help Joan could give him. He had been an alcoholic, but managed to conquer his addiction. Hal had married and divorced twice, and he named his only child, Joan, after his sister.

WHILE *The Best of Everything* was marketed as a Joan Crawford picture, she had less screen time than usual. Producer Jerry Wald, finding the film overly long, ordered it cut heavily, so that many of Joan's scenes were deleted. It is a multi-story film, with some of the characters and stories only peripherally related to Joan's character. Joan was extremely disappointed by the cuts.

The Best of Everything (1959)

Amanda Farrow (Joan Crawford) is an overbearing magazine editor who affects the lives of everyone working for her. Her unsatisfactory relationship with a married man often causes her to take out her anger and frustration on her assistants, Gregg Adams (Suzy Parker) and Caroline Bender (Hope Lange), who are involved in their own unpromising situations with men. Gregg, an aspiring actress, is having an affair with David Savage (Louis Jourdan), a Broadway director, and Caroline has turned to co-worker Mike (Stephen Boyd) after having broken up with her boyfriend.

Reluctantly, Amanda's boss, Mr. Shalimar (Brian Aherne), accepts her resignation when a widower with children proposes marriage to her. She finds herself unsuited to married life and returns to her old job at the magazine. Gregg and Caroline have moved on, having found success in their careers and happiness in their private lives. Amanda realizes how much her work means to her.

On May 5, 1959, Joan and Steele were in Washington to present a citation to Senator John F. Kennedy for his work with the Multiple Sclerosis Society. It was the last part of a two-month promotional tour for Pepsi-Cola. On their way back to New York, Steele complained of chest pains.

That night, he died in his sleep of a coronary occlusion.

"Many people would say that sudden death, peaceful death," Joan said, "when you are at a good place in your life, is the best. Well, maybe it's the best for the person, but it's the most terrible thing for the people who love you. The sudden shock.

"One day, I had a wonderful life and the next day, a broken heart.

"And then there are those what-ifs. Why didn't I force Al to take it easier? Why didn't I make certain he had the best doctor and went more often? Why didn't I see some symptoms? I should have noticed when he felt tired."

In the days just before Al Steele died, Joan was thinking about what gift she would give her husband on their approaching fourth wedding anniversary. She knew she wanted it to be something special and something personal that he would wear often. She had pretty much decided that gift would be a pair of Cartier cuff links.

"When Alfred died, I thought of all of the things I wanted to tell him that I would never be able to. I didn't know if I had said I loved him enough.

"I looked at the telephone and realized I would never hear his voice calling me again. I wished we could have skipped a few business trips and social events and just stayed home alone together. He seemed so healthy, and he wanted to work. I wished that I had made him stop working so hard."

Joan was devastated, but it was only the beginning.

Her assumption that Steele was a highly successful business executive and that he would have handled his personal money well and provided for Joan was not correct. Joan had believed it and believed in him, but his sudden death left her not only bereaved, but in a perilous economic position, with more debts than assets, especially since she felt responsible for any taxes and debts owed by her deceased husband. Pepsi-Cola had loaned him money with Steele's future salary as collateral.

Joan moved to a smaller nine-room apartment at the Imperial House, only a few blocks from their apartment at 70th Street and Fifth Avenue. She said that she was embarrassed to admit that nine rooms seemed small because of the way she had been living. She had to give away much of her furniture and other possessions. Some of the furniture was too large, on the grand scale of the remodeled apartment. She sent her dining room table to the residence of Cardinal Spellman in New York City.

"I knew my table would have a good home, would be a part of marvelous entertaining, and would contribute to those occasions. It was a fantastic table. I was so grateful that the cardinal wanted it."

Joan had never considered herself a materialistic person, so it amazed her how much she had accumulated. She found she had little difficulty in giving up most of her furnishings, as she planned for a different kind of life.

"I never felt I made a mistake, or missed something I had given away. I had enjoyed acquiring the things and using them, and I hoped the people I gave them to would have pleasure from them. I was never an extremely sentimental person about things. I remember someone told me, 'Never love anything that can't love you back.'

"I kept my clothes and shoes and jewelry, as those things were a part of me, a part of the public Joan Crawford. Some of the jewelry was gifts from Alfred. He knew I enjoyed wearing jewelry, and he enjoyed buying it for me. Wearing it made me feel close to him sometimes when I was all alone."

Shortly after Steele's death, Pepsi-Cola appointed Joan a member of the board. She was paid $50,000 a year, for which she would make promotional appearances for Pepsi. Although she hoped to continue making films in Hollywood, she decided to sell her Brentwood home and make New York her permanent base. "But she still had an apartment in Los Angeles, and she would come out here to make movies," Betty Barker told me. "She would come to Los Angeles much more than people realized."

"I really had no more use for my Brentwood home," Joan told me. "I wasn't planning to be in California that much, and the house was too big for me. Besides, I needed the money. But it wasn't without some emotion that I parted with it.

"I remembered how much it had meant to me when I bought it. It was where *Joan Crawford* had lived her life. Once I sold it, I did not want to see it again, except in my good memories."

"JOAN NEVER EXPRESSED a word of bad feeling about her last husband," John Springer told me, "not to anyone close to her, never. She only had good things to say about him. His death made her very sad. She spoke about what good times they had had, and how much she would miss him.

"It was unfortunate that he spent so much money, his and hers. Steele enjoyed living well, and Joan enjoyed living well with him.

"He used a lot of money to buy her gifts, and Joan, who loved buying gifts, would reciprocate. He bought gifts for her children. They took wonderful trips and entertained. What really got them into trouble was the decision to renovate her lovely apartment, which didn't look to me like it really needed anything much.

"They got heavily involved and it took many months. It was enough work for the neighbors to complain. It cost much more than the original estimate, the way those things do, and it went on and on and on. So, Al Steele borrowed against his future salary, and then he died. He was spending into a future he didn't have, only they didn't know that.

"Joan was glad to have a man to handle the finances, and she believed she had a rich husband who was earning a lot of money. He *was* a rich man, but he had other responsibilities, too, and his salary didn't go far enough, it seemed, after the fact.

"Joan was generous, but she was still careful about money because she said she'd been poor already and didn't like it and didn't want to do that again.

"As I understand, Joan's last marriage left her with debts, but like the honorable person she was, she set about paying them off and did.

"But she never said she blamed Al Steele for anything, and I really think she didn't. And I know she missed him. Maybe it wasn't the great love affair that she'd had with Douglas [Fairbanks, Jr.], or Clark [Gable], or Franchot [Tone], but he was a good companion for her. She didn't think she'd find another anymore, someone she could care about and trust, and she didn't."

"I HAD FUN with Al Steele," Joan told me. "Before he came into my life, I hadn't been having much fun and felt lonely. It's hard to have fun alone when you feel lonely.

"Earlier in my life, I had been able to enjoy things by myself, but I was beginning to feel that from now on, alone might be my permanent state of being.

"Then there was Al, who made everything fun. He enjoyed life so much, it was a real privilege to enjoy life with him. Perhaps I was more appreciative of fun than I had ever been before because less of it had been coming my way. Never underestimate the importance of fun."

After the death of her husband, Joan did not need such a large apartment as the one she and Steele had shared and remodeled. She would be living there alone. It was too expensive for her to maintain, not only because her film income was disappearing, but because there were also debts incurred by her deceased husband who had borrowed against his future salary to create what he felt would be their showplace home, where they would entertain for Pepsi-Cola, as well as for their personal pleasure. His unexpected death had left her with those debts and others, and she felt honor-bound to repay anything her husband owed. Because her standard for meticulously keeping the apartment in perfect condition was so high, that also imposed an additional burden.

"I had another reason, too," she told me. "Our home was filled with wonderful memories of our life together. I wanted to preserve those carefully treasured in my mind. Happy memories are so precious and nothing should be allowed to damage them. I felt, if I lived on there alone, my life could not live up to what I had shared with Al. The reality would be in contrast with what we had hoped and dreamed our future together would be. Those dreams were finished, but I wanted to keep my memory of our past. If I could have, and had chosen to, I suppose I would have lived on in that lovely apartment for years, but the lonely memories would have crowded the joyous times, and perhaps because they came later, I would have been less likely to remember the wonderful ones that had come before."

9

Joan Alone
(1961–1970)

J OHN SPRINGER remembered calling Joan Crawford in New York City a few years after her last husband's death. He had phoned to wish her a happy New Year. "Did you have a nice New Year's Eve?" he asked.

"No, I didn't," she replied. "I was just here at home, alone."

Springer couldn't understand it. He assumed if she had stayed home alone on New Year's Eve, it could only have been by her own choice.

"Was it because that was what you wanted?" Springer asked her.

"No, no, no. I *wanted* to go to a fabulous party, all dressed up, and be with wonderful people as the old year passed away and left us with hopes and dreams for the next. But I had to make my own toast and drink it all alone."

"But you must have been invited to many parties . . ."

"Oh, I had more than my share of invitations to parties, and I would have liked to have gone to all of them, but no one asked me out for New Year's Eve, and I certainly couldn't have gone to a New Year's Eve party alone, unescorted. Can you imagine what people would have said?"

Springer asked about "Butch" Romero. Cesar Romero was an old friend of hers, having escorted her to many parties.

"'He hasn't called me for a while,' she said, 'so I certainly couldn't call him.'

"'Everyone wants you, Joan,' I said. 'No one would have cared if you came alone or who you brought with you. You're a great star.'

"'Yes, Johnny. That's exactly why I couldn't go alone. I couldn't betray the image of Joan Crawford, the star.'"

IN WHAT MIGHT well be considered a Bette Davis type of line, Joan said, about working with her on *Baby Jane*:

"Bette is a survivor. She survived herself."

"It was Miss Crawford who brought me *What Ever Happened to Baby Jane?*" Bette told me. "I was rather surprised to see her. She came backstage after a matinee of *Iguana* and told me about a book which had parts for both of us in it. Robert Aldrich had bought it and thought he could get backing if we agreed to be in it. He was in Italy, and he'd asked Miss Crawford to approach me."

In October of 1961, Aldrich sent Joan a screenplay based on the novel *What Ever Happened to Baby Jane?* by Henry Farrell. She was so enthusiastic about the project that she visited Bette backstage at Broadway's Royale Theatre, where Bette was starring in Tennessee Williams's *The Night of the Iguana*. Bette was at first skeptical, then after she read the novel, she was enthusiastic.

"Without Joan's initial enthusiasm," Aldrich told me, "there would have been no *Baby Jane*. I never had anyone else in mind but Joan and Bette for the picture. And then Joan talked Bette Davis into being Baby Jane."

"When Bob Aldrich and I met in New York," Bette said, "I only needed to know I was Baby Jane and that he was not involved with Miss Crawford. It wasn't that I cared about his private life, or hers either. That's a matter of taste. I didn't want him favoring her with more close-ups."

Aldrich's laughter answered her second question. His assurance that he couldn't imagine anyone else except Bette being Jane sufficed.

Then came the struggle for financing. "They didn't want to put their money on two old broads," Bette said. Finally Seven Arts furnished enough backing to allow the film to be made.

"Miss Crawford and I each gave up part of our salaries in return for a percentage of the profits in order to make the project possible. After *Baby Jane* opened, it made each of us rich, for a while." The film opened in November 1962 in New York and New Jersey, where it recouped its production costs in eleven days.

Robert Aldrich recalled Joan's reaction to Victor Buono when the twenty-six-year-old actor arrived on the set to film *What Ever Happened to Baby Jane?*

"Joan had finished filming her part for the day, and she was getting ready to leave when Victor Buono arrived. Do you know what she did? She went right back into makeup and had her gaunt, tortured victim face put on, and she came and got right into bed, even though she wasn't being photographed.

"She did it just for him, for Victor Buono. She knew the picture was very important to him, because he was just starting out, and she felt he didn't have the experience to just look at a roll of blankets on the bed and see her and register the proper reactions.

"Buono was perfect, and he told people how beautiful Joan was for what she had done. He was really grateful to her."

Bette Davis, however, hadn't liked Aldrich's choice of Buono, whom he had seen in an episode of the popular television series *The Untouchables*. Peter Lawford had originally agreed to play the part, but dropped out.

"Bette came to me and said that Mr. Buono was too big and fat and too revolting to appeal even to her Jane character," Aldrich said. "I held my ground, and she accepted my decision. She was always polite to Buono, but not warm, and though I think he sensed the way she felt, he never said anything about it to me. He was very young, and this represented a big career opportunity for him, so any displeasure on her part would have had to make him even more nervous.

"Bette was a real lady and not only a professional, but a very honorable person, a square shooter. After her first scene or two with him, when we stopped shooting, she strode toward him in that way she had, and she said, in my presence, looking up at him, 'I confess that before we began, I did not care for Bob's choice of you, and I tried to persuade him not to use you. He was right, and I was wrong. I hope you will accept my apology, because you are absolutely marvelous.'

"Of course he was, but this recognition of his performance by Bette Davis made him very, very happy!"

For *What Ever Happened to Baby Jane?* Bette did her own makeup. She didn't feel any makeup man would dare to go as far as she would. "Miss Crawford did exactly the opposite," Bette said. "She did everything she could to make herself look as beautiful as possible. True, her character was a former beauty, but the emphasis should have been on *former* rather than on *beauty*.

"I was very grateful that she wanted *that* part, of Blanche. She never even considered wanting to do the part of Baby Jane, though I'm sure she understood very well that Jane was the juicier part. I would never have accepted anything *but* Baby Jane, who was one of the great characters and who allowed me to play her to the hilt. Miss Crawford was more concerned with the positioning of her falsies."

Joan never understood why Bette disliked her. "I didn't feel that way about her," she told me. "While we were doing *Baby Jane* together, I sent her flowers, and then I sent her some chocolates. No response."

Bette said what she valued most was sincerity, "a word Miss Crawford did not know. I hated it when she would send me flowers or little gifts, or gooey notes on that baby blue notepaper of hers. She would send anyone who gave her their address a thank-you note. She sent thank-you notes for thank-you notes. She carried this saccharine politeness to such an exaggeration of courtesy that it was disgusting and irritating. I believed her attempts to butter me up were absolutely *in*-sincere. Absolutely.

"And I have never enjoyed being buttered up. Give me a dash of sincerity anytime."

Some thought the feud resulted from Joan having won Franchot Tone when Bette wanted him. Bette admitted that she was "absolutely smitten" with Tone while they were co-starring together in *Dangerous*. "Bette was quite honest in what she said," Joan told me, "even when she was wrong. Some of what she said to people was hurtful. I never wanted to hurt anyone's feelings."

• • •

BETTY BARKER SPOKE with me about her experiences on the *Baby Jane* set, to which she accompanied Joan throughout the shooting.

"In all of that time," Barker said, "I never heard Joan say a bad word about Bette Davis, never a word against her. Well, maybe a slight undercurrent."

Barker recalled the first day of *Baby Jane*, when Joan asked her to go with her to the set.

"Joan introduced me to Bette Davis. I thought she was nice and very friendly, and I liked her."

"The next day, I said, 'Hello, Miss Davis,' and something like, 'How are you today?' And she seemed to be mad at me, that day.

"She was a very difficult person. She was very inconsistent. She was changeable and you didn't know where you were. She was completely different from Joan. With Joan, you always knew she was on your side. She was so nice, easy, and pleasant, and Bette was an angry person.

"One day Bette would be very, very nice to me. Then, the next day, she didn't like me anymore. A few days later, she would like me. I never knew from one day to another. I stopped bothering to say hello first.

"Well, it's all over now."

"PEOPLE ALWAYS ASK me about my feud with Bette Davis," Joan said. "Well, it won't take long to tell about *that*. I can't speak for her. I can only speak for myself, and doing that, I can only say, *I* didn't have a feud with her. Maybe she had one with me, but a one-sided feud isn't much of a feud.

"I admired her as an actress. I thought we should be friends. I assumed we *would* be, even though actresses who worked as much as we did didn't have much time to build friendships.

"We were so different, and each of us had her own strong style. During most of our great careers, we were at different studios. There was no reason for us to be competitive or jealous. Later, there were a few parts for which we might have competed, but I never knew exactly the reason why she seemed to dislike me—no, *hate* me.

"It may have been the press buildup of a so-called feud, and she believed what she read. Or, it may have been something that she thought was a good way to act, being angry at me to get attention for herself or even to gain sympathy against that 'terrible monster, Miss Crawford.' She said '*Miss* Crawford' not with a tone of respect, but with more of a sneer. I thought of her as Bette, but she never once called me Joan."

The legendary feud between the two may have been just that—a legend. They both read so much about hating each other that they ended up believing it themselves.

"I can tell you why I enjoyed poking a little fun at Miss Crawford," Bette told me. "It was because she had absolutely no sense of humor. Absolutely none, if you can believe that. I noticed it right away. She didn't understand my jokes. Not that they were all that funny, but she didn't even understand that they *were* jokes. It wasn't a matter of pulling her leg. In her case, she didn't notice.

"At first, I couldn't understand that she *didn't* understand. Maybe she thought irony had something to do with ironing.

"Then, I must say, I noticed poking some fun was a good attention-getting device, and I was never adverse to getting a little extra attention.

"And then, I found out it was expected of me. I was being interviewed before a group of press and someone called out, 'And now, tell us what you think of Joan Crawford.' That got a big laugh; in fact, it was a bigger laugh than any I could expect if I cracked wise. He'd topped me even before I opened my mouth, so I figured I had no place to go except to go straight and say something as boring as I could manage. And that was pretty boring. 'She's a very talented actress, etc., etc., etc.' Needless to say, I didn't get quoted. I had disappointed because the bar had been set too high. It's very hard if you have a performer's heart to know that you have let your audience down."

What Ever Happened to Baby Jane? (1962)

The Hudson sisters, Jane (Bette Davis) and Blanche (Joan Crawford), once child show-business headliners, are growing old together, but not compatibly, in a run-down Hollywood mansion. As a child, Jane was an acclaimed vaudeville star and later a mediocre film actress, while Blanche became a Hollywood superstar. After an accident crippled Blanche, Jane, believing she was responsible and not being able to support herself, was obliged to take care of her invalid sister.

Jane, who has come to resent her status as nurse and caretaker, begins to display symptoms of mental instability. Blanche becomes alarmed when she notices her sister's mental deterioration and decides to sell the mansion. Afterward, she plans to put Jane into a sanatorium. Learning this, Jane begins torturing her helpless sister, at first in small ways, like serving her sister a large broiled rat on a chafing dish.

All the while, Jane dreams of a show-business comeback for herself. She hires an unemployed pianist, Edwin Flagg (Victor Buono), to help prepare her act.

Their part-time cleaning lady, Elvira (Maidie Norman), notices a downturn in Jane's already alarmingly eccentric behavior, and Jane fires her.

When Jane's treatment of Blanche becomes intolerable, Blanche tries to escape, but is stopped by her sister, who is now definitely going mad. A suspicious Elvira, returning to investigate, finds Blanche bound and gagged. In a panic, Jane picks up a hammer and kills Elvira.

Edwin finds Blanche half-dead and rushes out of the house terrified. Fearing he will return with the police, Jane drives Blanche to Malibu. As she is dying on the beach, Blanche confesses to Jane that it is *she* who was responsible for the accident that left her crippled and that she lied to Jane to keep her sister a prisoner of guilt, obligated to take care of her.

As spectators watch and the police arrive, Jane happily imagines herself performing again, as, reliving the joys of her childhood, she dances on the beach.

Director George Cukor believed that Joan and Bette had a lot in common. "Neither one was a cunning person," he told me. "Intelligent, but not cunning. They didn't plot. Bette was not a Planny-Annie, and Joan wasn't a Planny-Annie, either."

Cukor did not personally like Bette all that much nor did he have much contact with her. He had fired her from her first job, which Bette never forgot, or forgave. He was a great fan of Joan's, professionally, and a great friend of hers, personally. He called Joan "a noble person."

"I loved both those ladies," John Springer told me. "Joan and Bette. And I like to think they loved me. I know they did. Those were both relationships I treasured. So they couldn't have been so different from each other, could they? They weren't. They were more alike than they were different."

Betty Barker recalled that Joan was disappointed when the Baby Jane character got all of the attention. "She had selected the part which suited her, and she thought it was a good part and that she did a good job and that Blanche was just as important to the film, but people all talked about Baby Jane."

Director Curtis Harrington remembered an occasion when he and his producer had lunch with Bette Davis at the Universal commissary. "My producer asked Bette—he wasn't totally serious—if she would be interested in doing a sequel to *Baby Jane*, with Joan Crawford.

"'Yes,' Bette retorted. 'And I'll tell you about the first scene. It'll be a scene of *this* one,' pointing at herself, 'putting flowers on *that* one's grave.'"

Bette was nominated as best actress for *Baby Jane*. Joan had hoped she would be nominated and was quite disappointed when she wasn't.

Joan, however, was one to take a constructive approach, if at all possible. She arranged with Anne Bancroft, who could not be in California on the night of the Oscars, to receive the Oscar for her if she won. Anne Bancroft won for *The Miracle Worker*, and Joan accepted the Oscar for her. Bette was definitely annoyed.

Baby Jane also received Oscar nominations for best supporting actor, Victor Buono; best black and white cinematography, Ernest Haller; and best sound, Joseph Kelly. It won an Oscar for Norma Koch's costume designs.

The film marked a turning point in the careers of both actresses, who were suddenly seen in a new light, that of gothic horror queens. For a while, this new image extended their careers as above-the-title stars. *The Caretakers* cast Joan in a rather unsympathetic role.

The Caretakers (1963)

Dr. Jubal Harrington (Herbert Marshall), the director of a mental hospital, is confronted with two opposing methods of treating the insane. The conventional method, backed by head nurse Lucretia Terry (Joan Crawford), advocates isolation and restraint. Terry has established judo classes for her staff in order to protect them from the violently insane. Supporting her harsh approach is Nurse Bracken (Constance Ford), who sadistically enforces the harsh methods.

An innovative new method, endorsed by young Dr. Donovan MacLeod (Robert Stack), stresses the value of individual treatment within a more normal environment, especially with less serious cases.

Walking a political tightrope, Dr. Harrington endorses the traditional methods espoused by Nurse Terry while trying to give the appearance of having an open mind toward new developments in the mental health field.

Dr. MacLeod's group therapy sessions bring about positive responses from some of the patients. One of those who improves is a young wife, Lorna Melford (Polly Bergen), who had a nervous breakdown after her child was killed in an automobile accident in which she, the driver, was at fault. Other patients who show promise are a neurotic prostitute, a displaced person from Europe, a young runaway, and a disoriented older teacher.

A temporary setback occurs when Lorna wanders into the male violent ward and is attacked. In spite of this, more compassionate treatment of the insane seems to promise better results.

Joe Franklin, New York's celebrated talk show host, told me how from time to time he would receive a call from someone who said, "Hello, this is Joan Tone. I'd like to be on your show." She was, of course, Joan Crawford, using her second husband's last name. When she appeared on Franklin's television program, she arrived with a bottle of Pepsi-Cola, which she placed in front of her so that it was always on camera.

The guests and crew also received Pepsi, but they had to return the empty bottles, to be collected at the end of the show. "You have no idea how much money we lose on bottles that aren't returned," Joan said.

Franklin, in his introductions, always said, "I knew her when she was Joan Tone."

Billy Wilder remembered Joan as being the most persistent person he'd ever known when it came to Pepsi-Cola. "I was filming *One, Two, Three* with James Cagney playing the part of a Coca-Cola executive, and Joan got wind of this, and she wanted equal time for Pepsi-Cola, *more* than equal time. I can imagine what it must have been like if she'd wanted a part in your movie.

"She was on the board of Pepsi, and her husband, who had died, worked for Pepsi. I was telling my wife, Audrey, about it, and then I got this idea. At the end in the airport, Cagney goes to a Coca-Cola machine and gets Pepsi-Cola."

W. J. Curran wrote to me from Canada about Joan's Canadian promotional tours for Pepsi-Cola, which allowed her to visit Franchot Tone at his chalet on Muskoka Lake, near Ottawa. "I knew a gentleman who worked with Pepsi," Curran said, "and he told me that Joan Crawford would have him check out public places where she would appear in Canada so that she could be color-coordinated."

WILLIAM CASTLE'S SPECIALTY was low-budget horror films that were often promoted entertainingly. At one premiere, he arrived at the theater in a hearse, from which he was transported to the stage in a coffin. Then, paper bats and spiders seemed to fill the theater. For another film, he offered $1,000 to the first person to die of fright while watching it.

Strait-Jacket, however, was not marketed in this way. It was, unlike most other Castle films, presented seriously and with restraint, causing critics to comment that he didn't *have* to use such garish promotional methods. The film was an enormous box office success, and Joan had a new, younger audience.

Strait-Jacket (1964)

For the crime of the axe murder of her husband and his young mistress, Lucy Harbin (Joan Crawford) was committed to the state mental hospital for the criminally insane. After twenty years have passed, she is considered cured, and is released.

She is taken in by her grown daughter, Carol (Diane Baker), who has been living with foster parents, Bill and Emily Cutler (Leif Erickson and Rochelle Hudson), since the murders. After being shut off from the world for two decades, Lucy seems quaint and out-of-date, and Carol encourages her to dress more fashionably and become a part of the contemporary world.

Soon, Lucy is presentable enough for Carol to introduce her to her fiancé, Michael Fields (John Anthony Hayes). Lucy makes it known to Michael that she is also attracted to him.

Carol is then humiliated when Lucy becomes hysterical in front of Michael's socially ambitious mother (Edith Atwater).

When there is a series of axe murders, Lucy is the natural suspect, but she isn't guilty. The murderer is Carol, who had witnessed her own father and his mistress being hacked to death by her mother. This traumatic image affected her profoundly, though it did not show up as psychotic behavior until her mother returned and stirred up those horrible memories and images of the past.

Joan was a good sport about the parts she was offered after *Baby Jane*. It never concerned her that some people thought she was degrading the image of Joan Crawford.

"There were gossips who speculated on why I didn't retire gracefully after my long career. There were two reasons.

"The first was I genuinely loved working. The only problem was that there weren't so many parts, and I didn't have much choice at my age. Stars of my age weren't in constant demand. If it was a good part that suited my talents, I took it.

"I felt lucky to be asked, though I did feel I was being asked more often for my name value of the past than for my talent in the present.

"Beggars can't be choosers, and while I wasn't exactly reduced to being a beggar, I didn't know how long I would live, and what the future held.

"I had very real financial problems, and I could see them getting worse, not better. Work had always saved me, and work could save me again, as long as I could work, and as long as I could get work.

"I feared the dark specter of poverty, not imminent, but lurking.

"I knew others who faced a decline in their fortunes and didn't like it, but there was probably none among them who knew as intimately as I did what it was like to be poor. I was frightened, but I couldn't let it show."

For *Strait-Jacket*, Joan received $50,000 plus a percentage of the profits.

JEREMIAH NEWTON, Motion Picture and Television liaison at New York University, wrote Joan a fan letter when he was in his early teens, and she answered him personally with a handwritten note.

When she replied, she asked about his classes, what he was studying, and what he wanted to be. He wrote that he would like to be an actor.

She wrote back to him that there were two films he had to see: *Citizen Kane*, because Orson Welles was "so intriguing," and Lon Chaney's *The Phantom of the Opera*, to see what a real actor can do without even talking.

"There were no VCRs or DVDs at that time," Newton said, "but I did get to see them at an old movie palace in Queens that did revivals."

They exchanged letters, and Newton had the opportunity to meet her a few times. He recalled the last time he saw her.

"She was making some personal appearances in theaters on Long Island and in Queens for a film she'd just done, *I Saw What You Did*.

"I went to see her at the Hillside Theater, and this huge art deco aluminum bus pulled up. The door opened and there she was, Joan Crawford.

"I came early and was standing right at the front of the crowd, watching. I was just a kid, about sixteen, and I wasn't dressed up, so one of the policemen, who was there to keep the fans back, sort of pushed me back.

"Joan saw that as she was coming out. She was very alert and she saw everything.

"She came right over to me. She was so tiny, even in high heels, holding her head up, the way she did, but she had a great air of authority. She said to the policeman, 'How dare you treat my son like that! Who do you think you are, anyway? You're just a bully.'

"The policeman said, 'I'm sorry, Miss Crawford. I thought he was just a fan.'

"I knew that outraged her, but she didn't say much. She just said, 'Yes, he's a fan, too!'

"I saw the film and her appearance. And that's the last time I saw her.

"I wish I could have told Joan Crawford how much she helped me. When you're younger, you don't see things in perspective. I didn't even know at the time that it would mean so much to me later. She treated me with such respect and dignity, and she didn't talk down to me, and I try to always treat people like that."

I Saw What You Did (1965)

Steve Marak (John Ireland) receives an anonymous phone call just after he has murdered his wife. A female voice says, "I saw what you did, and I know who you are." He fears a neighbor has witnessed the murder.

The caller, however, is just a teenage girl playing a prank. Kit and Libby (Sara Lane and Andi Garrett) are amusing themselves by dialing phone numbers at random and then speaking their menacing message.

Marak traces the call and tells his next-door neighbor and lady friend, Amy Nelson (Joan Crawford), what has happened. She sees that he has gone mad, and rushes to protect the girls and Libby's younger sister (Sharyl Locke), who has been left in their care by Libby's parents.

Marak kills Amy with a bread knife, but she has protected the girls long enough for the police and parents to arrive and save them.

Robert Aldrich planned to co-star Joan and Bette again in a film called *What Ever Happened to Cousin Charlotte?*, also written by Henry Farrell. Bette liked the treatment, but didn't like the title, and suggested *Hush . . . Hush, Sweet Charlotte*, drawn from a lullaby that had already been written for the film. She also didn't like the idea of working with Joan Crawford again, but grudgingly accepted it, if she received more money. Joan countered by demanding her name be first in the main titles.

Shooting began on location in Baton Rouge, Louisiana, on June 4, 1964. The cast included Joseph Cotten, Agnes Moorehead, Mary Astor, and Victor Buono.

No one met Joan at the Baton Rouge airport when she arrived. She believed that a star should look and act like a star at all times, and was a bit ruffled by not having been properly received on her arrival. Bette mingled freely with the cast and the crew. To travel any distance on location, Joan moved by golf cart while Bette walked. In the evening, Joan would leave the set with her maid and chauffeur in a limousine while Bette left in a station wagon with fellow cast members.

Joan was frequently ill, slowing down production or even forcing it to stop. Aldrich fought for every day he could by shooting around Joan's scenes.

When the production unit returned to Los Angeles, Joan checked into a hospital. Finally, Robert Aldrich reluctantly had to replace her. "I would have done anything I could to keep Joan," Aldrich said. "But my backers were nervous. Joan saw her part as playing second fiddle to Bette Davis, and whether that contributed to her not feeling well, I don't know."

"I was very hurt," Joan said, "that anyone could imply I was pretending to be ill. I understand that's what happened. It was, for anyone who knew me, totally contrary to my character to agree to make a film and then fake an illness. I had given my word, signed a contract, and my word was more important to me than a piece of paper."

Bette was not upset when she heard that "Miss" Crawford would not be returning to the film. She felt she had the perfect replacement in mind, her great friend Olivia de Havilland.

In Paris, some years later, de Havilland told me, "I did it to please Bette and not disappoint her. Given the choice, I wouldn't have deprived Joan Crawford of the honor."

AMONG JOAN'S post–*Baby Jane* movies, *Berserk!* was the most pleasurable experience. It was shot in England, and Joan was treated like the reigning cinema queen she had been at M-G-M and, to a lesser extent, Warner Brothers. To show her appreciation, she gave a party at the Grosvenor House for the crew and their wives. She especially liked the producer, American-born Herman Cohen.

Berserk! (1968)

Monica Rivers (Joan Crawford) and Dorando (Michael Gough) own a traveling English circus. Monica acts as the ring mistress, and Dorando is the business manager.

When Gaspar the Great (Thomas Cimarro) falls to his death, it appears that his tightrope might have been purposely weakened. Monica's unemotional reaction to the tragedy alarms Dorando. When she suggests it will be good for business, he asks her to buy him out, which she refuses to do.

Monica hires a new high-wire walker, Frank Hawkins (Ty Hardin). Not only is he handsome, he is daring. He does his act over a carpet of sharp spikes. Monica is impressed, especially by his physical appearance.

Shortly after an argument with Monica, Dorando is found dead, possibly murdered. Suspicion of Monica's guilt grows. Frank in particular suspects her. He saw her leaving Dorando's trailer before Dorando's body was discovered. He confronts Monica with this information, demanding a share in the circus for his silence.

Monica's daughter, Angela (Judy Geeson), having been expelled from school, shows up at the circus. Not knowing what to do with her unruly daughter, Monica pairs her with Gustavo the knife thrower (Peter Burton).

> During his high-wire act, Frank falls onto the spikes and is
> killed. It was not an accident. Angela was seen throwing a knife
> at him before he fell. Then she tries to kill her mother with a knife,
> but misses. As Angela attempts to escape, she is electrocuted by an
> exposed wire during a rainstorm. Monica sobs inconsolably over
> her daughter's body.

Because the budget for the film was so low, Joan told producer
Herman Cohen that she would save him some money by wearing
her own clothes. She was glad to help him, and she preferred wearing
dresses selected from her own wonderful wardrobe.

The only exception was the most important outfit, that of fishnet
stockings, short, fitted black leotard with a short red jacket, and long
black gloves worn by Joan as the circus mistress-of-ceremonies. The
design was Edith Head's gift to Joan. Head was a designer the production could never have afforded. Joan still had the beautiful legs and
fine figure that allowed her to wear the skimpy outfit.

AN IMAGE John Springer recalled vividly was going to Joan's New
York apartment and seeing an old, sickly-looking man in a wheelchair.
Though his face was different and his legs were covered by a blanket,
Springer recognized a very ill Franchot Tone. "Joan was in the kitchen
fixing something for him."

This was many years after their marriage and after their marriages
to others, but Joan was there for him, taking care of him. He lived
nearby.

She helped to support him financially, as well. Springer told me that
Tone would often be at her apartment in a wheelchair having dinner.

Springer commented to Joan that Franchot didn't look well at all.
Joan looked surprised. "Well, I know he's not feeling well these days,
but I think he *looks* quite well."

Springer said to me, "I understood then that all those years they
had an 'enchanted cottage' relationship." He was referring to the 1945
John Cromwell film in which a couple in love forget that the man is
disfigured from the war and the woman homely until people from the

outside remind them of the truth. Even so, the outsiders cannot shatter the view the young people have of each other.

"It was terribly hard for Franchot to have lost his money and not even be able to take care of himself," Joan told me. "He had always taken money for granted, and he didn't think about it. That's a wonderful luxury if you can afford it.

"He thought he would always be able to earn whatever he needed, but his career never went the way he had hoped."

Years before, Tone's fortunes had taken a sudden downturn when he suffered severe facial injuries in a fight with actor Tom Neal over a woman. Even with extensive plastic surgery, his handsome features were not fully restored. Some of his hospitalization and medical care was paid for by Joan.

Within a year of his divorce from Joan, Tone had married actress Jean Wallace, and they had had two sons. He remained married to her for seven years, after which they divorced and he married again two times. He appeared successfully on the stage in New York and made some films in Hollywood, including *Phantom Lady*, *Jigsaw*, and *The Man on the Eiffel Tower*, and did a great deal of television.

He and Joan had remained good friends. She visited him at his house on Muskoka Lake in Canada. When he developed lung cancer, he often came to her apartment in New York for dinner.

He died in 1968. He asked Joan to see to it that he was cremated. He wished to have his ashes scattered over the Canadian lake he loved, and she arranged it.

JOAN WAS ONE of the few stars who immediately saw the possibilities of television. "Mommie did the first *Johnny Carson Show*," daughter Cathy said. "But they didn't save the program because they didn't think he was going to last." Joan frequently appeared on quiz shows, game shows, and interviews, as well as guest appearances on series such as *I Love Lucy* and *The Man from U.N.C.L.E.* By 1969, she had also appeared in several television dramas, so when she agreed to appear on a new dramatic series, she was not a neophyte.

Newly under contract to Universal, twenty-one-year-old Steven

Spielberg was assigned his first project. It was to be one-third of a pilot for a new television series the studio was preparing for NBC. Spielberg had been chosen as director of the segment by Sid Sheinberg, head of production at Universal-MCA, who was number two at the studio to Lew Wasserman. The series, called *Night Gallery*, was intended for a November 1969 telecast.

Rod Serling was writing and hosting the show. His dream was to repeat the success of his acclaimed and extremely profitable *Twilight Zone*, to which Serling had sold all rights to CBS.

The format of the new series was similar to that of *The Twilight Zone*. Serling, as host, would stand in front of a painting in a darkly ominous art gallery, and the picture would come alive as a story while he talked about it.

The stories inspired by the paintings on *Night Gallery* could be classified as supernatural or science fantasy, with surprise endings. While *The Twilight Zone* usually presented only one such story in a half-hour format, *Night Gallery* did three in an hour, each featuring a well-known actor. In 1969, many stars from the golden age of Hollywood were available.

Spielberg's segment, "Eyes," was the second of the three in the pilot show. It is about a blind businesswoman who wants a corneal transplant even though her doctor has warned her that she will gain only twelve hours of sight.

She buys the eyes of a desperate man and the operation is performed. As it turns out, her twelve hours of sight coincide with the city-wide blackout of 1965. Seeing nothing but darkness, she stumbles out onto the penthouse terrace, falling to her death on the Manhattan sidewalk below.

Spielberg was disappointed. He didn't "feel" the script. When asked for his advice, Sheinberg cautioned the young man to set aside his misgivings about the script and accept the assignment. At that point in his career, he said, Spielberg would be unwise to risk getting a reputation for being difficult. Spielberg took Sheinberg's advice and found out he would be directing Joan Crawford for his first assignment.

He would be directing Mildred Pierce!

He would also be directing someone who had been directed by

George Cukor, Michael Curtiz, Howard Hawks, Otto Preminger, Joseph Mankiewicz, William Wellman, Lewis Milestone, Tod Browning, Frank Borzage, Jules Dassin, Jean Negulesco, and Robert Aldrich, among others. "It was like being told to make love to Marilyn Monroe," Spielberg told me. "She couldn't help but make comparisons. How could I compare?"

Though only a small project for Universal, it was big for Spielberg, because he knew, "They'd be taking a hard look to see what I could do." It could determine his future at the giant studio.

Even worse for him, he feared he would be staying on to do television programs that offered limited opportunity. Spielberg looked even younger than he was, which meant Miss Crawford might feel as if she had a teenager as director. Thus, it was with at least a little trepidation that Spielberg met his star.

ON HEARING THAT she was going to be directed by a twenty-one-year-old newcomer, Joan had at first been "speechless, and then horrified."

"He couldn't possibly have enough experience," she moaned. "How could I feel reassured the way an experienced director is supposed to make you feel? The producer said, 'Wait'll you meet him.' I thought, 'Yeah, sure. He's probably a very mature-looking twenty-two.' Actually, he looked about twelve.

"Why was this happening to me? I was unhappy, but I've never liked to show temperament, and I respected Sheinberg's judgment. Besides, the segment was only about fifteen minutes long."

Her first impression of Steven Spielberg was only of his voice, because she didn't see him at all. She was wearing a mask over her eyes, practicing being blind.

Without taking off the mask, she explained, "Mr. Spielberg, this is how a blind person walks though a room. The key is, she gropes."

She took off her practice mask. Though she did her best not to show it, she was clearly unimpressed by his appearance, or if impressed, negatively so. They went out to dinner.

Spielberg felt she probably had something to say, perhaps through

her agent, to the powers-that-be at the Black Tower, as the build–
ing that housed the executive offices was called. Spielberg knew that
Joan had previously been represented by Lew Wasserman, head of
Universal-MCA.

He worried that she may have ranted or had a tantrum when she
learned that she had been assigned so inexperienced a director, with no
features to his credit. It might have seemed to her that she was being
treated with no respect.

Respect or not, when the eight-day shoot began, Joan was as punc-
tual as she had always been, and the director was there waiting. The set
was cool, many would have said cold, because Joan had continued to
insist in her contract, as she always had from the time she became a star,
that the set temperature be kept at 55 degrees.

She arrived with a small retinue of hairdresser, makeup person, wardrobe assistant, and dresser. She also brought cases of Pepsi-Cola and
small refrigerators. Cans of the drink were distributed to all of the crew.

Spielberg knew, as did Joan, that only one of them could be in
charge on the set. With a star of the importance of Joan Crawford, the
star was always in control unless she deferred to the director. Sometimes that happened, but this was not one of those times.

It became quickly clear to all that Joan Crawford was totally in control, but once she was in control, she could afford to be magnanimous.
She could also afford to relax.

"When I began to work with Steven," Joan told me, "I understood
everything. It was immediately obvious to me, and probably to everyone else, that here was a young genius. I thought maybe more experience was important, but then I thought of all of those experienced
directors who didn't have Steven's intuitive inspiration and who just
kept repeating the same old routine performances. *That* was called
'experience.'

"I knew then that Steven Spielberg had a brilliant future ahead of
him. Hollywood doesn't always recognize talent, but Steven's was not
going to be overlooked. I told him so in a note I wrote him. I was
happy about my part in his career, as well as in 'Eyes.'

"I wrote to Rod Serling, too. I was so grateful that he had approved
Steven as the director. I told him he had been totally right.

"But I have to say that once I agreed to do the part, I was very careful to give the young director my total respect, even before he had earned it. I didn't want to intimidate him or make him feel nervous, so I was as cooperative as I could be. Not that I don't always try to be cooperative, but in this case, my being a major star could have intimidated him. Knowing him better now, I understand that he knew what he wanted. He was always polite and respectful, but he would not have let anyone spoil what he was doing. I respect that. He had *that* kind of dedication."

Once Joan got over being tense and mistrustful, once she had established that he would not make her do what she thought was wrong, she noticed that he had some interesting ideas. She almost wished that she had encouraged him to have a freer hand. But she couldn't have done that because she had even more to lose than "Steven," as she had begun to think of him. "He had his whole life ahead of him. He could afford a mistake at that age."

She had decided he was even younger than she had been told, about nineteen maybe. She had observed his determination in the face of compromise. "I've never thought compromise was a good idea. I think it's better that one person or the other has his or her way. Compromise always seemed to me to have the greatest chance of making a muddle, and then you never know who was right."

SPIELBERG BELIEVED THAT Joan Crawford had been important for him at the beginning of his career. As a novice director, he had learned a great deal from directing an actress of her talent and experience.

Appearing at the annual luncheon of the American Film Institute, Spielberg began his speech by saying, "Joan Crawford was my *mohel*."

The audience laughed.

A *mohel* is the person who performs ritual circumcisions, and Spielberg meant that Joan Crawford had done this for him—symbolically, of course.

"They'll probably cut that for television," he added, and the audience laughed again.

• • •

IN OCTOBER 1969, Christina, who was featured in *The Secret Storm*, a CBS daytime serial, fell ill and required major surgery. Joan stepped in and played her part for five episodes. No one seemed to mind that Christina was twenty-nine and Joan was sixty. Ratings went up for Joan, then down when Christina returned. Far from being grateful, Christina was resentful.

JOHN SPRINGER'S SON, Gary, who carried on his father's publicity business, Springer Associates, remembered his father having a terrible cold. "He stayed home from work, which he didn't often do.

"When Joan Crawford called him and learned about this cold, she rushed right over. She lived near us on the Upper East Side of Manhattan.

"She went straight past my mother [June] to my father, who was sitting in his chair. 'I'm going to take care of you,' she told him, 'and we'll have you well soon.'

"Addressing my mother, she said, dismissing her, 'You can go out,' and never using her name, which she knew very well after all those years, she said, 'I'll take care of Johnny.' My mother always called my father John.

"My mother left. She wasn't angry. She was accustomed to that sort of thing, though not from Joan.

"It was expected from Marlene Dietrich, who would rush over as soon as she heard my father had the slightest ailment, and she would come equipped with powerful medicine, a large jar of her secret-recipe chicken soup."

IN THE LATE summer of 1969, Joan flew to England to do what would be, as it turned out, her final feature film. "It was my chance to do a science fiction film," Joan said. "I'd never played a scientist before."

The director, Freddie Francis, was a famous cinematographer who from time to time, also directed low-budget films, such as *Trog*. He won the best cinematography Oscar in 1961 for *Sons and Lovers*. His participation in *Trog* is what persuaded Joan to accept the part.

Joan had recently appeared in two other films, *Della* (1964) and *The Karate Killers* (1967), both intended for television. *Trog* was shot at Bray Studios in England on such a low budget that Joan had to share her dressing room in a van with the other actors. Her co-star was an eight-foot troglodyte or cave-dwelling creature. She did not have to share her dressing room with the trog.

Trog (1970)

Two cave explorers in England encounter a troglodyte. The half-man, half-ape creature kills one of them, and the other escapes. In a hospital, the survivor describes the creature to a research doctor (Joan Crawford), who sets out to capture "Trog," as they call him.

Trog is captured and brought back to a laboratory, where the scientist studies him. Her attempts to communicate with him are successful, and she develops a relationship.

The townspeople, however, fear Trog and come to kill him. He escapes from the hospital and goes back to the cave, taking a young girl with him as hostage. He threatens to kill her if they don't leave him alone. The doctor talks him into releasing the girl. He is then killed in a battle with the townspeople.

In Chicago, Myrna Loy was performing in Neil Simon's *Barefoot in the Park*, when some of the cast and the stage manager were called to New York after the great success of the Broadway opening of Simon's *The Odd Couple*. Because of all the changes, Loy had the opportunity to work with her friend Joan's daughter Christina.

Loy said that when she heard the news, she was very pleased to be working with Christina, but that didn't last long.

"Christina," Loy told me, "wouldn't stand where she was supposed to, she said her lines any way she wanted to, and she upset everyone in the cast, especially me. I tried to speak with her. I had wanted to help her, if I could, but it was clear she resented me.

"When I asked her if her mother would be coming to her opening, she said, 'No,' angrily. I didn't know at whom she was angry. Her mother? Me? The world? I guess all of the aforementioned. I tried to get some help from Harvey Medlinsky, who had come in to direct the new production of *Barefoot*. Christina had arrived with Medlinsky.

"Well, that didn't work out at all. He didn't seem to listen to me. Then he never said a word to Christina except to glow over her with approval, even when she came late. He seemed to regard that as cute. I didn't find out till later that they were romantically involved, even if it didn't last that long. It lasted more than long enough to upset our production and well beyond that.

"I called Robby Lantz in New York, who represented Neil Simon, and I asked Robby if he could come out and see what was happening. I think he thought I was exaggerating or being temperamental or something, but he came right away from New York to Chicago, and he watched the show. Then he called Neil Simon, and Neil flew in.

"Christina was fired.

"As you can imagine, Christina never liked me after that. Actually, I don't think she liked me even before that. She saw me as her mother's friend, and it was clear to me *she* wasn't her mother's friend.

"My own personal theory was she wasn't just *jealous* of Joan, she wanted to *be* Joan."

DURING THE VIETNAM War, Joan was particularly active with the New York City USO. She gave what money she could afford, and she gave generously of her time in the spirit of her Hollywood Canteen days during World War II.

"It had nothing to do with how I felt about that war. I hate wars, but I always love the brave young men who go to fight, risking and sometimes giving all they have for our country, and I wanted to do anything I could."

· · ·

WHEN JOAN REACHED sixty-five, she was retired by Pepsi-Cola. She still received the same income from the company, but she lost most of the perquisites of the position, which represented more money than her salary.

Joan's last professional appearance as a performer was on the ABC series *The Sixth Sense* in 1972. She did not, however, announce her retirement.

The next year, she appeared onstage in a New York Town Hall series organized by John Springer called "Legendary Ladies of the Movies." Also in the series were Bette Davis, Rosalind Russell, Sylvia Sidney, Lana Turner, and Myrna Loy.

Knowing how Bette felt about "*Miss* Crawford," Springer asked her if she would object to Joan Crawford appearing in the same series. "I thought about it," Bette told me. "I knew it was good for him. So I said, 'All right. Ask Crawford. You can have her as long as it's a different night and we're not on the same stage at the same time. And I'll sit in the first row, and knit.'"

Joan was greeted by a long standing ovation, to which she replied, "I never knew there was so much love."

Contrary to her reputation for being nervous at live personal appearances, Joan appeared at ease before the large audience. One person noticed this and commented on it, saying that he had always heard that she was a nervous wreck at the mere thought of a personal appearance, to which she replied quite calmly: "What the hell do you think I am tonight?"

Someone in the audience asked her, in the light of her own experience with four children, how she viewed the problems of bringing up children in the 1970s. She answered: "I believe that the reason most of the kids are on pot and other junk is because they don't have enough love and enough discipline." (She had always said to me, "Discipline is one of the ways of showing love.")

At the end of the evening, members of the audience threw flowers of tribute up on the stage, and during the applause, she knelt to pick up every flower. As she was leaving the stage, she noticed a flower she had missed. She stopped, turned, and gathered it up, too.

• • •

JOAN INVITED HER friend, author, teacher, and film historian, Jeanine Basinger, to visit her in her New York apartment. "She said she would be free the next Wednesday afternoon, which was the only time possible," Basinger told me.

"I hesitated. Then I said I was so sorry, but I wouldn't be able to come on Wednesday.

"She asked why. It was my little girl's birthday.

"Her tone warmed, and she said, 'I understand. Please come on Sunday.'

"She sent my daughter a lovely note and a birthday gift, and when Joan moved to a smaller apartment, she sent some of her wonderful dresses to my daughter to play 'dress-up.' The dresses went to the museum at Wesleyan [University].

"I was a teacher at Wesleyan, and I had asked Joan Crawford if she would come to speak at my class. Even though she dreaded appearing in front of an audience, she agreed.

"She wanted to know all about the entrance to the auditorium, such as, were there a lot of stairs on her approach? I said, yes, there were. She asked me how many. I went and counted. When I called her back, she said, 'Impossible!' She would be wearing a fitted evening dress and very high heels, and she couldn't take the chance of stumbling in public view. 'It would be too embarrassing,' she said. 'There must be another way.'

"I asked and searched but couldn't find a way, and then somebody said, 'There's the garbage elevator.' When I told her, she said, 'Oh, perfect! As long as I don't get any garbage on my dress.' And she didn't.

"The students and everyone there never forgot it. It was the only time she ever appeared before a class, because she suffered so when she had to make a live appearance."

"JOAN WAS TERRIBLY shy about appearing as herself," Springer told me. "As long as she had her character to hide in—not behind, but *in*—

Joan was not nervous. Appearing live, as herself, she was so nervous and tense, I had to almost drag her to Town Hall, verbally, anyway.

"Joan was always strong on preparation. Preparation made her feel more secure, but she still never felt totally secure.

"She loved her life and her career. She loved her audience, her public, more than any other star I ever knew. But she would say, 'Oh, Johnny, don't ask me to appear before live audiences. Those butter-flies!'

"She was always afraid of disappointing her fans. She didn't want to lose their love. She felt she hadn't held the love of her husbands. She felt she hadn't held on to the love of her two older children, who not only didn't love her, but, she felt, *hated* her.

"That was her older daughter, Christina, and her son, Christopher. I would try to reassure her that one day it would all be straightened out. I really thought it would be. She said to me, 'No, never.' I was wrong. She was right.

"She said, 'Johnny, you're so lucky. You have three such wonderful children. I really envy you.

"'You know the troubles I've had with my two older children. I can't understand why it turned out so badly. I tried to give them every-thing. I loved them and tried to keep them near me, even when they didn't return my love. Well, I couldn't *make* them love me, but they *could* have shown some respect. I couldn't insist on love, but I could insist on respect.

"'I suppose I spoiled them, but I wanted them to have everything I never had. When you're a child, you don't know how everyone else lives. You adjust to what life is like for you. As a small child, I knew we were poor, but I didn't know what the word 'poverty' meant, and we really, at least part of the time, lived in poverty. When I went to school, to keep my place, I had to serve all of the other girls their meals and make their beds. Fourteen of them.

"'Lately, I've been thinking more about the childhood I missed. I thought I'd left it far behind me, but I suppose it stayed a part of me, along with the desire for what I hadn't had. I was able to buy all the material things I wanted after my success. But I didn't want a doll anymore. I'd missed an early education because I was always too tired from chores to be able to learn. And I missed all of the early friendships I might have had because of my poor background and, actually, poor foreground. I suppose those weren't real friendships, the ones I would have had with girls who were only fair-weather friends. Well, so what? I didn't know the difference, and it certainly would have made me happy at the time. Happiness in its moment is worth quite a lot, even if it doesn't hold up forever.

"'All of my money couldn't buy back my childhood.

"'I remember my mother's words, and I hear her voice in my head saying, 'It's for your own good.' She would say that when I was cleaning or doing the laundry. She'd say it when she hit me because I hadn't pleased her. I never knew what to expect. I just knew one thing: It wasn't for my own good. I wanted my children never to experience what I had experienced. I wanted them to have wonderful birthday parties, toys, holiday trips. I don't know if I didn't give them enough discipline, or if I gave them too much."

Al Steele had been able to control Christopher. Betty Barker said that she felt Christopher resented women. "He wouldn't take orders from women."

He was sent to a military school for his high school education. As soon as he could, he left home. This time, Joan did not try to stop him, nor did she try to find him.

He joined the army during the Vietnam War. After he was discharged, he brought his wife and child to see Joan. She didn't see them.

"I remember most clearly," she told me, "when a teenage Christopher spat in my face. He said, 'I hate you.' It's pretty hard to overlook *that*. I couldn't.

"The last time Christopher left, he returned to being an orphan."

"I'D HEARD ALL the arguments about heredity versus environment," Joan told Springer and me, "and I believed environment was everything.

"It's not nature, but nurture. Environment, not genes. That's what I originally thought.

"Well, obviously, environment doesn't produce blond hair, except if you have a bottle of peroxide in your environment.

"But for what really counts, what a person is made up of inside— mind, heart—I *knew* it was a matter of environment. I knew if you put children into the right happy, loving home, they would flourish. It was only important to give them enough love and for them to know how loved they were.

"Well, I was wrong."

10

Goodbye, World
(1971–1977)

J OHN SPRINGER WROTE a book about film actresses of the 1930s
called *They Had Faces Then*. It was published in 1974 by Citadel
Press.

"When she heard about the book," Springer said, "Joan called me,
and said, 'Johnny, I want to give you a book party. I'll take care of
everything. I insist. You must let me do it.'

"You can imagine how thrilled I was. I was terribly flattered, and
very happy.

"Then, after I hung up, I began to feel worried. I was used to pub-
licizing other people, not myself. I began to feel a little self-conscious
and nervous about the idea. I couldn't face it. I guess you might say I
had an attack of modesty.

"I tried speaking to Springer the writer as I, Springer, the publicist,
had done with so many clients. I told myself how good it would be for
my book and how much fun I would have. What a happy memory it
would be, how proud my wife, June, would be. My children. No use.
It didn't work. I couldn't convince myself.

"I began to panic. I tried to figure out how I could escape, how to
get out of it. I'd already told my editor, and the publisher was, as you
can imagine, very keen on a book party with Joan Crawford presiding
as hostess. Joan wanted to pay for everything, too, which made it even
more desirable for the publisher. They wanted to use her name on the
invitation, and she said yes.

"It wasn't easy to say no to Joan. She always took no as a personal rejection. Well, I suppose we all do. How could I tell her I didn't want the book party, when I had been so excited about it? And in my heart, I didn't really want to say no.

"I got an idea which seemed to me a very good one. It would get me off the hook, but save the party. It turned out to be one of the worst ideas of my life, but I didn't know that then. Ever since, I've wished I could take back the whole thing, undo it, skip the book party, but I couldn't go back in time and do it.

"Since Roz Russell was still in New York after doing my 'Legendary Ladies' series the night before, it seemed it would take some of the pressure off Joan if I asked Roz to co-host the evening with her, so I asked Joan what she thought about the idea. I knew that she knew Roz and liked her, although they didn't see much of each other, since Roz lived in California and Joan had come to New York. They'd both appeared in *The Women*, a long time ago. I thought it would be kind of a courtesy to Roz.

"As soon as I said it, I was sorry. There was a pause. Too long a pause. What could Joan say? She said it. Yes. But I think she'd wanted to do it alone, for me, and I'd spoiled it.

"Joan met me at the party before the guests arrived, and she stood at the door and greeted everyone. She was beautifully dressed and was wearing a lot of diamonds. She had her makeup carefully done to emphasize those full lips and to exaggerate those tremendous eyes. She was stunning. She still looked like Joan Crawford.

"When I called Joan the next day, I knew she would be upset by some of the pictures of her that were in the newspaper, pictures of her leaving the party with Roz. I knew they were unflattering, though they didn't look as terrible to me as they did to her.

"The photographs of Roz were especially unflattering. Her face appeared puffy because of Roz's need for cortisone for her painful arthritis.

"I tried to reassure Joan. 'Anyone can take a bad picture,' I said. I didn't say it to her, but I thought the pictures of Roz were so much worse. Standing together for the photographer the way they were, I think it made the pictures of Joan look even worse. Nothing I could say had any effect. She'd always listened to me, but this time, I could tell she wasn't listening. She wasn't angry with me, which she might have been, or even as angry at the newspaper as I thought she should be. She seemed to be angry at herself.

"I guessed the pain of it would fade with time, and she would see it in perspective. But the pain never went away. It lasted the rest of her life. She never got over those pictures, because she was convinced they showed her the way she really looked. She became increasingly reclusive.

"I said, 'Forget about the bad pictures. Look at all the beautiful pictures you have of yourself.' I knew she had saved a great collection of the most wonderful portraits of herself.

"'No, Johnny,' she said, 'I don't look at those because the comparison makes me feel even worse.

"'I don't want to meet the press anymore, because the interesting part of me is over.'"

AFTER JOHN SPRINGER'S book party, Joan saw fewer people. Her occasional meetings were private; she no longer appeared for public events. "She didn't want to see old friends, people she hadn't seen for a long time, because she didn't want to see a look of shock on their faces as they saw how she had changed," Springer said.

She preferred to meet new people. They didn't see those changes.

Above all, she did not want to meet photographers taking candid pictures. She missed going to '21' for lunch, but she felt she couldn't go where she was expected.

"When Helen (Gurley Brown) and I went to '21' with Joan," producer David Brown told me, "everyone greeted her and loved her, from the maître d' to the dishwashers."

"MY PUBLIC LIFE really ended at Johnny's book party, though I didn't know it until the next day," Joan told me. "My life as I had enjoyed living it was largely over because my life as Joan Crawford was over. I had to retire Joan Crawford from public view. What was left of me could only destroy that image.

"I couldn't bear people saying, 'Oh, look, she used to be Joan Crawford!' I would rather stay in my home and answer my fan mail.

"Sometimes I looked at an old film of mine. I've had such a wonderful career, which lasted so long. I always knew it had to end someday.

"The day after the book party, I was just preparing to go out when I saw the papers with those horrifying pictures of myself. Horrifying!

"At first, I couldn't bear to look. A glance was *more* than enough. But then, I took a deep breath and with all of the courage I could muster, I took a long look at the pictures, so I would never have to look at them again. I never did. But I had to see what everyone else would see.

"I took off my jacket, put down my purse, and I canceled my appointment. I couldn't face people. They would have seen the pictures.

"I couldn't do anything to stop the pictures. I couldn't do anything to stop people from seeing them.

"I couldn't control other people's actions. I could only control my own.

"I did the only thing I could do.

"I said, 'Goodbye, world.'"

IT WAS CLEAR as I listened to Joan and Springer at a lunch almost a year before the publication of Christina Crawford's book, *Mommie Dearest* (which did not yet have that title), that they knew the book was forthcoming. They believed it would be published soon, and they spoke about it with a sense of foreboding.

Christina had not told Joan that she was writing a book, indicating for Joan and Springer that it was not going to be a book to which Joan could look forward.

"I think she's using my name strictly to make money," Joan told us. "I suppose she doesn't think I'm going to leave her enough or that I'm going to disappear soon enough."

Joan sighed. Obviously referring to her adoption of Christina, she said, "No good deed goes unpunished."

Springer asked her if she planned to read Christina's book when it came out.

"I plan *not* to read it," she replied. "Why spoil days of your life reading a book that can only hurt you? Once you've read it, the specific words stay with you and torture you. The book produces a bad aura, which costs days of your life. It's against my beliefs. You know, Johnny, I've become a Christian Scientist. I find it very positive and comforting and a kind of protection. You're a Catholic, and I know your faith does that for you.

"I've learned that there are people who will hurt you, if you let them—even if you *don't* let them. I prefer to cut off people who can only hurt me, who *want* to hurt me, rather than to continue to give them power over me to go on inflicting pain.

"I think this book will be full of lies and twisted truths. She would not be writing it if she hadn't found someone to pay her to do it. Her main reason is for the money. If she thought I had more money than I do, and I probably have even less than she thinks I do, and that I would be leaving it to her, she could at least wait for my total disappearance before any news of a book leaks out.

"I don't think my adopted daughter is writing the book just to hurt me. If her purpose were to hurt me, she has already accomplished it without going to the trouble of writing a book.

"If Christina had good things to say about the person who adored her, tried to be a good mother to her, she would have told me about the book. I would have helped if I could, if she wanted my help.

"I've come to think that what she has wanted is to be *me*. Or at least to have what I have. I wanted to share everything I had with her, but I couldn't reach or influence her.

"She is her own person, and that person has brought me a lot of pain. I feel it is enough, more than enough pain, as with her brother. She is a grown woman, and I did my duty as best I could. Now, I wish her well, but *not* as part of *my* life.

"I said this about Christopher and now I say it about Christina. The problem was I adopted her, but she didn't adopt me.

"I feel that 'Tina' is looking for a character to play. I hope she finds her character and is happy with it."

After Joan's death and the subsequent publication of *Mommie Dearest*, Springer told me, "The character Christina found to play was 'daughter dearest.'"

Film historian Sean Sobeck observed, "That book created a caricature of Joan Crawford that took on a life of its own and stood apart from the person, but it was often confused with the person."

"Do you know when you're really old?" Joan asked me. "You're old when you get bitter.

"The worst thing about getting old is going to all those funerals. Instead of being invited to parties, you're invited to funerals. Your old friends disappear, and even worse, you see them suffer. I know how I *don't* want to go. I don't want to do it slowly, and I certainly don't want to do it publicly.

"I would fight with all my strength to my very last breath to preserve a life that was worth living, to conquer an illness from which I might get better.

"I've seen my friends fight for every terrible day, prolonging their suffering. I love life and want to hang on as long as it's enjoyable or has any promise of being enjoyable again, but I know I don't want to spend my last days being tortured."

Springer told me that he did not learn of it until afterward, "but if I had known at the moment it happened," he said, "I'd have known that Joan was very near death—when she gave away Princess Lotus Blossom.

"She really loved that dog, and she would never have parted with her unless she knew she had to find a place for her helpless companion in order to safeguard Princess's future. Joan was like that, planning for the future, trying to help those she cared about. If she gave Princess away, it had to mean she knew she couldn't take care of her anymore.

"Joan only survived a matter of days after she'd given Princess Lotus Blossom away."

. . .

"I've heard many actors, and others as well, say, 'I hope I don't outlive my money,'" Joan told me. "I never thought that way because I thought I'd always be young. It sounds silly now, but when you're young, life seems forever. A day, a week, a month, a year all seem long. That's before you get older and time speeds up, and you can't imagine how it can be going so fast, but I still believed I'd always be able to work. That lasted until I couldn't.

"I wouldn't say that I hope I don't outlive my money, but rather that I hope I don't outlive my pride, of which my vanity is a part."

When Joan learned that she had cancer, very few people were told. It was her choice not to speak about it because it was a private matter. She did not want sympathy, and she had said, "I would like to be like an old wolf, or an old gorilla. I have heard that when they know they have reached their last days, they go away to be alone and just disappear. As far as I'm concerned, they have the right idea.

"I don't know *when* I will die or of *what* I will die, but I do know *where* I will die. At home, in my bedroom. I don't have control over the other two factors, but I do have control over where, unless I have an accident. Otherwise, it will be in my own bed in my own home."

That was exactly where she died.

Though very ill on the morning of her death, Joan rose early. She had no appetite for breakfast, but she wanted to prepare the meal for a longtime faithful fan who had stayed the night, keeping the vigil along with Joan's housekeeper. Joan wanted them to have a good breakfast. She insisted.

As they sat down and began their breakfast, she retired to her bedroom. She had been up early, before the others, in order to prepare the breakfast for two.

She had fixed her hair, put on some lipstick and one of her favorite robes. She knew she didn't look well. She was too thin. She hadn't slept all night, and she was in pain.

She turned on the television set, neatly pulled back the cover, and got into the bed. She did not see what was on the screen.

On May 10, 1977, Joan Crawford died in the bedroom of her New York City apartment.

It was announced that Joan had died of a heart attack, a coronary occlusion. It was what Joan had preferred, "not a discussion of my insides." The heart attack may have been brought on by her deteriorating health.

Her obituary appeared on page one of *The New York Times*. No one would have appreciated their words on her position in film history more than Joan herself:

"Miss Crawford was a quintessential superstar—an epitome of timeless glamour who personified for decades the dreams and disappointments of American women."

Douglas Fairbanks, Jr., said that he was asked frequently by interviewers if he believed Joan Crawford had ended her own life, as had been rumored. Did she commit suicide?

Fairbanks's answer was an unequivocal no. "She had the strong will to be able to do it, if it was what she had wanted to do, but nobody could convince me she would want to do that. Even in pain, even with no hope of ever getting better, I feel it was against her religious and ethical beliefs. It took the greater strength for her to go on.

"She liked to be in control of her life as much as possible, and she didn't like to feel out of control. I believe that when she heard the bad news, no hope, she waited for a natural death without trying to prolong a life she didn't consider would be worth living. She wanted to die in a dignified way, looking as well as she could. I know that."

Myrna Loy told me, "When I got the call saying Joan had died, I saw I had written on the pad next to the phone, 'Call Joan.' I hope she arrived in heaven, where she deserved to be, the way she would have liked to, in a limousine, the way she felt Joan Crawford was expected to arrive."

According to Joan's instructions, there was to be a cremation, and her ashes were to be placed in an urn at Ferncliff Cemetery, Westchester County, New York, next to her last husband, Alfred Steele.

The funeral was held at Campbell's Funeral Home in New York City. Among those in attendance were Myrna Loy, who had known her the longest, Van Johnson, one of her favorite luncheon companions, Brian Aherne, Andy Warhol, John Springer, and Joan's four children.

On May 17, a memorial service was held at All Souls Unitarian Church. The 23rd Psalm was read by the Reverend Kring. Eulogizing her were Anita Loos, Geraldine Brooks, Cliff Robertson, and George Cukor, who flew in from California for the service.

Cukor characterized her as "the perfect image of the movie star." He spoke of her intelligence, her vitality, her will, her beauty. He said something he always said in one way or another when speaking about Joan: "The camera saw a side of her that no flesh-and-blood lover ever saw."

WHEN JOAN DIED, Jack Valenti, the president of the Motion Picture Association of America, asked the studios to observe a minute of silence to honor her. It wasn't something routinely done, but all of the studios agreed.

When I spoke with Valenti more than twenty years later, I asked him if he could have had the minute of tribute if Christina Crawford had published her book before her mother's death.

"I would have tried," Valenti said, "but I don't think I would have been successful. Words in print have an enormous effect.

"I don't think anyone will ever be able to undo that book her daughter wrote, and I'm not going to dignify it by mentioning its title.

"Joan Crawford deserved the honor as an icon. It was a professional honor, paying tribute to her career and what it had meant all those years to Hollywood. But there was no way that the portrait that was painted of her by her daughter and received as truth wouldn't cast aspersions on her name. That blurred the personal *and* the professional.

"I knew this lady, and I know she had done many good deeds anonymously. She was always dependable for helping out with worthy charities and good deeds, and that's the way I remember her."

· · ·

A MONTH AFTER Joan Crawford's death in 1977, there was a tribute to her at the Academy of Motion Picture Arts and Sciences in Hollywood, organized by George Cukor. Among the speakers were Cukor, John Wayne, Myrna Loy, Robert Young, and Steven Spielberg.

Myrna Loy remembered seeing Christina there with her husband, "though to the best of my knowledge, I don't believe anyone invited her.

"But what was so striking was that wonderful representation among the Academy members, not only the famous names but there were many guild and union people, especially from M-G-M, hairdressers, wardrobe people, makeup artists, lighting people, grips, because all of those people loved her. She had gone out of her way to know and recognize everyone who worked on each of her pictures. No one else had ever made that kind of effort, not only to know the people, but to know the names of their wives and families."

JOAN'S WILL LEFT about $2 million. On October 28, 1976, less than a year before her death, she had made a new will. She left trust funds of $77,500 to each of her adopted twin daughters, and $35,000 to her longtime friend and secretary, Betty Barker, and smaller bequests to a few other people.

She left money to her favorite charities: the USO of New York; the Motion Picture Home, of which she had been a founder; the American Cancer Society; the Muscular Dystrophy Association; the American Heart Association; and the Wiltwyck School for Boys.

She stated specifically that Christina and Christopher had been knowingly and deliberately left out of the will. "It is my intention to make no provision herein for my son Christopher or my daughter Christina for reasons which are well known to them."

At a Christie's auction, Andy Warhol was the major purchaser of Joan's costume jewelry. She already had sent many of her books and papers to Brandeis University. "I want my books to be placed in a good home because they were my friends," she said.

"I bet you can't guess what my favorite book is," she asked me once. "It's the dictionary. I'm very self-taught."

At the Plaza Galleries Auction house, a box filled with Joan's false eyelashes went to a pleased Crawford fan. It was an affordable purchase. The unsorted lashes were not in pairs, but that didn't matter.

It was George Cukor who told me about Joan's secret charity. He said it was "something she had done for many people over the years, and some of those people lived good lives which they owed to Joan. They might not have lived at all if not for her, but she didn't want even the people she did it for to ever know.

"In 1926, she had gone to a young doctor, Dr. William Branch, for some ailment or other, and she was thrilled with him. He had the kind of dedication to his work that she had to hers. He was also very fair and said, 'I'll just charge you whatever you think you can afford to pay because you're a young actress and can't afford very much now.' And she said, 'But you're a young doctor starting out, and you must need the money.' Joan had decided very early that she wanted to share her good fortune with others, and she had this idea which she couldn't afford then, but she was certain she was going to be able to afford.

"She said, 'Sometime soon, I'm going to be earning more money than I need, and I would like to help people. I work with people who make the movies, the ones who have all of those little jobs without which there couldn't *be* movies. They are so important, and they do such wonderful work. When they get sick and need medical help, some of them don't have the financial means they need, so I want to see that they have the help they deserve. I want to pay for a room in the hospital and other costs. Dr. Branch said he would work free." Later, as she could afford it, Joan extended it to two rooms.

"They did this for many years, and Joan was always resolute, determined that the few people who knew should never tell anyone.

"I'm only telling you now because Joan is gone, and I'm interpreting my promise as lasting for her lifetime. That seems fair. Besides, I think people should know what kind of person Joan was, an extraordinarily fine person."

• • •

BECAUSE JOAN HAD won the USO's "Woman of the Year" award, Christina Crawford titled her book about her mother *Mother of the Year*. The title was later changed to *Mommie Dearest*. The book was published by William Morrow in 1978. In it, Joan was portrayed as an abusive mother who had no understanding of, nor feeling for, her children, and whose only real attention to them was to discipline and punish them. It was generally believed that the publication was delayed in order to allay any suspicions that Christina had written it because she had been left out of Joan's will. The book immediately made the bestseller list and stayed there for months.

In 1981, a film was made based on the book, starring Faye Dunaway as Joan. A number of actresses had turned down the part. Christina Crawford wished to write the screenplay, but the screenplay she offered was rejected.

Lee Strasberg told me that he had advised Dunaway not to take the part even though it seemed like a good one. He felt that accepting the role would be a bad step in her career. She had always followed her mentor's advice, but this time she went against it. Later, according to Strasberg, Dunaway admitted, "Lee, you were so right."

The film has contributed to the *Mommie Dearest* stigma.

There were people, among them even some who knew Joan, who believed what Christina said. Some felt Joan had mistreated her two older adopted children. Many of those closest to her, however, were vehement in their denunciation of the book and of Christina for writing it.

Joan Crawford was not Bette Davis's favorite person, as Bette told me in one way or another during the years I knew her, but she was outraged by the book. "I was not Miss Crawford's biggest fan, but wisecracks to the contrary, I did and still do respect her talent.

"What she did not deserve was that detestable book written by her daughter. I've forgotten her name. Horrible. What a vile way to cash in on her mother's name. Miss Crawford wasn't my close friend, but what her daughter, who I understand was adopted, did was absolutely vile.

"I looked at that book, but I did not need to read it. I wouldn't read trash like that, and I think it was a terrible, *terrible* thing for a daughter to do. An abomination! To do something like that to someone who saved you from the orphanage, foster homes, who knows what. If she didn't like the person who chose to be her mother, she was grown up and could choose her own life.

"I felt very sorry for Joan Crawford, but I knew she wouldn't appreciate my pity because that's the last thing she would have wanted—anyone being sorry for her—especially me.

"The daughter had waited until her mother was dead and couldn't speak for herself. What a coward she was, *is*.

"I can understand how hurt Miss Crawford would have been. Well, no, I can't. It's like trying to imagine how I would feel if my own beloved, wonderful daughter, B.D., were to write a bad book about me. Unimaginable. I am grateful for my children and for knowing they would never do to me anything like what Miss Crawford's daughter did to her.

"Of course, dear B.D., of whom I'm so proud, is my natural child, and there always are certain risks in adopting. Gary [Merrill] and I adopted two babies because when we married, I was too old to have our own. We were very pleased with our little boy, Michael, but our adopted daughter, who was a beautiful baby, was brain-damaged. I never have had regrets, though, because I think we provided for her better than anything else that could have happened to her, and we gave her some happiness in her life. You can't return a baby like you can a carton of cracked eggs."

Joan had said, "There was one thing where Bette was one up on me. She'd had a baby, a child of her own. I wanted one, and Bette was so lucky to have been able to have own daughter, B.D., I think she called her."

With *Mommie Dearest* as her inspiration, B.D. would later write *Her Mother's Keeper*, her attack on her own mother, Bette Davis.

Douglas Fairbanks, Jr., considered the Joan Crawford portrayed in *Mommie Dearest* to be totally different from the person he knew.

"If you want to know someone, you must see emotions off guard," he told me. "That's how I know Joan Crawford could never have been cruel to her children. I really *knew* her when she was still Billie, as Joan liked to be called in those days. In a relationship as close as ours, I had the chance to see her in every kind of personal situation. She was never out of control. The most she was guilty of ever was a few sharp words and not many of those. We had our rows, but she never showed any sudden bursts of temper."

Cathy Crawford, who had lived in the same family, though later, said she and her twin sister, Cindy, were devastated by the book and the film. Cathy told me, "There *were* no coat hanger beatings. There were no *beatings*."

"We lived in the same house as Christina, but we didn't live in the same *home*, because she had her own reality. Cindy and I had a different reality, the opposite. I don't know where she got her ideas. Our Mommie was the best mother anyone ever had."

One of Joan's best friends was Van Johnson, who told me: "Some people said that Joan was better off being dead when *Mommie Dearest* came out because it would have broken her heart, and this way, she was spared all that pain.

"I'm not one of those people. I totally disagree. They didn't know Joan. I wish she had been alive when that terrible piece of garbage came out.

"I wish the book had never happened. But if it happened when Joan was still alive, and not too sick, I know her well enough to know she would have fought back in her way. She had a quiet strength, but she was strong, and she was determined. Nothing wishy-washy about her.

"I think if she could have, Joan would have protected her life and her body of work against that viper she had taken to her bosom."

"What bothers me," Myrna Loy said, "is that there were book buyers who bought that book and read it and people who believed it. It goes without saying that Christina was vicious, ungrateful, and jealous, but what perplexes me and makes me profoundly sad was that people wanted to spend their money that way, on such trash, and worse yet, believed it. The readers who believed it were the ones who did the damage."

John Wayne had known Joan from her last days at M-G-M. He remembered how much he liked working with her in *Reunion in France* and how she had done everything to help him at the studio where she reigned.

"She deserved the best, which she didn't always get," Wayne told me. "There's no one I'd rather have on my side."

"A lot of criticism has been leveled at Joan since the publication of her daughter's book," Vincent Sherman told me. "Christina hurt her mother's image a lot, but at least not while Joan was still alive. Bette Davis wasn't so fortunate, or maybe I should say she was *more* fortunate. She had to endure the hurt, but anyway, she was there to defend herself and to go on the offensive.

"Bette was not a lady to depend on being on the defensive. Her métier was the attack. I think I knew Joan as well as anyone ever did, but I honestly don't know how Joan would have handled *Mommie Dearest* if Christina had published it while she was still alive. She would have been heartbroken. Who wouldn't be? I can't even begin to imagine how I would have felt if one of my children had written a book like that one about me.

"Joan would have been in disbelief, but of course she couldn't have remained that way because the printed word was there and a best-seller.

"Maybe she would have written her own book in answer to it, the way Bette did, but I don't think she would have just fallen apart. She was strong, but the Joan I knew was a very, very vulnerable person. I think it would have depended on her health, because she cared so much about what her fans thought, she would have done something if she could."

Douglas Fairbanks, Jr., added, "Her daughter knew how to hurt her. Joan was punished for her good deed. She had worked so hard for her place as a star and an icon. She gave up her chance for a good marriage and personal happiness. She was willing to give up everything. She gave up *me!*"

· · ·

"THEY SAY YOU shouldn't live your life for other people, caring what they think, but I don't see what's so wrong about that," Joan said.

"My fans write to 'Dear Miss Crawford' or 'Dear Joan.' These are wonderful words, so now my favorite name isn't Lucille or Billie. My only name, as long as I live, and as long as my movies live, is Joan Crawford.

"I *am* Joan Crawford.

"Do you know what I would put on my tombstone?

"'I care what my fans think of me—now and forever.'"

"Mommie Wasn't a Movie Star in Our House"

A Postscript

I WAS ABOUT SIX," Cathy Crawford LaLonde told me, "and my sister Cindy and I were at school at Marymount, in Palos Verdes, and we were playing a game, 'Tisket a tasket, a green and yellow basket,' and I fell down and broke my elbow and my wrist in a few places.

"The school called Mommie. Joan Crawford ran off the set in the middle of filming, out of the studio and into her car, wearing her full makeup that she was wearing for the camera.

"When Mommie arrived for me, having raced to the school, she was still in her makeup. She got me and took me to the doctor and then we went home. She was still wearing makeup that she had on for the film.

"That's how I remember her when I think about her, which I do every day. There is no better way to tell about the kind of mother I had.

"I was a teacher of children with special needs for twenty-five years but when my own children were young, I told their schools that if one of my children ever felt sick or had an accident, they were to call me where I worked and I would leave immediately to go to them, the way Mommie had done for me.

"When I was little, I didn't know my mother was a movie star. She wasn't a movie star in *our* house.

"I'll never forget the night Mommie invited friends in to see a film of hers. It was called *Humoresque*. I was very excited.

"Mommie had a separate theater in a building in the back of our house. It was nice, and the chairs were so comfortable. It was a very nice place to watch a movie. I was about three or less, and I crawled up into the chair.

"I got the seat next to Mommie, so I was very happy until at the end of the movie, I was watching the screen, and I saw Mommie walking into the ocean. She was going to drown.

"I was so frightened. I started to cry. I grabbed Mommie's arm. I held on to it, I was clutching her sleeve.

"She smiled at me and reassured me. 'Honey, don't cry. Here I am, Cathy. I'm right here.

"'Nothing happened to me. It was a movie. It wasn't real.'

"But I was still holding on to her, because I was worried.

"That's how I found out what Mommie did."

HEARTBROKEN AFTER THE attack on their mother in *Mommie Dearest*, neither Cathy nor Cindy Crawford has given interviews. Christina's book left her younger sisters feeling embarrassed and humiliated.

"It makes me very sad," Cathy told me. "Every time Mommie's name is mentioned, 'that book' is mentioned. I don't want to give it any more publicity than it's already had. Even when people say or write good things about my mother, 'that book' gets linked to her name. It's so unfair."

The twins were born on January 13, 1947, in a Byersburg, Tennessee, hospital. Cathy was eight minutes older than Cindy. Cathy was Catherine and Cindy was Cynthia. Joan's adoption certificate was dated January 16, 1947.

The babies were premature and had to stay in the hospital for several weeks. Cathy remembered Joan telling her that she had weighed only a little more than three pounds.

Their mother, who had given them up for adoption, was very ill and died less than a week after the twins were born. She hadn't been married.

The adoption arrangements were made with the baby broker before the twins were born. Joan agreed to adopt them knowing they would be twins, but not knowing they would be premature.

Cathy told me that she and her sister always considered Joan their mother, and they had no interest in knowing who their biological mother was. In the early 1990s, however, Cathy went back to Tennessee to find out about her family.

"I learned my grandmother had seen a picture in a movie magazine of my sister and me with Mommie. She thought we were her grandchildren, so she saved the picture and carried it around in her purse. She never found out for sure that she was right."

Cathy told me her first memory was the image of herself and her twin sister, Cindy, doing the dishes.

They began doing them when they were so little they couldn't reach the sink. Two chairs were provided so they could climb up on the chairs and wash the dishes. The only question was who would dry? Cathy remembered liking to wash. "It was more interesting."

Cathy said they had responsibilities and chores, like making beds and keeping their rooms neat, but that they saw them as part of their mother's caring about them. Sometimes Joan did the chores with them, such as pulling weeds, and Cathy remembered that as "great fun."

Her mother explained to them that it would give them the independence to face hard times in life.

Cathy said her mother had been right, and when in her own life she had difficult times, she was especially grateful to her mother, who had not believed in spoiling children by simply giving everything to them. Her mother said it was easier just to give to your children, rather than being strict and trying to teach them good values.

"Mommie was very affectionate. My twin sister and I used to crawl into bed with her in the morning, and she would like that, and we did, too.

"I always liked riding with her on our holiday trips to Carmel. I would snuggle up to her while she drove up there. We always had wonderful times during our visits to Carmel. Mommie didn't have to go to work, and it was so beautiful there.

"Once when I guess I was about four, Mommie was working, and she hurt her shoulder, and she came home with her arm in a sling. I was so frightened and worried about her. That night I had to sleep in bed with her.

"Two of her best friends, who came over and talked with us and played with us, were Uncle Van [Johnson] and Uncle Butch [Cesar Romero]. Uncle Van always wore red socks. We knew they weren't really our uncles, but Mommie taught us to treat adults with respect who were her good friends and came to our house.

"As a special treat, sometimes my sister and I got our sleeping bags and we 'camped out,' sleeping on the floor by Mommie's bed in our sleeping bags.

"I remember when we went to the theater in New York, a lot of times after the play Mommie was introduced. I was personally shy, but I didn't mind it because Mommie enjoyed it, and I understood it went with the territory.

"Mommie took us to *Peter Pan* with Mary Martin, and when we went backstage to her dressing room, she was waiting for us with stardust and the sparkly stuff she had gathered on her stage flight, which she gave to us. I still don't know how she flew that way."

Joan was careful not to divulge any information that would spoil the magic for her children.

"I have so many happy memories with Mommie. One I always remember is going to see *Hello, Dolly!* with her and Cindy. Carol Channing was a friend of Mommie's. We had house seats, and she knew we would be coming backstage. She gave me, and my sister, too, each of us, a beautiful bracelet of small diamonds. They weren't really diamonds, but we thought they were. When I found out they were rhinestones, I loved it just as much.

"I remember," Cathy said, "going to Chasen's with my sister and Mommie. We sat in one of those very big booths in the small front section where everybody Mommie knew liked to sit. Chasen's was the great place to go, and Mommie and her friends always sat in those big booths. In the front there, it looked kind of like a diner. The big back part was like a separate restaurant.

"We were eating our lunch, and I saw Judy Garland come in. I recognized her because she was a friend of Mommie's who came to our house.

"I tugged at Mommie's sleeve, and I said, 'Look, Aunt Judy is here.' Mommie didn't seem to hear me.

"Just as we were leaving, I told her again, 'Look, Mommie. It's Aunt Judy over there.'

"This time, Mommie heard me, and we went to the table where Judy Garland was sitting.

"Mommie and Aunt Judy hugged each other, and Mommie told Aunt Judy, 'Cathy was trying to tell me you were here.'

"I was proud.

"Sometimes Mommie had to go to work, and my sister and I were left with our governess, who was with us many years and who we loved.

"After we went to school, we knew my mother was famous and successful and that she went to the movie studio to work.

"She took me to the set. Sometimes she took one of us, sometimes both of us, with her, and we watched her acting. She was making *The Best of Everything*. I remember I saw her once, and I couldn't stop looking at her eyes. They were so blue.

"Mommie was strict. She believed in discipline.

"I remember once doing something when I was little for which I had to stand in the corner. I don't remember anymore what it was. I guess we all stood in the corner some time in our lives.

"I remember another time when I said I didn't like my dinner and I didn't want to eat it. I didn't *have* to eat it, but I didn't get something else. I had to go to bed without dinner. I don't think it was such a terrible punishment."

When Cathy and Cindy were teenagers, they went to lunch with Joan at '21.'

"After we were seated," Cathy said, "the maître d' brought over a bottle of Coca-Cola and put it at Mommie's place. We didn't understand.

"Mommie waved at a man across the room, and he waved back, acknowledging the bottle of Pepsi-Cola she had sent to his table.

"Mommie explained to us that he was the president of Coca-Cola, and whenever they were at the same restaurant at the same time, they exchanged colas.

"After Mommie married Al Steele, she went with him on Pepsi-Cola business trips to Europe or she went to make a movie in England. Whenever we weren't in school, they sent for us.

"We had one trip for the Christmas holidays to St. Moritz, and I liked Gstaad, and we had a wonderful trip to Italy. In Rome, I loved seeing all of the churches and cathedrals. They thrilled me, experiencing the life of another time.

"I was the luckiest child in the world to have Mommie choose me, I wouldn't have chosen any other mother in the whole world because I had the best one anyone could ever have. She gave me backbone and courage and so much I could never say it all, but—oh, my gosh—the most important gift she gave me was all of the wonderful memories to last and take me through my life."

An emotional Cathy remembered one of her last visits with her mother at her New York City apartment. "There was a lot of pastel yellow and green and white in the apartment. Mommie always took as much California with her as she could."

She had brought her young children, Carla and Casey, to see their grandmother. Cathy had continued her mother's practice of giving her children names that started with C. They were five and four years old.

"They called Mommie 'JoJo.' She liked that. They really loved their grandmother, and she really loved her grandchildren.

"They were in the next room playing, and Mommie asked me, 'Do they really think of me as their grandmother?' She wondered if they understood about adoption. Did they understand the difference in her being their natural grandmother or their adopted grandmother?

"I said, 'They only think of you as their grandmother.'

"She smiled. Mommie looked very pleased.

"Then, we heard a sliding noise in the next room. I knew immediately what it was. Mommie had these wonderful parquet floors. She kept them perfectly, the way she always kept everything.

"Before we'd gone into the building, I'd said to my children, 'Remember, no sliding. Absolutely no sliding.' But my children found those parquet floors irresistible.

"I started to get up and I said, 'Oh, I'm so sorry. I'll tell them to stop.' Mommie motioned to me not to get up to stop them.

"'No, it's all right, Cathy. They're enjoying themselves. Let them slide.' She paused. Then, she said:

"'I've mellowed.'"

Filmography

Miss M-G-M (M-G-M) 1925
   Advertising short featuring Lucille LeSueur

Proud Flesh (M-G-M) 1925
   Directed by King Vidor

Lady of the Night (M-G-M) 1925
   Directed by Monta Bell, uncredited

The Only Thing (M-G-M) 1925
   Directed by Jack Conway

The Merry Widow (M-G-M), 1925
   Directed by Erich von Stroheim and Monta Bell

Pretty Ladies (M-G-M) 1925
   Directed by Monta Bell

The Circle (M-G-M) 1925
   Directed by Frank Borzage

Old Clothes (M-G-M) 1925
   Directed by Eddie Cline

Sally, Irene and Mary (M-G-M) 1925
   Directed by Edmund Goulding

The Boob (M-G-M) 1926
   Directed by William A. Wellman

Tramp, Tramp, Tramp (First National) 1926
   Directed by Harry Edwards

Paris (M-G-M) 1926
  Directed by Edmund Goulding

The Taxi Dancer (M-G-M) 1927
  Directed by Harry Millarde

Winners of the Wilderness (M-G-M) 1927
  Directed by W. S. Van Dyke

The Understanding Heart (M-G-M) 1927
  Directed by Jack Conway

The Unknown (M-G-M) 1927
  Directed by Tod Browning

Twelve Miles Out (M-G-M) 1927
  Directed by Jack Conway

Spring Fever (M-G-M) 1927
  Directed by Edward Sedgwick

West Point (M-G-M) 1928
  Directed by Edward Sedgwick

Rose-Marie (M-G-M) 1928
  Directed by Lucien Hubbard

Across to Singapore (M-G-M) 1928
  Directed by William Nigh

The Law of the Range (M-G-M) 1928
  Directed by William Nigh

Four Walls (M-G-M) 1928
  Directed by William Nigh

Our Dancing Daughters (M-G-M) 1928
  Directed by Harry Beaumont

Dream of Love (M-G-M) 1928
  Directed by Fred Niblo

The Duke Steps Out (M-G-M) 1929
  Directed by James Cruze

Our Modern Maidens (M-G-M) 1929
  Directed by Jack Conway

The Hollywood Revue of 1929 (M-G-M) 1929
  Directed by Charles F. Reisner

Untamed (M-G-M) 1929
  Directed by Jack Conway

Montana Moon (M-G-M) 1930
  Directed by Malcolm St. Clair

Our Blushing Brides (M-G-M) 1930
  Directed by Harry Beaumont

Paid (M-G-M) 1930
  Directed by Sam Wood

Dance, Fools, Dance (M-G-M) 1931
  Directed by Harry Beaumont

Laughing Sinners (M-G-M) 1931
  Directed by Harry Beaumont

This Modern Age (M-G-M) 1931
  Directed by Nick Grinde

Possessed (M-G-M) 1931
  Directed by Clarence Brown

Grand Hotel (M-G-M) 1932
  Directed by Edmund Goulding

Letty Lynton (M-G-M) 1932
  Directed by Clarence Brown

Rain (United Artists) 1932
  Directed by Lewis Milestone

Today We Live (M-G-M) 1933
  Directed by Howard Hawks

Dancing Lady (M-G-M) 1933
  Directed by Robert Z. Leonard

Sadie McKee (M-G-M) 1934
  Directed by Clarence Brown

Chained (M-G-M) 1934
  Directed by Clarence Brown

Forsaking All Others (M-G-M) 1934
  Directed by W. S. Van Dyke

No More Ladies (M-G-M) 1935
  Directed by Edward H. Griffith and George Cukor

I Live My Life (M-G-M) 1935
  Directed by W. S. Van Dyke

The Gorgeous Hussy (M-G-M) 1936
  Directed by Clarence Brown

Love on the Run (M-G-M) 1936
  Directed by W. S. Van Dyke

The Last of Mrs. Cheyney (M-G-M) 1937
  Directed by Richard Boleslawski

The Bride Wore Red (M-G-M) 1937
  Directed by Dorothy Arzner

Mannequin (M-G-M) 1937
  Directed by Frank Borzage

The Shining Hour (M-G-M) 1938
  Directed by Frank Borzage

Ice Follies of 1939 (M-G-M) 1939
  Directed by Reinhold Schünzel

The Women (M-G-M) 1939
   Directed by George Cukor

Strange Cargo (M-G-M) 1940
   Directed by Frank Borzage

Susan and God (M-G-M) 1940
   Directed by George Cukor

A Woman's Face (M-G-M) 1941
   Directed by George Cukor

When Ladies Meet (M-G-M) 1941
   Directed by Robert Z. Leonard

They All Kissed the Bride (Columbia) 1942
   Directed by Alexander Hall

Reunion in France (M-G-M) 1942
   Directed by Jules Dassin

Above Suspicion (M-G-M) 1943
   Directed by Richard Thorpe

Hollywood Canteen (Warner Brothers) 1944
   Directed by Delmer Daves

Mildred Pierce (Warner Brothers) 1945
   Directed by Michael Curtiz
      Academy Award for best actress

Humoresque (Warner Brothers) 1946
   Directed by Jean Negulesco

Possessed (Warner Brothers) 1947
   Directed by Curtis Bernhardt
      Academy Award nomination for best actress

Daisy Kenyon (20th Century-Fox) 1947
   Directed by Otto Preminger

Flamingo Road (Warner Brothers) 1949
  Directed by Michael Curtiz

It's a Great Feeling (Warner Brothers) 1949
  Directed by David Butler

The Damned Don't Cry (Warner Brothers) 1950
  Directed by Vincent Sherman

Harriet Craig (Columbia) 1950
  Directed by Vincent Sherman

Goodbye, My Fancy (Warner Brothers) 1951
  Directed by Vincent Sherman

This Woman Is Dangerous (Warner Brothers) 1952
  Directed by Felix Feist

Sudden Fear (RKO) 1952
  Directed by David Miller
    Academy Award nomination for best actress

Torch Song (M-G-M) 1953
  Directed by Charles Walters

Johnny Guitar (Republic) 1954
  Directed by Nicholas Ray

Female on the Beach (Universal International) 1955
  Directed by Joseph Pevney

Queen Bee (Columbia) 1955
  Directed by Ronald MacDougall

Autumn Leaves (Columbia) 1956
  Directed by Robert Aldrich

The Story of Esther Costello (Columbia) 1957
  Directed by David Miller

The Best of Everything (20th Century-Fox) 1959
  Directed by Jean Negulesco

What Ever Happened to Baby Jane? (Warner Brothers) 1962
  Directed by Robert Aldrich

The Caretakers (United Artists) 1963
  Directed by Hall Bartlett

Della (Four Star Pictures) 1964
  Directed by Robert Gist (TV film)

Strait-Jacket (Columbia) 1964
  Directed by William Castle

I Saw What You Did (Universal) 1965
  Directed by William Castle

The Karate Killers (M-G-M) 1967
  Directed by Barry Shear (TV film)

Berserk! (Columbia) 1968
  Directed by Jim O'Connolly

Trog (Warner Brothers) 1970
  Directed by Freddie Francis

Television Dramatic Appearances

"Because I Love Him" (CBS) *The Revlon Mirror Theater*,
  September 19, 1953

"The Road to Edinburgh" (CBS) *General Electric Theater*,
  October 31, 1954

"Strange Witness" (CBS) *General Electric Theater*,
  March 23, 1958

"And One Was Loyal" (CBS) *General Electric Theater*,
  January 4, 1959

"Rebel Ranger" (CBS) *Zane Grey Theater*,
  December 3, 1959

"One Must Die" (CBS) *Zane Grey Theater*,
January 12, 1961

"Same Picture, Different Frame" (CBS), *Route 66* (series),
October 4, 1963

"Eyes" (NBC) *Night Gallery* (series), November 8, 1969
(directed by Steven Spielberg)

The Secret Storm (CBS), (daytime serial), October 1969
(Joan replaced Christina Crawford in five episodes)

"Nightmare" (NBC) *The Virginian* (series), January 21, 1970

Journey to the Unknown (NBC), June 15, 1970

"Dear Joan: We're Going to Scare You to Death" (NBC),
The Sixth Sense, September 30, 1972

Radio Appearances

I Live My Life, October 7, 1935, *Lux Radio Theatre*

Paid, October 9, 1935, *Lux Radio Theatre*

Within the Law, October 14, 1935, *Lux Radio Theatre*

Chained, July 27, 1936, *Lux Radio Theatre*
(with Franchot Tone)

Mary of Scotland, May 10, 1937, *Lux Radio Theatre*
(with Franchot Tone)

Anna Christie, February 7, 1938, *Lux Radio Theatre*

A Doll's House, June 6, 1938, *Lux Radio Theatre*

Train Ride, July 5, 1939, *CBS Silver Theatre*

None Shall Part Us, October 15, 1939, *Screen Guild Theatre*

Baby, March 2, 1940, *Arch Oboler's Plays*

Two, November 22, 1940, *Every Man's Theatre*

Dark Victory, March 17, 1949, *Screen Guild Theatre*

The Ten Years, June 2, 1949, *Screen Guild Theatre*

Document A/777, April 17, 1950, *United Nations Radio*

Flamingo Road, May 26, 1950, *Screen Directors Playhouse*
(directed by Michael Curtiz)

Statement in Full, January 15, 1951, *Hollywood Star Playhouse*

Three Lethal Words, March 22, 1951, *Screen Directors Playhouse*

The Damned Don't Cry, April 5, 1951, *Screen Directors Playhouse*

Secret Heart, May 10, 1951, *Screen Guild Theatre*

I Knew This Woman, October 6, 1951, *Stars over Hollywood*

When the Police Arrive, March 1, 1952, *Stars over Hollywood*

INDEX

305

Index

Index

**POCKET
BOOKS**

Charlotte Chandler

The Girl Who Walked Home Alone: Bette Davis

Of Human Bondage, Jezebel, All About Eve, Whatever Happened to Baby Jane? Just this short list of Bette Davis' films gives an unmistakable sense of the role she played in twentieth-century cinema as one of the finest performers in Hollywood history.

Based on an extensive series of conversations that took place during the last decade of Bette Davis' life, *The Girl Who Walked Home Alone* is a startling portrait of an enduring icon.

ISBN 978-1-41652-222-5